RENEWALS 458-4574
DATE DUE

**WITHDRAWN
UTSA Libraries**

Developing Alliance Capabilities

Developing Alliance Capabilities

Koen H. Heimeriks

Foreword by
Jeffrey J. Reuer

© Koen H. Heimeriks 2008
Foreword © Jeffrey J. Reuer 2008

All rights reserved. No reproduction, copy or transmission of this publication may be made without written permission.

No paragraph of this publication may be reproduced, copied or transmitted save with written permission or in accordance with the provisions of the Copyright, Designs and Patents Act 1988, or under the terms of any licence permitting limited copying issued by the Copyright Licensing Agency, 90 Tottenham Court Road, London W1T 4LP.

Any person who does any unauthorised act in relation to this publication may be liable to criminal prosecution and civil claims for damages.

The author has asserted his right to be identified as the author of this work in accordance with the Copyright, Designs and Patents Act 1988.

First published in 2008 by
PALGRAVE MACMILLAN
Houndmills, Basingstoke, Hampshire RG21 6XS and
175 Fifth Avenue, New York, N.Y. 10010
Companies and representatives throughout the world.

PALGRAVE MACMILLAN is the global academic imprint of the Palgrave Macmillan division of St. Martin's Press, LLC and of Palgrave Macmillan Ltd. Macmillan® is a registered trademark in the United States, United Kingdom and other countries. Palgrave is a registered trademark in the European Union and other countries.

ISBN-13: 978–0–230–20169–9 hardback
ISBN-10: 0–230–20169–5 hardback

This book is printed on paper suitable for recycling and made from fully managed and sustained forest sources. Logging, pulping and manufacturing processes are expected to conform to the environmental regulations of the country of origin.

A catalogue record for this book is available from the British Library.

A catalog record for this book is available from the Library of Congress.

10 9 8 7 6 5 4 3 2 1
17 16 15 14 13 12 11 10 09 08

Printed and bound in Great Britain by
CPI Antony Rowe, Chippenham and Eastbourne

**Library
University of Texas
at San Antonio**

To Carine, Lara and Pepijn

Contents

List of Tables	viii
List of Figures	ix
Foreword	x
Preface	xiii
Acknowledgements	xv
1 Introduction	1
2 A Literature Review of Alliance Research	17
3 Describing the Phenomenon: Alliance Capabilities	43
4 Towards a Micro-level Understanding of Alliance Capabilities	60
5 An Analysis of the Alliance Capability Development Process	91
6 Conclusions, Implications, Limitations and Future Research	111
Appendices	125
Notes	147
References	151
Index	181

List of Tables

2.1	Prior research on alliance capabilities	23
2.2	Contributions of theories applied to alliance research	40
2.3	Overlap in concepts and terminology used in different theories	41
3.1	Levels of alliance experience	54
4.1	Eigenvalues	68
4.2	Wilks' lambda	68
4.3	Structure matrix	70
4.4	Exploratory factor analysis and reliability of factor-based scales	74
4.5	Test of equality of group means	77
4.6	Eigenvalues	77
4.7	Wilks' lambda	77
4.8	Structure matrix	78
5.1	Descriptive statistics and correlation matrix	103
5.2	Results of ordinal regression analysis	104

List of Figures

1.1	Comparing firms' current and future market value generated via alliances	2
2.1	Reasons for strategic alliance failure	19
2.2	Early (inter-firm) versus recent (intra-firm) alliance research	21
2.3	Theoretical framework	27
4.1	Use of alliance mechanisms in percentages	66
4.2	Role of mechanisms in alliance capability development	84

Foreword

Strategic alliances have become ever more important for firms to globalize, innovate and ultimately generate value. As individual firms have accumulated scores, if not hundreds, of partnerships over the years, many have developed very extensive portfolios of collaborations that now represent a substantial proportion of the firms' overall activity. Firms' ability to manage alliances on a portfolio-wide basis has therefore gained in importance, yet the tools and practices that firms might use in the process have not received enough attention or systematic analysis.

Academic research on capability building in general, and alliance capability building in particular, has long emphasized the role played by the accumulation of experience and the resulting trial-by-error learning. Firms such as Corning and others have developed many alliances over a long period of time and have used this organic, informal approach of cultivating the managerial and organizational capabilities needed to manage collaborative agreements. For firms such as Corning, alliances represent an important part of their culture and history, and involvement in joint ventures is also a key component of managers' career paths and their development of general management skills.

Yet for other firms, there are important limitations, and even potential problems, associated with reliance on experience in the capability-building process. For one, many firms are seeking to build up extensive alliance portfolios in very short order, so they therefore lack the time necessary to build up and leverage experience across deals. Learning can also be 'superstitious', or the practices used in an early successful deal can be inappropriately applied to future collaborations having very different motives, features, or challenges. The marked heterogeneity of alliances can impede learning by doing, as can the simple fact that it is difficult to measure the performance of individual alliances and draw comparisons across deals. It can also be quite difficult to make correct attributions as to why certain collaborations were successful or not when deciding which practices to transfer to future collaborations. Alliance learning processes also do not occur in a vacuum, so it can be the case that lessons learned from other, related corporate development activities (e.g., M&A) might be transferred inappropriately to certain alliances with very different strategic and organizational requirements. All of this suggests that learning might be an imperfect, and in some cases seriously flawed, means of developing capabilities for alliances.

Practice quickly began to get a good distance ahead of academic scholarship on alliance capability building. A number of years ago the popular press reported that firms such as Hewlett-Packard, Cisco, and Eli Lilly were using various tools to formalize alliance practices and engage in learning in a more deliberate manner. Specifically, firms began to use some best practices from knowledge management to codify and share their lessons learned and specify processes and criteria for future collaborations (e.g., investment, partner selection, governance etc.). Some firms also began to use alliance managers as well as dedicated staff groups at the corporate or business level to assist in the development and management of alliances throughout the organization. Professional organizations such as the Association of Strategic Alliance Professionals also emerged to share best practices and enhance alliance management in participating firms.

This is where Heimeriks's contributions fit in. His work enumerates and investigates the various practices and tools that firms might use to facilitate alliance capability building and improve the effectiveness of alliance portfolio management. One of the primary contributions of his research on this topic is that he provides detailed insights on these various tools and practices in a fine-grained fashion. For example, he not only evaluates some of the functional or staffing solutions just mentioned, but he also examines an impressive array of knowledge management tools, internal and external training solutions, and third-party solutions (e.g., legal, consulting, and other services).

His careful categorizations of these tools and practices are used to understand how firms develop alliance capabilities, and he uses both quantitative analyses as well as fieldwork at some leading international firms to do so. For instance, he offers accounts of alliance capability development processes at companies such as Oracle, Philips, GlaxoSmithKline, and KLM. The result is a movement away from experiential learning as the dominant source of alliance capabilities to an identification of some of the more micro-level origins of alliance capabilities. He also shows how firms' usage of the various tools are contingent upon their experience levels, suggesting that not all firms should simply copy the tools and practices used by others. Heimeriks's findings will be useful to very recent work and conversations shifting focus away from individual alliances to the management of portfolios of alliances, and his work is of more general interest to scholars doing work on competence-based perspectives in strategy as well as in organizational learning. His combination of contemporary theories in strategy and organization with his knowledge of managerial practice in the alliance domain makes for an interesting and worthwhile addition to an already large literature on alliances.

JEFFREY J. REUER

Preface

Over an extended period, from April 2001 to October 2004, I have worked on this PhD thesis. This period has been challenging and turbulent both professionally and personally. Professionally, it has been Geert Duysters who has helped me succeed. Geert, your supervision introduced me into the topic and I am sincerely thankful for all your stimulations. In particular, your ability to create 'a butterfly effect' helped me transform. Your professional friendship has always been open and has at various instances given me the energy to fulfil the mission. I hope we will jointly bear the fruits of our 'strategic alliance' in the future! I am also very thankful to Martin Wetzels for contributing his empirical expertise and Wim Vanhaverbeke's comments, which provided an enduring challenge to touch the void. The other members of my PhD committee, Bart Nooteboom and Niels Noorderhaven, I would also like to thank for their comments and cooperation to read my PhD thesis at such short notice.

I would like to thank my colleagues at the department of Organisation Science and Marketing. In particular, Ard-Pieter de Man, Charmianne Lemmens, Ad de Jong, Ad van den Oord and Bonny Beerkens. Ard-Pieter, as an expert in the field and chairman of the European chapter of the Association of Strategic Alliance Professionals, you have greatly contributed to the insights realized by helping define the critical components of this study. Charmianne, thanks for always listening to and answering my questions with regard to the PhD! Ad, thanks for helping me with the measurement scales! Adje, you are the one who was always willing to think along, adjust the questionnaire and ask me when the first print of the manuscript would be available. Moreover, my colleagues from Strategy Academy have been supportive during the excessive lunches we enjoyed. The conversations Bob de Wit and I had, provided me with some key insights into 'how to manage promoters'.

Personally, others helped me sustain. My dad Jacques who remained a source of encouragement due to his enthusiasm and pride in me. Moems Els, we have come to understand that words can be shared in many different ways. Although we have experienced that perseverence is no guarantee for success, I am sure your strength and vision enlighten this PhD. And my mother-in-law Coco also gave me joyful encouragements and put into perspective my drive and motivation. As a very special friend I am happy to have shared and talked about the many bumps that are inherent to a promotion with Jan-Mathijs Schoffelen. Our telephone calls were sometimes pessimistic. Nevertheless, you were the one that really understood the hurdles to be overcome. I am proud to have you as a friend!

I would also like to thank Virginia Thorp, editor at Palgrave Macmillan, who helped me to get the thesis converted into a book. Also, wonderful(ly), stimulating colleagues such as Stephen Gates, Elko Klijn, Jeff Reuer and Maurizio Zollo helped me progress in my research and my understanding of the topic. Thank you for that! Mostly though, I am thankful for the support my family gave me throughout this period. Carine, your continuing belief, understanding and patience are personal skills I have come to deeply admire and cherish. I will not forget all those times you turned down- into upturns. Your, Lara's and Pepijn's contribution may not be evident from outside, but it makes this PhD a product of both insight and *love*; an ingredient essential to make any mustard seed flourish. Perhaps that skill is the source needed to develop the ultimate alliance capability...

KOEN H. HEIMERIKS

Acknowledgements

Figure 2.1. Reasons for strategic alliance failure, from *Crafting Strategic Technology Partnerships*, G. M. Duysters, G. Kok, M. Vaandrager, copyright 1999 R&D Management. Used by permission of Blackwell Publishers Ltd.

Figure 2.2. Early (inter-firm) versus recent (intra-firm) alliance research, from *Alliantievaardigheid: een bron van concurrentievoordeel*. J. Draulans, De Man A-P, H.W. Volberda, copyright 1999 Holland/Belgium Management Review. Used by permission of Reed Business Information BV.

Figure 3.1 Levels of alliance experience, from *Alliantievaardigheid: een bron van concurrentievoordeel*. J. Draulans, De Man A-P, H.W. Volberda, copyright 1999 Holland/Belgium Management Review. Used by permission of Reed Business Information BV.

Chapter V is partly based on *Alliance capability as mediator between experience and alliance performance: an empirical investigation into the alliance capability development process*, K. Heimeriks and G. Duysters, copyright 2007 Blackwell Publishing. Used by permission of Blackwell Publishing Ltd.

Every effort has been made to trace all copyright-holders, but if any have been inadvertently overlooked the publishers will be pleased to make the necessary arrangement at the first opportunity.

1
Introduction

In their struggle to adapt successfully to the rapidly changing environment, many firms increasingly rely on strategic alliances as an expedient to overcome resource limitations, crack new markets, share costs or to provide platforms to remain strategically flexible. Strategic alliances (hereafter referred to as 'alliances') are defined as temporary cooperative agreements in which two or more firms share reciprocal inputs to realize improved competitive positions for the partners involved, while maintaining their own corporate identities. Both the number of newly established strategic alliances per year (Hergert and Morris, 1988; Narula and Hagedoorn, 1999) and the percentage of revenues that stem from strategic alliances (Harbison and Pekar, 1998b; Margulis and Pekar, 2001) have increased significantly in recent years. However, scholars and practitioners alike have pointed at the poor track record of alliances that over time continue to report high failure rates, ranging from 40 to 60 per cent (see for an overview Duysters et al., 1999a).

A striking fact is that some firms within and across different industries, sizes and nations are more successful in their overall alliance activity than others (Madhok and Tallman, 1998; Anand and Khanna, 2000). It appears that these 'consistent high performers' have developed alliance capabilities thereby relying on an ability to learn from their prior experiences and subsequently internalize these lessons (Harbison and Pekar, 1998a; Kale and Singh, 1999; Kale et al., 2000). Consequently, scholars and practitioners have been eager to learn more about this issue. Nevertheless, evidence with regard to critical antecedents of alliance performance is scattered and little specific as to how to solve the problem (Park and Ungson, 2001). Consequently, despite unprecedented attention for this topic and the persistent and eminent difficulty of many firms to perform, the hallmark of successful alliance management has not yet been clearly or fully defined.

1.1 Developments in the field of strategic alliances

Since the beginning of the 1980s, a spurt in alliance activity has occurred (Hladik, 1985; Hergert and Morris, 1988; Anderson, 1990; Khanna et al., 1998; Narula and Hagedoorn, 1999; Bekkers et al., 2002). As Peter Drucker recently stresses, 'Today a multinational is a network of alliances for manufacturing, distribution, technology and so on.... These companies are held together by strategy and information, not ownership' (*Financial Times*, 2004c). Research confirms what this remark suggests: not only has the number of alliances increased, but also the percentage of revenues coming from alliances (Harbison and Pekar, 1998a, b; Margulis and Pekar, 2001). This is confirmed by results of this study, as our respondents indicate an expectation of a vast increase in market value (which is defined as the share price times the number of shares) accruing from alliances in the next five years. Figure 1.1 shows that whereas currently an average of 38 per cent of the respondents' market value is generated via alliances, they expect 51 per cent to be generated via alliances in the next five years. Hence, in the coming years, firms in our study expect alliances to account for over half of their annual revenues.

These figures are in line with earlier findings (Freidheim, 1998; Harbison and Pekar, 1998b; Margulis and Pekar, 2001) and are indicative of the growing importance of alliances for many firms. In addition, prior

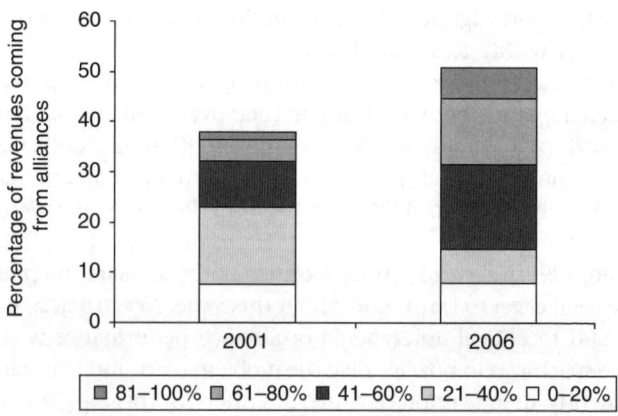

Figure 1.1 Comparing firms' current and future market value generated via alliances (N = 192)

research shows that successful inter-firm activities outperform industry averages in terms of return on investment (ROI): alliance-experienced companies achieve 20 per cent for ROI compared to 11 per cent as a US industry average (Harbison and Pekar, 1998b). As the value generated via strategic alliances can thus be significant (Dyer and Singh, 1998), cooperation seems to be used at an increasing rate to fulfil complex strategic demands. This is confirmed by recent surveys among top managers from large companies worldwide, who state that managing the alliance activities has become a key management issue (Kalmbach and Roussel, 1999; Rule, 1999; Corporate Strategy Board, 2000; Accenture, The Conference Board, 2001; Arthur D. Little, 2001; Accenture Consulting, 2002).

Although research has shown that the strategic benefits in terms of potential revenues are compelling, the challenges of successfully managing alliances have proven to be daunting. The number of alliances formed and the revenues generated via alliances have accelerated over the past decades. However, failure rates of strategic alliances have remained at a very high level (Duysters et al., 1999a). Most scholars report failure rates that vary between 40 and 60 per cent (for an overview see Das and Teng, 2000b; Park and Ungson, 2001). The 192 firms involved report an average success rate of 52 per cent, which is comparable to other studies (e.g. Harrigan, 1985, 1988b; Kogut, 1989; Bleeke and Ernst, 1993).[1] Given the fact that revenues derived from alliances have also increased steadily over the past decade (Margulis and Pekar, 2001), it becomes a key managerial challenge for firms to understand how to enhance overall alliance performance. Hence, firms that are able to succeed in their alliances can derive advantage over competitors who continue to fail in managing their alliances.

1.2 Developments in alliance research

Over the past decades, numerous researches have been triggered by the growing importance of alliances (see e.g. Contractor and Lorange, 1988, 2002; Lorange and Roos, 1990; Harvard Business Review Press, 2002; Ireland et al., 2002). Besides the increased alliance activity, it is the potential for a distinct competitive advantage created through effective alliance management that underlines the necessity to investigate the critical antecedents of alliance performance (Kanter, 1994). A firm is said to have a competitive advantage when it is implementing a value creating strategy not simultaneously implemented by any current or potential competitors (Barney, 1991: 102). As a consequence, literature on alliances and concomitant performance antecedents has blossomed over the past decades.

Over time, the main research emphasis of scholars committed to uncovering the antecedents of alliance performance has shifted. Whereas early studies on alliances generally centred on inter-firm or dyadic factors influencing alliance performance, more recent studies focus on intra-firm antecedents of alliance performance. Traditionally, relying on literature such as transaction cost theory and industrial organization theory, scholars primarily focused their attention on factors influencing alliance performance in individual alliances. As this literature suggested, firms essentially function as independent units (Sanchez and Heene, 1997) and alliances were considered to be second-best options to going-alone or full hierarchical integration of companies (Contractor and Lorange, 1988). As a result, firms were expected to have a tendency to rely on internal development of know-how rather than opt for inter-organizational constellations (Duysters, 2001). If undertaken at all, cooperation with other firms was seen as a dyadic phenomenon. Viewing alliances as distinct business transactions, scholars devoted particular attention to the critical inter-firm factors that should be taken into account when managing the individual alliance (see e.g. Steiner, 1968). For instance, trust and complementarity were supposed to be critical in enhancing alliance performance (Johnson et al., 1996; Nooteboom et al., 1997; Parkhe, 1998; Luo, 2002a). Another example is commitment, which refers to the ease with which a partner will end the relationship in case unforeseen difficulties arise (Medcof, 1997). These factors have collectively been referred to as collaborative advantages (Kanter, 1994) and relational advantages (Dyer and Singh, 1998). In particular, collaboration-specific rents (Madhok and Tallman, 1998), relational rents (Lane and Lubatkin, 1998), common benefits (Khanna et al., 1998) and relational capital (Kale et al., 2000) can result from these advantages. These studies make up a vast amount of academic literature on alliance-specific and inter-firm factors that are supposed to optimize alliance performance. However, the dyadic or inter-firm factors analysed in this literature often remained anecdotal in origin and little specific as to how to solve the issue (Park and Ungson, 2001). This is a result of the fact that these analyses concentrate on identifying critical dyadic factors between the partners. Although these dyadic factors are important, they tend to remain generic and leave undiscussed the intra-firm process of alliance capability that also seems relevant to gain a comprehensive understanding of the antecedents of alliance performance. Thus, traditionally, leaving some notable exceptions aside (Littler et al., 1995; Sivadas and Dwyer, 2000; Tsang, 2002b; Draulans et al., 2003; Sarkar et al., 2004), scholars have paid little attention to the role intra-firm antecedents play and how these help firms outperform competitors in their alliance activities (Takeishi, 2001).

In other words, although studies into inter-firm antecedents of alliance performance have generated interesting contributions, they have only provided a partial solution to the persistent differences in alliance performance between firms. In order to better understand why some firms persistently outperform competitors in terms of alliance performance, another stream of research has emerged which is distinct from inter-firm antecedents research and looks at factors that promote alliance performance at the intra-firm level (e.g. Sims et al., 2003). In this respect, Hamel (1991: 84, in Grant and Baden-Fuller, 2002) notes, 'The crucial distinction between acquiring such skills in the sense of gaining access to them...and actually internalizing a partner's skills has seldom been clearly drawn'. The need to complement early alliance research that centred on inter-firm antecedents of alliance performance is also evident from Ireland et al. (2002: 114), who underscore the need for firms to simultaneously concentrate on both content and process elements to enhance alliance performance. In their view, it is insufficient to understand the critical issues at the dyadic level without addressing the internal processes and mechanisms that underlie successful alliance management at the firm level. Other studies, such as Simonin (1997), Dyer and Singh (1998), Kale and Singh (1999) and Hoang (2001), confirm the need to pay attention to the role of intra-firm factors in order to provide a better understanding of antecedents of alliance performance. Thus, these studies suggest that internal or intra-firm factors are of key importance to come to a better understanding of the factors involved in enhancing a firm's alliance performance.

Recently, referring to theories such as evolutionary economics, the resource-based view, dynamic capability view and organizational learning theory, scholars proposed that alliance capabilities can be viewed as a rare, valuable and difficult-to-imitate resource at the company level (Gulati, 1998) which has an important impact on rent generation in alliances (Khanna et al., 1998). In an attempt to fill the gap left open by early studies, researchers have recently started to analyse managerial processes, tools and routines in order to explain the reported fixed-firm effects in alliance performance. For instance, Kale et al. (2002) confirm that a dedicated alliance function, which is a unit responsible for the strategic coordination of a firm's alliance activities and the capturing of alliance-related knowledge, can positively influence a firm's alliance performance. To this end, these studies concentrate on internal or intra-firm factors rather than dyadic or inter-firm factors as antecedents of alliance performance. Consequently, they posit that firms that consistently generate above-average rents in alliances possess specific alliance capabilities (Alliance Analyst, 1996b; Kale and Singh, 1999; Anand and Khanna, 2000; Kale et al., 2002; Bamford and Ernst, 2003). Overall, these studies underscore the need to develop an alliance capability in order to enhance the performance of a firm's alliance portfolio. Consequently, following Lorenzoni and Baden-Fuller (1995), Anand and Vassolo (2002), Bamford and Ernst (2002) and Parise and Casher (2003), a firm's alliance portfolio rather than the individual alliance becomes the unit of analysis. Whereas dyadic or inter-firm antecedents literature by nature centres on critical factors influencing the individual alliance, intra-firm antecedents literature investigates the influence of firm-specific alliance capabilities that by nature are likely to influence a firm's entire portfolio of alliances. Hence, no longer are the antecedents of performance optimization in the individual alliance the topic under investigation. Rather, it is the influence of firm-specific capabilities on a firm's alliance portfolio that has become of central concern.

A remarkable observation made in recent contributions to the intra-firm antecedents literature is that firms develop alliance capabilities in different ways. Some firms have proven to be able to better capitalize on their alliances than others as they consistently generate above-average rents (see e.g. Kanter, 1994; Harbison and Pekar, 1998b; Madhok and Tallman, 1998; Anand and Khanna, 2000). Furthermore, in this respect, research has shown that firms can commit to various mechanisms depending on the task at hand (Zollo and Winter, 2002). Different mechanisms, such as grafting, congenital learning, searching and noticing, experiential and vicarious learning are available to firms to foster learning (Huber, 1991, cited in Tsang, 2002a). Although these mechanisms differ in their effectiveness, each of them can be at the root of a firm's alliance capability (Reuer et al., 2002a). This is confirmed by numerous examples of firms that successfully manage alliances in very different ways (see e.g. Alliance Analyst, 1994, 1999b; Spekman et al., 1999; Takeishi, 2001; Bamford et al., 2003). Some firms prefer to use firm-specific material, while others use generalized alliance knowledge in their quest for increased alliance performance (Alliance Analyst, 1994; Margulis and Pekar, 2001). For instance, on the one hand, pharmaceutical firms such as Eli Lilly and Alza are known for their dedicated efforts to promote alliance management as critical element of business success. These firms have installed an alliance department and are highly committed to best practice dispersal using alliance trainings (Sims et al., 2003; Alza Corporation, 2004). Corning, which is a United States-based technology company, on the other hand, mainly uses informal communication to leverage alliance experience (Alliance Analyst, 1994). Hence, it appears that investments made to increase a firm's alliance capability should fit a firm's specific needs (Alliance Analyst, 1994). This implies that the principle of equifinality may apply to the development of an alliance capability, since firms can develop alliance capabilities in different ways and this development is path-dependent (Eisenhardt and Martin, 2000). The way in which they develop alliance capabilities can differ depending on the firm's current resource endowments and historical commitments.

In line with the logic of this observation, alliance experience has become a central and recurrent theme in intra-firm antecedents literature. Experience stands for the firm's ability to manage alliances and to act upon unforeseen pitfalls using the skills developed as a result of prior experience. Maidique and Zirger (1985, cited in Garvin, 1987: 61) underline that 'the knowledge gained from failures [is] often instrumental in achieving subsequent successes...In the simplest terms, failure is the ultimate teacher'. In the same vein, Kleiner and Roth (1987: 137) suggest, 'insights are rarely shared openly...Why? Because managers have few tools with which to capture institutional experience, disseminate its lessons, and translate them into effective action.' These quotes underline the obvious need for firms to ensure that prior experiences are disseminated. Assuming that the proportion of a firm's experience is directly related to the number of alliances it has been involved in, a firm's alliance experience is often measured as the number of prior alliances. Some studies even assume alliance capabilities to be equivalent to alliance experience (see e.g. Kale et al., 2002; Li and Rowley, 2002). Similarly, Nti and Kumar (2001) reckon that the volume of alliance knowledge created is a critical aspect of a firm's capability. The more alliances a firm has been engaged in, the greater its exposure to potential instances to learn and gather knowledge on how to manage alliances. In these studies, experience serves as a proxy for a firm's alliance capability in order for scholars to be able to understand enduring and systematic alliance performance differences. In this way, research has been able to contrast firms with low and high experience levels in order to verify to what degree this variable has an impact on alliance performance.

Various theories frequently and explicitly refer to experience as a critical concept to understand persistent firm performance differences. For instance, organizational learning theory suggests experience to be a key variable in understanding learning curve differences among firms (see e.g. Lapré et al., 2000). Alliance experience is generally posted and found to positively influence alliance performance (Chan et al., 1997; Anand and Khanna, 2000; Hoang et al., 2002). However, firms do not necessarily continue to form alliances over time, which implies that experience does not need to follow a linear or upward trajectory (Oliver, 2001). Moreover, Hoang (2001) has found that other factors, such as the ability to integrate and leverage alliance knowledge, affect future alliance formation. Recently, this has been confirmed both conceptually (De Man, 2001) and empirically (Simonin, 1997; Kale and Singh, 1999; Kale et al., 2002; Draulans et al., 2003). These findings suggest that, in addition to experience, other factors are involved that influence a firm's alliance capability. However, although various scholars have put forth experience as a critical factor for alliance performance (e.g. Powell et al., 1996; Gulati, 1999), the links between critical concepts such as experience and alliance capability have not been clearly established (Dosi et al., 2000b; Rugman and Verbeke, 2002). Despite the fact that experience is often used as a proxy for a firm's alliance capability (Kale et al., 2002), it does not fully reflect the difficulty of developing such a capability since it does not stipulate the key ingredients needed to develop it (Simonin, 1997).

In spite of evidence that confirms accumulated experience can have a positive influence on learning (Pisano et al., 2001), to date little attention has been devoted to how firms can develop an alliance capability in order to leverage their alliance performance. Although studies have repeatedly pointed to experience as critical performance antecedent, these contributions lack micro-level specificity and scrutiny with respect to the internal process underlying the development of an alliance capability. Some recent exceptions specify a number of mechanisms that firms should employ in order to realize the potential learning effects that eventually enhance alliance performance (e.g. Nault and Tyagi, 2001; Hoang et al., 2002; Kale et al., 2002; Tsang, 2002b; Sarkar et al., 2004). For instance, Tsang (2002b) finds that sharing of joint venture experience among managers is a key instrument to raise the lessons learned from an individual to an institutional level. It is suggested that an alliance capability results from an internal process in which the use of such mechanisms enables firms to share and disperse experience-related knowledge. This internal process is often suggested

Introduction 9

to involve routines, which help firms to efficiently perform certain tasks (Nelson and Winter, 1982). An alliance capability then refers to the underlying institutionalized managerial mechanisms used to accumulate alliance knowledge inside the individual firm and which facilitates the alliance capability development process (Kale and Singh, 1999). Moreover, Anand and Khanna (2000) underline that the creation of an alliance capability demands formalization of processes by which a firm can systemize the acquisition or development of knowledge relevant to managing alliances.

Hence, although recent research has started to try and solve the causal ambiguity between alliance management practices and performance outcomes, little micro-level evidence has so far emerged. Detailed studies on the exact contents of an alliance capability and how firms can internally nurture it are virtually non-existent (Gulati, 1998). Most scholars deduce the existence of an alliance capability from a firm's prior alliance experience or from a higher level of performance between firms that frequently re-partner or other indirect measurements (see e.g. Anand and Khanna, 2000; Zollo and Reuer, 2003). The operationalizations and constructs of these studies often remain equivocal. Leaving some notable exceptions aside (Makhija and Ganesh, 1997; Nault and Tyagi, 2001; Zahra and Nielsen, 2002), so far scholars' attempts to discern how firms develop such a capability have remained scarce (Simonin, 1997; Sarkar et al., 2004) and little is known about the mechanisms that make up such a capability (Thomke and Kuemmerle, 2002). Moreover, the relationships between experience, capability and performance have remained complex and obscure (Dosi et al., 2000b; Rugman and Verbeke, 2002).

1.3 Problem definition

As mentioned before, scholars and practitioners alike have so far been largely unable to fully grasp the driving forces behind the edge generated by some firms as a result of their alliance capabilities. However, although firms use different practices when it comes to managing alliances (see e.g. Hill and Hellriegel, 1994), some firms consistently realize above-average returns on their alliances (Madhok and Tallman, 1998; Anand and Khanna, 2000). Therefore, articulating the key factors involved in alliance capability development has recently become a challenge to scholars in the field of alliances. Building on recent attempts by scholars committed to uncovering intra-firm antecedents of alliance performance, this book tries to seek for the building blocks of an alliance capability by focusing on the internal process through which a firm can share and institutionalize experience and to what extent this contributes to the development of an alliance capability. The central research question is therefore defined as: *How do firms develop alliance capabilities?*

This book tries to answer this question by examining the internal process underlying the development of an alliance capability for the individual firm. Although we know that for instance an alliance department can play a central role when firms develop alliance capabilities (Kale et al., 2002), little empirical evidence has been found to substantiate and extend the role of intra-firm mechanisms. To be able to answer the central research question, the following three issues will have to be analysed.

The phenomenon called alliance capabilities

The first issue relates to the question what alliance capabilities entail. Very little is known about what actually constitutes a so-called 'alliance capability' or how it comes about. The relative obscurity of the phenomenon leaves practitioners and scholars alike wondering how to develop such a capability (Gulati, 1998; Simonin, 1997; Dosi et al., 2000b). Hence, in order to lay the foundation for the main research question, the following question should be answered: *What are alliance capabilities?*

Over the years, some authors have stressed the need to look beyond mere alliance or collaborative experience in order to understand how some firms consistently outperform their peers (e.g. Lyles, 1988; Simonin, 1997). As a consequence, recently others have investigated intra-firm concepts involving knowledge and learning capacity, thereby seeking to define such issues as alliance competence (Spekman et al., 1999; Lambe et al., 2002), collaborative know-how (Simonin, 2002) or advantage (Dyer, 2000) and alliance capabilities (Alliance Analyst, 1996a; Harbison and Pekar, 1998a; Anand and Khanna, 2000; Draulans et al., 2003; Kale et al., 2002; Bamford and Ernst, 2003). These issues all relate to a firm's ability to absorb knowledge on alliance management or 'the capacity to learn' (Hamel et al., 1989) (see Table 2.1 for a complete overview). As firms continue to form alliances, the ability to successfully manage them becomes increasingly important. Therefore, the third chapter will elaborate on the nature of the phenomenon called alliance capabilities. This will be done relying on an extensive literature review which concerns both alliance-related studies and an analysis of the underlying theories.

Micro-level understanding of alliance capabilities

Having looked in detail at the phenomenon itself, the second issue concerns specificity at the micro-level of what alliance capabilities are. As both practitioners and scholars acknowledge that alliance capabilities are a major issue for firms to consider (Anand and Khanna, 2000; Corporate Strategy Board, 2000), it became increasingly clear that little was known about their origins (Singh, 2003). Even as interests in fundamental theories such as resource-based theory gained salience, little attention was paid to understand the micro-level elements that lie at the roots of capability development (Henderson, 1995; Kusunoki et al., 1998; Montealegre, 2002). Even more so, little is known about the specific nature of how firms develop *alliance* capabilities.

Intrigued by this topic itself, so far various authors have investigated capabilities as a distinctive resource explaining rent distribution (e.g. Prahalad and Hamel, 1990; Madhok and Tallman, 1998; Metcalfe and James, 2000), while others have looked at the impact of firm capabilities on industry evolution (e.g. Jacobides and Winter, 2004). However, as mentioned earlier, fairly limited insight has been gained into the development of alliance capabilities. We follow scholars such as Simonin (1997, 2002), Kale et al. (2002) and Knott (2003), who recently have performed advanced research in this direction. Their efforts have been directed to truly uncover the complexity of the micro-level nature of alliance capability development. In line with these studies, we argue that it is of great importance to investigate the intra-firm mechanisms firms use to manage alliances to understand how alliance capabilities are developed. The second sub-question is defined as: *What is the influence of (groups of) intra-firm mechanisms on alliance performance?*

In Chapter 4, we therefore examine the impact of intra-firm mechanisms such as functions, tools, control and management processes and external parties on alliance performance, arguing that these mechanisms help disperse alliance-related knowledge throughout the organization. Relying on expert input and panel reviews, a list of thirty intra-firm mechanisms was constructed. This list was then used to compare 192 firms worldwide. Subsequently, these mechanisms are tested both individually and in factor analytic ways. Moreover, twelve experts from practice and academia in the area of alliances and capability development were interviewed providing us with their insights on the subject. Doing this, we expect to contribute to the current literature in a number of ways. First, it highlights the ability to shape alliance success voluntaristically by installing intra-firm mechanisms that help disperse alliance-related knowledge. We argue that these intra-firm mechanisms play an important role in creating the firm's ability to successfully manage alliances in addition to dyadic issues such as commitment and trust. Second, and perhaps most importantly, it helps us resolve, as King and Zeithalm (2001: 75) put it, the conundrum of the relationship between alliance capabilities and alliance performance. Hence, it may provide a gateway to solving (some of) the causal ambiguity and obscurity surrounding alliance capabilities.

The alliance capability development process

Having looked at the (groups of) intra-firm mechanisms and their relationship with alliance performance, it remains unclear what the internal process looks like that helps develop alliance capabilities (Gulati, 1998; Kale and Singh, 1999). Given the causal ambiguity surrounding processes related to capability development, recently scholarly efforts and interests have been directed at substantiating what elements are involved in developing capabilities and how these interrelate. Despite a recent study by Simonin (1997), which analyses the way in which firms internalize collaborative know-how, and different conceptual studies (e.g. Crossan et al., 1999; Zollo and Winter, 2002), it remains unclear how firms can internally develop alliance capabilities. Therefore, the third and last issue that helps answer the research question pertains to the alliance capability development process: *What is the relationship between the critical concepts in the alliance capability development process?*

In Chapter 5, we suggest that alliance experience, alliance capabilities and alliance performance are linked. We will argue that alliance experience and alliance capabilities positively influence alliance performance and that alliance capabilities mediate between alliance experience and performance. We expect that firms that make extensive use of intra-firm mechanisms to disperse alliance knowledge will be more likely to successfully manage alliances due to the widespread availability of critical knowledge gained via prior experiences. On the other hand, firms with less alliance experience and which use only a couple of intra-firm mechanisms to disperse knowledge are expected to be less successful. The main contribution of this chapter lies in understanding the internal process of alliance capability development.

The three sub-questions serve to answer the central research question. However, before the first sub-question is investigated, the theories related to the topic of central concern are discussed in the Chapter 2. We follow the theoretical logic of recent contributions by Fujimoto (1999), Kale et al. (2002), Zollo et al. (2002) and Helfat and Peteraf (2003), who build on a multitude of theories. Therefore, we propose that, in order to grasp the micro-level elements of alliance capabilities, internal or intra-firms factors that foster knowledge sharing on critical alliance performance antecedents are investigated. This book's approach is novel in two ways. First, the role of alliance experience and mechanisms is investigated *across a portfolio* of alliances. So far, apart from exceptions like Anand and Khanna (2000), Anand and Vassolo (2002) and Sarkar et al. (2004) and apart from the literature on alliance networks (e.g. Nohria and Eccles, 1992), alliance research was directed at the dyadic level. Second, and more importantly, we follow a recent trend when it comes to measuring a firm's capabilities. In line with the logic proposed by Gittell (2002), Kale et al. (2002), Simonin (2002), Bamford and Ernst (2003), Knott (2003) and Miller (2003), an alliance capability is supposed to consist of the institutionalized managerial mechanisms a firm has in place to manage its alliances and optimize its alliance performance. These mechanisms facilitate the accumulation, codification and sharing of knowledge related to managing alliances gained through experience (Kale and Singh, 1999; Kale et al., 2002). While the logic underlying the measurement of a firm's capability has been suggested by various scholars (i.e. consisting of a composite of a firm's mechanisms), it has only been very scarcely applied. In this book, mechanisms are divided into a number of categories: (1) functions (e.g. alliance department, vice-president), (2) tools (e.g. alliance trainings, partner programme), (3) control and management processes (e.g. alliance metrics, reward and bonus systems) and (4) use of external parties (e.g. consultants, mediators). In total, thirty mechanisms are identified and defined that may influence alliance performance. Using this recently introduced way to operationalize the central concept of this study, we hope to gain additional insight into how firms develop alliance capabilities.

The central research question thus allows for a number of contributions, which are theory-oriented and contain a number of managerial implications (Verschuren and Doorewaard, 1999). First, with respect to the theoretical contributions, this book intends to extend the current understanding of intra-firm antecedents of alliance performance. Literature on intra-firm antecedents has only recently been initiated

(Hoang, 2001) and is in its infancy in comparison to inter-firm antecedents literature. It can thus be seen as the beginning of a new stream of alliance research, which proposes a new viewpoint on the critical determinants of successful alliance management. Therefore, since only a limited number of studies has recently investigated alliance capability development, the contributions of this book in that respect can be significant. Intra-firm mechanisms are used to quantitatively analyse the impact of a firm's alliance capability on alliance performance. Given the relative youth of this field of study and the complexity of the topic under investigation, this book relies on a mix of theoretical underpinnings to shed light on the alliance capability development process. It links different concepts that were previously treated as theoretically distinct and tested as unrelated constructs. In this way, the potential theoretical contributions are highly relevant as the book seeks to extend current understanding of the ingredients of the alliance capability development process.

Second, the insights of this book may contribute to managerial literature as it embodies a number of managerial implications. First, it may help understand the necessity of developing an alliance capability and the criticality of certain mechanisms in contributing to do so. Given the rise in the number of alliances formed over the last years and the increase in revenues generated via alliances, it will become ever more important for firms to understand the role alliance capabilities play and how they can develop alliance capabilities. In addition to insight into the process underlying alliance capability development, testing for the contribution of mechanisms also implies that management can directly distil what contribution each mechanism makes to enhance a firm's alliance performance. So, it can help underline the necessity for investing in certain mechanisms, while other mechanisms may prove to be less effective in realizing performance gains in alliances. In this respect, we expect to define various managerial contributions that may prove to be significant for a firm's alliance management strategy.

1.4 Study design

The qualitative analysis in this book consists of two aspects: (1) a literature review and analysis of theories relevant to the current study and (2) expert interviews. Given the complexity of the topic, the literature review and theory analysis comprise an important part of the analysis. A mix of theories is used to provide for solid theoretical underpinnings. Chapter 2 presents a framework of theories central to this book and discusses its contributions to alliance research. In Chapter 3, we discuss the critical concepts that follow from the theories central to this book and which are critical to understanding alliance capabilities. In deducting the main concepts necessary to comprehend the phenomenon called alliance capabilities from the theoretical framework, we reckon that this helps grasp the complexity of the phenomenon. Another qualitative aspect relates to the expert interviews performed. Twelve experts in the field of alliances and capability development were interviewed to verify our empirical results and extend the argumentation for our findings (Yin, 1994; Remenyi et al., 1998). Semi-structured interviews were used to interview these experts, of which seven were from a practical background and five from an academic background (see Appendix 2 for an overview of experts interviewed). These interviews primarily allowed us to better comprehend the nature of alliance capabilities and how firms handle alliance capability development in practice.

This book also relies on a quantitative analysis to achieve its objectives. A survey was sent out to 650 Vice-Presidents of alliances and alliance managers worldwide, who were responsible for managing and overseeing the firm's alliance portfolio. A database of the Association of Strategic Alliance Professionals (ASAP) and the Dutch Internet Society (ISOC) was used to direct our survey to these persons. The cross-sectional dataset consisted of 192 respondents and was analysed using SPSS 10.0, thereby applying various statistical methods such as discriminant analysis and logistic regression. Using these methods, we expect to get an insight into the intra-firm mechanisms that help disseminate alliance-related knowledge and the degree to which these capabilities influence alliance performance.

The remainder of this book consists of five chapters. After the introduction, Chapter 2 provides an extensive literature review on the antecedents of alliance performance and theories fundamental to these studies. This allows us to better understand why alliance capabilities are important to the firm's existence and introduce the main concepts critical to alliance capability development. Chapter 3 describes the main concepts and the nature of alliance capabilities. The description and discussion of these concepts rely on the theoretical underpinnings presented in Chapter 2 and provide the basis for the empirical analyses of this study. Chapter 4 presents the results of an empirical analysis of the influence of mechanisms on alliance performance. This analysis entails both an item-level as well as a scale-level analysis to understand how firms disperse knowledge gained in prior alliances. This, I argue, should give a clear impression of what role intra-firm mechanisms play in a firm's alliance capability. Chapter 5 analyses the relationships between the main concepts in this book. Whereas Chapter 4 investigates only the influence of (groups of) mechanisms, this chapter analyses the sequence of the entire model containing experience, capabilities and performance. The last chapter summarizes, concludes and puts into perspective the results by emphasizing its implications, limitations and possibilities for future investigations.

2
A Literature Review of Alliance Research

2.1 Introduction

Over the past decades, a vast amount of literature has evolved around the topic of alliances. Scholars have analysed this topic referring to different theoretical backgrounds thereby increasing our understanding of antecedents of alliance performance. Scholars from varying backgrounds, such as sociology, marketing, strategic management, operations management, economics and organization theory, have developed vast amounts of literature on this topic (Barringer and Harrison, 2000). Analysing early and more recent literature on alliances, a clear development over time can be identified. This chapter discusses the differences between early alliance research, which is mainly concerned with the role of inter-firm antecedents of alliance performance, and more recent alliance research that has been occupied with uncovering intra-firm antecedents. The remainder of this chapter will introduce and discuss the theories underlying this book as well as their contributions on the basis of which the theoretical framework of the study is constructed.

2.2 Early alliance research

Initially, traditional strategy perspectives such as transaction cost economics and industrial organization theory were used to understand the antecedents of alliance performance (e.g. Coase, 1937; Williamson, 1993; Madhok, 2002; David and Han, 2004). The logic that follows from these theories is one wherein firms were in general considered to be individual, self-fulfilling units (Williamson, 1975, 1991) that prefer going alone over cooperative agreements (Contractor and Lorange, 1988). Alliances were viewed as separate business cases that were to be studied primarily from a dyadic or firm-level perspective, which means looking at a single alliance (Duysters et al., 1999b; Kale and Singh, 1999). Consequently, most alliance research viewed alliances as single transactions that are pursued to overcome market failure and industrial constraints.[1] Typically, studies building on these traditional theories centre on critical success or failure factors related to competitive issues between the partners (Kogut, 1988; Bleeke and Ernst, 1991, 1995; Parkhe, 1993; for an overview see Das and Teng, 2000b). As alliances were viewed as distinct business transactions, researchers following this theoretical logic tend to focus on critical aspects idiosyncratic to the alliance (e.g. Koza and Lewin, 2000). More specifically, alliance-specific and relational or behavioral factors are often suggested to compose a group of critical antecedents of alliance performance. Different studies confirm that the choice of governance structure (Williamson, 1985; Pisano, 1989), partner fit or symmetry (Geringer, 1991; Medcof, 1997; Harrigan, 1988b) and trust and complementarity (Johnson et al., 1996; Nooteboom et al., 1997; Luo, 2002a) significantly influence the quality of the relationship between the partners. For instance, trust, or the expectation that partners will behave cooperatively, can substantially reduce transaction costs (Boersma, 1999). The degree of trust required varies by relationship (Parkhe, 1998: 222) and tends to also vary within the hierarchy; it tends to be stable at the top of the organization and more fluid at lower levels (Zaheer et al., 1998). Moreover, Luo (2002a) finds that trust becomes a more important performance determinator in case the alliance is relatively young; risks are evenly spread between partners; markets are less volatile; resource dependency between the partners is greater and commitment by the partners is higher. Trust then should be considered as an important determinant of alliance performance (Aulakh et al., 1996; Cullen et al., 2000). Various studies have tried to define a recipe for successful alliance management, thereby trying to uncover critical issues between the partners involved (Harrigan, 1988b). In general, concepts such as relational advantage (Dyer and Singh, 1998) or collaborative advantage (Kanter, 1994) have been suggested to explain for instance a firm's ability to generate collaboration-specific rents (Madhok and Tallman, 1998) or common benefits (Khanna et al., 1998) in single relationships. Overall, in this stream of alliance research the dyadic or inter-firm factors are the topic under investigation and are suggested to significantly impact alliance performance. Duysters et al. (1999a) provide an overview of failure reasons, which is represented in Figure 2.1. This figure shows what scholars have identified as a particular

Author \ Reasons for failure	Goals/strategy	Partner/partnership	Strong–weak/weak–weak partner	Culture (nationality/corporate)	Trust	Love at first sight	Geographic/operational overlap	Personnel	Commitment	Expectations/time pressure	Alliance evolution (no recognition)	Incentives (asymmetric)	Complexity	Learning aspects (uneven)	Financial aspects
Kanter		✓				✓									
Dacin & Hitt		✓					✓		✓						
Medcof		✓													
Khanna et al.											✓	✓			
Niederkofler	✓			✓	✓			✓	✓						
Bleeke & Ernst				✓			✓		✓						
Adarkar				✓											
Maljers	✓			✓	✓		✓								
Douma	✓	✓											✓		
Stafford	✓			✓	✓	✓				✓					
Wildeman & Kok	✓	✓			✓			✓			✓				
Chevallier	✓	✓							✓						
Schuler et al.			✓		✓	✓									
Brouthers et al.								✓							
Lorange & Roos	✓		✓					✓				✓		✓	
Beamish & Delios	✓														

Figure 2.1 Reasons for strategic alliance failure

Source: Duysters et al., 1999a.

reason for strategic alliance failure. The failure factors which result from this research tend to be little specific in providing explanations as to why some firms consistently outperform others in alliances (Park and Ungson, 2001). As most alliance research dedicated to uncovering inter-firm factors influencing alliance performance looks at alliances as single transactions, their contributions are especially aimed at uncovering critical success factors for managing individual alliances. Little attention has therefore been devoted to explicate how firms can internally nurture or institutionalize the knowledge embodied in these critical success factors so as to positively influence a firm's overall ability to successfully manage alliances.

In spite of the contributions made by these studies, they seem to fall short of stipulating how firms can internalize the ability to yield above-average returns on their alliance portfolio. Some scholars even suggested that a dyadic perspective was inappropriate or incomplete for scientific study in alliance research, as it leaves little room for understanding how firms can increase their alliance success in general (Anderson et al., 1994; Duysters et al., 1999b). In other words, studies following the traditional or dyadic logic are only able to partially explain the reported fixed-firm effects in individual firm's alliance performance. To fully grasp what the critical alliance performance antecedents are, we also need to understand the processes and mechanisms underlying successful alliance management. So, whereas inter-firm factors have received overwhelming scholarly attention over the past, intra-firm factors are only recently given attention. Moreover, while both groups of factors contribute distinct insights into the antecedents of alliance performance, they may complement each other (Ireland et al., 2002).[2]

2.3 Recent alliance research

As a result, scholars have recently extended the theoretical logic in alliance research. Lately some scholars have started to focus on firm-specific or intra-firm factors to explain fixed-firm performance differences. These recent studies have proven to be a suitable complement to traditional theories (Henderson and Cockburn, 1994), as they attempt to complement research on inter-firm factors or failure factors by investigating such issues as firms' assets or resources which aid in managing alliances over a longer period of time and which are not alliance-specific (see e.g. Draulans et al., 2003). These studies refer to the need to create an alliance capability (Kale and Singh, 1999; Anand and Khanna, 2000; Kale et al., 2002), which can act as a means to gain competitive advantage for the firm possessing them (De Man, 2001). Moreover, they posit that firm-specific alliance capabilities may allow firms to consistently generate above-average rents in alliances (Kale and Singh, 1999). Dedicated assets and mechanisms, for example, the use of an 'alliance function or department', are suggested to have a positive effect on alliance performance (Kale et al., 2002). The gradual shift in scientific logic underlying alliance research that has occurred over the past years is represented in Figure 2.2. This figure shows that, while early alliance research emphasized factors explaining rent optimization in individual alliances, recent scholars try to uncover firm-specific capabilities that help leapfrog the performance of the entire firm's alliance portfolio and therefore explain persistent fixed-firm differences in alliance performance.

As follows from Figure 2.2, recent alliance research investigates the role of internal organizational attributes, such as organizational structure, managerial processes and routines. These intra-firm factors form the basis for firm-specific capabilities that are difficult for other firms to buy or imitate (Leonard-Barton, 1992; Teece and Pisano, 1994; Henderson and Cockburn, 1994; Eisenhardt and Martin, 2000). More specifically, the internal infrastructure that supports alliance activities and the way

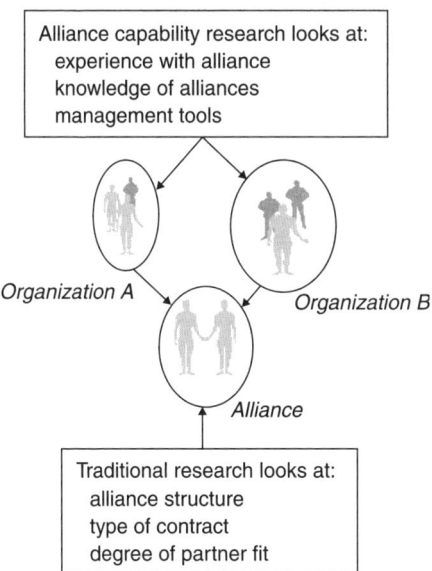

Figure 2.2 Early (inter-firm) versus recent (intra-firm) alliance research
Source: Draulans et al., 1999.

in which this infrastructure enhances alliance performance is a key issue in these studies (Kanter, 1994; Dyer, 2000; Bamford and Ernst, 2003). Besides conceptual or case-based evidence (*Alliance Analyst*, 1994; Harbison and Pekar, 1998b; Clegg, 1999; Kale and Singh, 1999; Sims et al., 2003), a limited number of recent studies empirically validate that the development of alliance capabilities can significantly accelerate a firm's ability to derive value from alliances (Simonin, 1997; Kale et al., 2002; Draulans et al., 2003). These studies allow for a better understanding of the influence of certain intra-firm mechanisms and routines on capability development and alliance performance.

Recent studies have opted for a different unit of analysis in comparison to earlier studies. Whereas in earlier studies the dyad was the topic under investigation, recently some scholars use the firm's alliance portfolio as unit of analysis. Looking at a portfolio of alliances not only helps firms to reduce complexity, but also enables them to share knowledge to leverage the performance of all its alliances. More importantly, taking the firm's alliance portfolio as a unit of analysis is more appropriate when trying to assess the impact of specific capabilities on performance than using individual alliance performance (Anand and Vassalo, 2002; Sarkar et al., 2004). Concentrating on alliance capabilities, these studies have used and applied different theories that are complementary to theories underlying early research investigating inter-firm factors. While early investigations mainly built on transaction cost economics and industrial organization theory, the vast majority of recent investigations have relied on a mix of theories in which a few theories have a dominant stake (see Table 2.1).[3]

2.4 Theoretical underpinnings of recent alliance research

Analysing the influence of alliance resources, assets, mechanisms or capabilities on alliance performance, recent studies investigating alliance capabilities mainly rely on theories such as the resource-based view, dynamic capability view, competence-based view, knowledge-based view, evolutionary economics and organizational learning.[4] Although distinct in origin (for a comparison see Das and Teng, 2000b; Sanchez, 2001a), the theories recently applied to investigate alliance capabilities are highly related (Foss, 1997b) and make specific contributions to understanding the intriguing phenomenon called alliance capabilities. As this book follows recent investigations into alliance capabilities by building on a multitude of theories, it is important to

Table 2.1 Prior research on alliance capabilities

Author(s)	Theoretical perspective	Concepts	Conceptualization	Empirical validation	Outcomes
Lyles (1988)	OL	Strategic capability	Past JV experience and the methods used for transference of learning	Interviews among 4 firms with JV experience	JV sophisticated firms make extensive use of decision rules, best practices, structures, reporting systems, management methods
Simonin (1997)	OL, DCV, CBV	Collaborative know-how	Five dimensions: collaborative management, negotiation, partner searching know-how, knowledge and skill transfer, exiting skills	Survey of 151 large and medium-sized US firms from different industries	The higher the level of collaborative know-how, the greater the tangible and intangible benefits obtained; experience does not directly influence benefits
Dyer and Singh (1998)	KBV, DCV	Relational capability	A firm's willingness and ability to partner	None, conceptual	Relational capabilities or relation-building skills are argued to be necessary to employ effective governance mechanisms, create relation-specific assets and develop knowledge-sharing routines
Gulati (1999)	RBV, economic sociology	Alliance formation capability	Experience as number of past alliances, diversity of governance modes and nationality of partners firms in past alliances	2400 alliances formed by 166 firms, 1980–1989	Experience was found to increase likelihood of alliance formation; diversity of alliances has no influence on performance

Continued

Table 2.1 Continued

Author(s)	Theoretical perspective	Concepts	Conceptualization	Empirical validation	Outcomes
Kale and Singh (1999)	OL, KBV, DCV	Alliance capability	Alliance capability measured as the coordinative capacity and processes for articulation, codification, sharing and internalization of alliance-related knowledge	Survey of 160 US firms in different industries where alliances are key to firm strategy	Coordinative capacity and knowledge management processes positively influence alliance performance; alliance experience also has direct effect, but significance reduces upon inclusion of the knowledge variables
Lorenzoni and Lipparini (1999)	OL, RBV	Relational capabilities	Changes in the lead firms supplier networks towards fewer but closer suppliers; development of specialized supplier network while building a smaller, more focused set of core competences	Exploratory, longitudinal case studies of three lead firm-network relationships in Italy	Relational capabilities help competence renewal and reduce resistance to change; lead firms can achieve valuable positions using multiple formal ties for knowledge access and transfer; collaboration is valuable to expand and improve core competences
Anand and Khanna (2000)	OL, DCV	Alliance capability	Estimation of firm-fixed effects over and above alliance experience to capture unobserved heterogeneity in firm-level alliance capability	Secondary data on 1976 JVs and licensing agreements	Results show strong and persistent differences across firms in their ability to create value in alliances; the authors interpret this as differences in alliance capabilities

Author	Theory	Construct	Definition/Operationalization	Sample	Main findings
Sivadas and Dwyer (2000)	TCE, CBV, innovation management	Cooperative competence	Composite variable of trust, communication, coordination, governance and administrative mechanisms, partner type, mutual dependence, innovation type and institutional support	Survey of 56 semiconductor and 50 health care firms	Results show significant impact of cooperative competence on performance measure (used NPD success)
Hoang et al. (2002)	Organization theory	Alliance capability	General and partner-specific alliance experience	Survey of 30 firms with 145 alliances in pharmaceuticals	While general experience does positively influence alliance performance, partner-specific experience does not.
Kale, Dyer and Singh (2002)	RBV, DCV	Alliance capability	The presence (X = 1) or absence (X = 0) of an alliance function	Survey of 78 firms and their 1572 alliances	Both experience and investment in a dedicated alliance function are found to positively influence performance
Lambe, Spekman and Hunt (2002)	CBV, RBV	Alliance competence	Alliance competence as organizational ability to find, develop and manage alliances: alliance experience, alliance manager development capability and partner identification propensity	Survey among 145 alliances from 71 different firms	Joint alliance competence is directly positively related to alliance performance and indirectly via the combination of complementary resources in an alliance and the creation of idiosyncratic resources in the alliance

Continued

Table 2.1 Continued

Author(s)	Theoretical perspective	Concepts	Conceptualization	Empirical validation	Outcomes
Zollo, Reuer and Singh (2002)	RBV, DCV, EE	Inter-organizational routines	Inter-organizational routines are stable patterns of interaction among two firms developed and refined in the course of action	Survey among 145 alliances from 81 biotech and pharmaceutical firms	Partner-specific outcomes positively influences performance; from this, the authors derive that this experience influences the extent to which partners accumulate knowledge, create new growth opportunities and achieve objectives

CBV – Competence-based view; DCV – Dynamic capability view; EE – Evolutionary economics; KBV – Knowledge-based view; NPD – New product development; OL – Organizational learning theory; RBV – Resource-based view; TCE – Transaction cost economics.

Source: (adapted from) Schreiner and Corsten, 2003.

clearly delineate the basic premises of each theory and what theory makes what specific contribution to understanding the phenomenon called 'alliance capability'. The following theories are important and are discussed in a more extensive fashion: (1) the resource-based view, (2) the dynamic capability view, (3) the competence-based view, (4) the knowledge-based view, (5) evolutionary economics and (6) organizational learning theory (see Table 2.2 for an overview of authors and contributions of the various theories).

Figure 2.3 presents the theoretical framework of this study in which the main theories are depicted. It shows each of the theories and provides the basis for this book's purposes. However, it does not pretend to specify all relationships between the theories involved. Before we stipulate what fundamental contribution each theory makes to the field of strategic management and organization science in general and how they interrelate, the particular contribution of each theory to this study is shortly described. First, the RBV is included in the main theoretical framework of this study because we reckon it delineates why resource endowments (i.e. tangible and intangible assets) cause performance differences and why firms exist (Williamson and Winter, 1993). Similarly, the DCV and CBV respectively point to how capabilities and competences cause competitive heterogeneity. These theories go beyond the

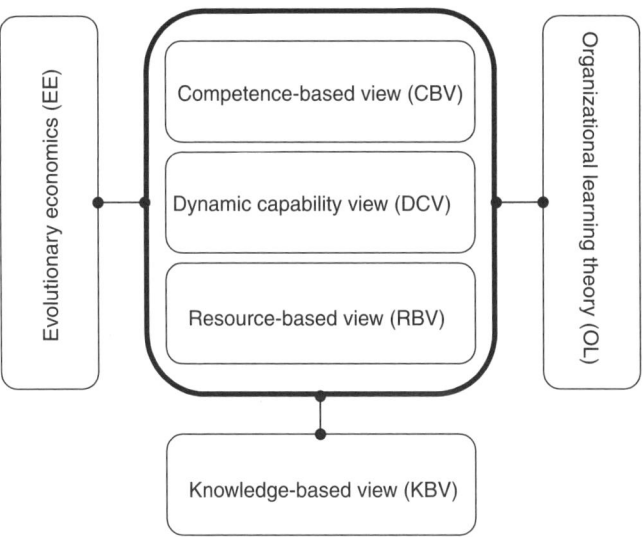

Figure 2.3 Theoretical framework

essential contribution of the RBV as they not only explain why markets and firms are different, but also why even firms in closely related markets differ (Wernerfelt, 1984; Barney, 1991; Foss, 1997b). In other words, whereas the RBV underpins the equilibrium or exchange aspect of the firm, the DCV and CBV are more related to the process or transformation aspect of the firm (Metcalfe and James, 2000). In this respect, we concur with Foss (2000: 12), who identifies a schism in contemporary resource-based thinking. Traditionally or in its purest form, the RBV does not encapsulate a learning or evolutionary aspect. For this reason, both OL theory and EE play a central role in this thesis.[5]

Organizational learning theory addresses the question of *how* firms learn and how it can best distil and disseminate lessons from prior experiences (Vera and Crossan, 2003). Evolutionary economics, on the other hand, expands on the view that firms are largely heterogeneous entities, whose evolution depends on unique resource bases and routines and the tacit knowledge they accumulate (Nelson and Winter, 1982; Aldrich, 1999). It helps understand how firm-specific advantages are created through a portfolio of differential skills and routines that are sometimes hard to transfer and may create inertia and is therefore highly conducive to this book's purpose. Last, the KBV as a theory contributes to the purpose of this study, as it is knowledge that is the basic ingredient of intangible resources, capabilities and routines and hence essentially is the key inimitable resource of the firm (Leonard-Barton, 1992; Grant, 1996a; Lewin and Volberda, 1999).

The theoretical framework is designed in a certain way, which relates to the logic of the individual theories and to the purpose of this study. With respect to the logic of the framework a number of issues should be mentioned. First of all, Figure 2.3 shows that the theories of central concern (i.e. RBV, DCV and CBV) are presented in a hierarchical fashion. It is designed in such a way, because numerous scholars suggest that resource, capabilities and competences (i.e. a firm's endowments) are related as such (Hunt and Morgan, 1996; Mahoney and Sanchez, 1997; Sanchez and Heene, 1997; Makadok, 2001). Whereas a 'capability' is often suggested to reflect the ability of the firm to utilize its resources, a 'competence' (or dynamic capability) is related to the firm's ability to adjust the utilization of their resources and processes (e.g. Makadok, 2001).

Second, the KBV, OL theory and EE are linked to the hierarchy formed by the three theories of central concern. The framework links the KBV to these theories (i.e. RBV, DCV and CBV) because knowledge is a critical underpinning in each of these theories (Kogut and Zander, 1992; Zander and Kogut, 1995; Langlois, 1997; Teece et al., 1997). In her seminal work,

Penrose (1959) confirms this by stating: 'knowledge is probably the most important asset that firms possess- a key source of both Ricardian and monopoly rents' (in Rugman and Verbeke, 2002: 773). Knowledge is an essential element independent of the type of firm endowment investigated (i.e. resource, capability or competence), thereby linking together the RBV, DCV and CBV (Grant, 1995). The remaining two theories that are related to the hierarchy are OL theory and EE. In general, OL theory and EE are often used and applied to investigate developments or changes in a firm's endowments (see e.g. Inkpen and Dinur, 1998; Zollo et al., 2002). For instance, some studies apply OL theory to understand to what extent firms can absorb knowledge obtained from alliance partners (Khanna et al., 1998; Inkpen, 2000, 2002). Another example is a recent study by Zollo et al. (2002), who investigate the role of routines between alliance partners, which relates to the sharing of knowledge and resources, in explaining alliance performance differences among firms.

Third, besides potential direct links between the different theories in this study's eclectic framework, there are a number of examples of more complex interactions between theories as has been shown in numerous studies (Foss, 1997a). For instance, the RBV, DCV, CBV, KBV, EE and OL theory essentially are all related to the use and application of a firm's endowments. In doing so, they all refer to two key factors influencing competitive advantage: resources and organizational processes. Consequently, these five theories all propose a direct link between a firm's endowments and its competitive advantage (Takeishi, 2001). In this context, various scholars have maintained that the relationship between the KBV and DCV is apparent, as it is knowledge that makes up capabilities (Grant, 1996a; Langlois, 1997; Sanchez, 2001b). Another example relates to the DCV, EE and OL theory, which all share a dynamic or evolutionary aspect (see e.g. Zander and Kogut, 1995). Organizational learning theory suggests that learning is a process that through repetition and experience allows firms to perform better and improve production opportunities. This can be directly linked to the DCV and EE, since organizational processes need to be built (Teece et al., 1997) and new routines or patterns of interactions can emerge (Nelson and Winter, 1982; Nelson, 1997) which may represent successful solutions to problems apparent in the firm (Kogut and Zander, 1992).

Hence, as Figure 2.3 suggests, we view the firm as a collection of unique resources, capabilities, competences, mechanisms and routines that help explain performance differences and rent generation capacity in alliances thereby following recent studies by for instance Fujimoto (2000) and Knott (2003). We therefore rely on the theories mentioned, which we will now discuss in greater detail. First, the body of literature called the RBV plays a central role in the analysis of alliance capabilities as it does in strategic management literature in general.[6] Within the field of strategy research, the RBV states that the microeconomic equilibrium can be overcome by firms which hold superior resources and who have the isolating mechanisms in place to prevent diffusion of their resources (Rumelt, 1984). It emphasizes the role of resources in structuring the way business is performed (Madhok, 2002; Rugman and Verbeke, 2002). Its origins date back to Penrose (1959), which characterizes the firm as a collection of resources. A firm can gain competitive advantage by pursuing an effective selection of its collection of resources, also referred to as an effective resource-picking mechanism (Barney, 1986). However, in order to be able to provide for competitive advantage, resources should meet certain criteria (Peteraf, 1993). First, they should be heterogeneous, since homogeneity would not allow firms to differentiate (Williamson, 1985; Barney, 1991) nor to obtain above-market or Ricardian rents (Montgomery and Wernerfelt, 1997). Second, as a consequence of that, there should be ex ante limits to competition, which implies that resources have to be acquired at a price which is lower than its discounted net present value (Barney, 1986). Third, valuable firm resources are usually imperfectly imitable and characterized by a lack of direct substitutes (Lippman and Rumelt, 1982; Dierickx and Cool, 1989). Fourth, resources should be imperfectly mobile or relatively specific to the firm (Caves, 1980; Wernerfelt, 1984). Consequently, a firm's unique set of resources allows it to differentiate itself from competitors and therefore is paramount to a firm's competitive position (Foss, 1997a; Montgomery and Wernerfelt, 1997; Teece, 1997).

In addition to these characteristics of resources, a number of isolating mechanisms are at play which create barriers for competitors (Rumelt, 1984; for an overview see Mahoney and Pandian, 1992). These mechanisms are critical to understand that, although resources do not lack common features, causal ambiguity and a firm's inability to change strategic direction are a result of accumulated resources or 'stickiness' which create path dependency and firm heterogeneity (Hunt and Morgan, 1996; King and Zeithaml, 2001). Moreover, accumulating productive resources takes time and investments do not need to pay off in the very short run (Pacheco-de-Almeida and Zemsky, 2001). Overall, although it touches on some aspects put forward by organizational economics (Williamson, 1975; 1991; Porter, 1980; Foss, 1997a), the RBV can be said to be an 'introverted' perspective of the strategic management literature (Combs and Ketchen, 1999; Barney, 2002), as it emphasizes the role of specific (investments in) resources and the barriers these create, which allow firms to yield above-average rents. Alliance research has built on the RBV in two ways. First, alliances are seen as a vehicle to gain access to certain assets or resources (e.g. Hamel et al., 1989). This means that, if firms wish to nullify resource scarcity, trading and accumulation of resources become strategic necessities (Eisenhardt and Schoonhoven, 1996). Given the fact that certain resources are not perfectly tradable because of structural inertia (Thomke and Kuemmerle, 2002) or because they are difficult to separate from other resources or are embedded in organizations, market transactions, strategic alliances and mergers and acquisitions will be variously employed (Vanhaverbeke et al., 2002). Second, alliance research has outlined the role of dedicating specific resources to the alliance, which can positively influence alliance success and rent-yielding capacity of the alliance at hand (Madhok and Tallman, 1998; Das and Teng, 2000a; Harrison et al., 2002; Robins et al., 2002). This contribution in particular has aimed to resolve the causal ambiguity issue in relation to alliances by shedding light on the contribution of certain resources to improve alliance performance. Consequently, the RBV contributes to the theoretical underpinning of this study, since it underlines the basic need to pick or invest in the right resources in order to successfully manage alliances.

Second, the DCV stresses the importance of firm-specific capabilities as a source of inimitable and thus sustainable competitive advantage (Spanos and Lioukas, 2001). Introduced in the early 1980s, it points to the necessity for firms to build higher-order resources or capabilities (Makadok, 2001) and deploy resources in an efficient manner to create sustainable competitive advantage (Amit and Schoemaker, 1993). In this way, the productivity of these 'basic' resources can be improved by a special type of resource or capability. It adds that basic resources should interact with embedded organizational processes, which require continuous nurturing in order to provide competitive advantage (Oxtoby et al., 2002). Therefore, the very nature of a 'capability' diverges from that of a 'resource' in two ways (Makadok, 2001): (1) capabilities are difficult to obtain and copy, which makes them firm-specific and (2) they are accumulated through learning and therefore path-dependent. A capability is firm-specific because it is inherently linked to organizational processes and can therefore only be built and not acquired without acquiring the (entire unit of the) firm (Markides and Williamson, 1994; Teece et al., 1997). Capabilities can not therefore be easily assembled through markets (Teece, 1982; Kogut and Zander, 1992). Thus, although distinct, the DCV parallels the RBV as it underlines the firm's ability to deploy and renew its resources (Sanchez, 2001a).

The DCV stresses that competitive advantage arises from the distinctiveness with which a firm coordinates and combines its assets or endowments and succeeds in advancing these along a dynamic and evolutionary path (Sanchez, 2001a). The critical element of 'dynamism' inherent in the dynamic capability literature underlines the fact that capabilities are not static and therefore do not necessarily guarantee sustained competitive advantage (Eisenhardt and Martin, 2000). Although certain mechanisms can enhance performance at some stage, conditions of technological change can negate a firm's efforts to imitate or trade certain capabilities (Thomke and Kuemmerle, 2002). The very essence of capabilities is that they need to be built and can only be developed over time through complex interactions among the firm's resources (Amit and Schoemaker, 1993). In doing so, the DCV is especially devoted to uncovering the mechanisms that help firms integrate, build and reconfigure internal capabilities (Teece et al., 1997; Fujimoto, 1999, 2000).

The DCV has contributed to alliance research in a number of ways. First, most prominent in this research have been analyses which centre on the influence of a firm's experience on its alliance performance. In these studies, experience is presumed to represent a firm's ability to successfully manage alliances. Consequently, many of these studies use experience as a proxy for a firm's alliance capability (Anand and Khanna, 2000; Hoang et al., 2002; Kale et al., 2002; Reuer et al., 2002a, b).[7] The vast majority of these studies finds a positive relationship between experience and performance, suggesting that the development of an alliance capability is responsible for this positive relationship (Kale and Singh, 1999). Second, as experience itself provides little specificity on any underlying internal organizational processes fostering the development of an alliance capability, other studies have analysed the influence of certain mechanisms on alliance performance (Nault and Tyagi, 2001; Büchel and Killing, 2002). In doing so, they try to create insight into how firms leverage their experiences and what internal processes underlie the development of alliance capabilities. The logic of the DCV is useful to this study as it allows for a more comprehensive understanding of the complex interactions needed between a firm's experience, its organizational processes and mechanisms in order to develop alliance capabilities.

Third, introduced in the early 1990s, the CBV can be seen as an extension of the resource-based and dynamic capability views (Hamel, 1994;

Heene, 1994; Sanchez and Heene, 1997). Although competences themselves are often seen as resources (Prahalad and Hamel, 1990, 1993), they contain an ability on the side of the firm to sustain the coordinated deployment of assets so as to achieve a firm's goals over a prolonged period of time (Sanchez et al., 1996b). In order to counter fragmentation and disconnection of strategic management theories, the CBV relies on both internal and external factors to analyse competitive realities (De Leo, 1994; De Wit and Meyer, 1994; Verdin and Williamson, 1994; Sanchez and Heene, 1997; Barney, 2002). It explicitly stresses the need for firms to develop a more dynamic way of management, thereby relying on idiosyncratic firm capabilities as prime determinants of fixed-firm performance differences.[8] This theoretical perspective increases the conceptual complexity of strategic management as it addresses the interplay between resources, capabilities, organizational processes, managerial cognitions and social interactions within and between firms (Sanchez et al., 1996b; Chiesa and Manzini, 1997; Sanchez, 2001a,c, 2002). Therefore, a competence is often said to represent the specific constellation of resources, organizational processes and capabilities unique to the firm.

Rumelt (1984: 15–16) summarizes four key characteristics of a core competence. First, core competences span across products or business units. This characteristic emphasizes the fact that a core competence consists of an integrated bundle of unique skills (Hamel, 1994). Second, a firm's core competence changes more slowly than for instance the products they bring forward. As a consequence of the first characteristic, a change in core competence will demand an amendment in skills of employees, but also a change in organizational processes and routines (see e.g. Flaherty, 2000). It requires a transformation of the very building blocks of a firm's core competence. Third, core competences arise and can be developed through organizational learning, as it demands coordination and integration of skills and technological capabilities (e.g. Appleyard et al., 2000). Fourth, succeeding in sustaining a competence-based advantage requires continuous development of a firm's unique set of skills. This demands an adaptation of complex interactions between skills, organizational processes and routines (Karnoe, 1995). Although directly related, competences are different from resources and capabilities as they entail a capability to change capabilities, also referred to as a meta-capability (Henderson and Cockburn, 1994; Fujimoto, 1999).

The application of the CBV to alliances has resulted in a number of contributions. First of all, on basis of the CBV, a number of studies have tried to develop more comprehensive constructs of an alliance capability (e.g. Spekman et al., 1999; Dyer, 2000; Lambe et al., 2002; Schreiner, 2003). In doing so, scholars proposed to integrate different levels of analysis, such as the cognitive level, alliance level and firm level (e.g. Van de Ven and Ferry, 1980; Lorenzoni and Baden-Fuller, 1995; Sivadas and Dwyer, 2000; Schreiner, 2003). Second, using multidimensional constructs, these studies allow for a more holistic and potentially more realistic version of how firms develop capabilities in reality (e.g. Simonin, 1997, 2002). Therefore, applying CBV to alliance research has enabled scholars to give a better representation of the complexity involved in managing alliances. It shows the interrelatedness and interaction needed between a firm's resources to develop an alliance capability (see e.g. Appleyard, 2002). Given the relative infancy of this theory, the aspirations to apply the integrative nature of this theory to alliances have remained limited so far. The integrative nature makes it suitable to serve as a basis for more comprehensive insights on the development of alliance capabilities in future research. The specific contribution of the CBV to this study is inherent in its ability to integrate various theoretical backgrounds and provide a more comprehensive representation of the importance for firms to be able to develop a firm's capabilities over time in order to remain competitive in the long run. Obviously, the 'meta-capability' or competence to continuously adapt a firm's endowments also holds for the development of alliance capabilities.

Fourth, the KBV has been deemed essential to our understanding of the firm because of the role of knowledge in production and exchange processes (Demetz, 1991; March, 1991; Kogut and Zander, 1992; Schoonhoven, 2002; see also Harvard Business Review Press (1987) on Knowledge Management; *Strategic Management Journal* Special issue on Knowledge and the Firm 1996 17(S2); *Organization Science* Special issue on Knowledge and Organizations 2002, 13(3)). Knowledge is considered to be a key competitive resource (Nonaka and Takeuchi, 1999). However, in order to be successful, firms should ensure efficient transfer and creation of knowledge (Kogut and Zander, 1992). Nonaka (1994: 19) specifies four modes of knowledge conversion, which refer to four patterns of interaction between tacit and explicit knowledge. First, *socialization* converts tacit knowledge through direct interaction between individuals and shared experiences. Second, *combination* involves the transformation of explicit knowledge into new knowledge through combination of different bodies of explicit knowledge via social processes such as meetings. Third, *externalization* or articulation is the conversion of tacit into explicit knowledge (Hedlund, 1992). Fourth, *internalization* refers to the conversion of explicit into tacit knowledge. The fourth mode of knowledge conversion has traditionally been linked to the notion of learning, which refers to a firm's ability to share and institutionalize knowledge. The different types of knowledge creation underline the importance for firms to develop a capability 'to create new knowledge, disseminate it throughout the organization, and embody it in products, services, and systems' (Nonaka and Takeuchi, 1995: 3). Senge (1990a) and Nonaka (1991) add that firms need to efficiently extract knowledge from prior experiences. In the end, it is the access to and integration of specialized knowledge held by individuals that forms the basis of a firm's capabilities (Grant, 1991, 1996b; Zollo and Winter, 2002).

With respect to alliance research, the KBV underlines that transfer and integration of knowledge is critical to optimize value creation in alliances (Inkpen, 1996; Khanna et al., 1998; Almeida et al., 2002; Grant and Baden-Fuller, 2002). Still other studies have emphasized the need to protect and avoid leakage of sensitive knowledge to external parties (Kale et al., 2000; Tucci, 2002). Loss of knowledge or asymmetrical learning and knowledge acquisition can become important impediments to successful alliances and the long-term survival of the firm (e.g. Inkpen and Beamish, 1997; Lorange, 1997). Since knowledge sharing stimulates organizational learning (Huber, 1991), it becomes important for firms to leverage knowledge across a firm's alliances by considering alliances as a portfolio rather than a separate activity (Lorenzoni and Baden-Fuller, 1995, in Duysters et al., 1999b: 184). The logic of the KBV is relevant to this study, since a firm's ability to gather and leverage knowledge from prior alliances can be an important driver of its alliance performance. Moreover, the KBV directs attention to the internal mechanisms that help firms disperse and leverage existing knowledge.

Fifth, EE draws upon behavioural and economic traditions to explain a firm's competence as a consequence of its routines (Reuer et al., 2002a; Barnett and Burgelman, 1996; for an overview see Schendel, 1996). A central issue in EE is the way of doing things in firms, which has a strong element of continuity. The notion of 'routines' originates from EE and refers to the relatively constant dispositions and strategic heuristics that shape the approach of a firm to the non-routine problems it faces (Nelson and Winter, 1982; Bruderer and Singh, 1996). This implies that differences in organizational routines tend to persist for a longer period of time, making 'routines' a plausible concept to explain persisting performance differences among firms (Teece et al., 1997). Another important notion in EE is 'coordination', which refers to the management of interdependencies among tasks (Malone and Crowston, 1994).

Various studies confirm that variation in how firms in the automotive industry coordinate and manage activities with respect to new car models (Clark and Fujimoto, 1991; Fujimoto, 1999, 2000) and activities with respect to alliance management (Dyer, 2000; Takeishi, 2001, 2002; Dussauge et al., 2002; Garcia-Pont and Nohria, 2002; Ghosn, 2002; Kotabe et al., 2003) is indicative of its performance. Moreover, organizational routines facilitate the transfer of knowledge within firms (Dyer, 2000). It suggests that a firm's routines evolve with experience, thereby engendering incremental improvements in tasks and assignments (see e.g. Nelson and Winter, 1982). Hence, a firm's ability to vary, select and retain resources will determine its viability in the long run. The ability to adapt routines explains the survival of the firm, which is derived from biology that describes the genetic developments in organisms to explain long-term survival (Sanchez and Heene, 1997). Inherent to EE is a dynamic aspect, which differentiates successful from unsuccessful firms. Whereas intentionality and deliberate action are essential to theories such as RBV, EE is primarily concerned with the quasi-automatic and repetitive character of behaviour and performance (Coriat, 2000).

Evolutionary economics has contributed to alliance research by specifying the role of routines established either inside the firm or between partners. It suggests that certain stable or repetitive patterns of interactions influence alliance performance (e.g. Zollo et al., 2002). These studies investigate as to what extent accumulated experience and knowledge influence alliance performance. Cyert and March's (1963) view of the firm as being 'an adaptively rational system that basically learns from experience' (Kim, 1993: 41) underlines the contribution EE makes to this study. Hence, the contribution of EE to this study resides in the fact that it highlights the need to understand the process involved in leveraging accumulated experience and knowledge embedded in stabilized patterns of interactions in firms.

Sixth, scholars have relied upon OL theory to explain how firms learn (Pisano, 1984; Lapré et al., 2000; Levin, 2000). In general, OL theory refers to rises in productivity as a consequence of experience gains (Hirschmann, 1964; Argote, 1999). Dutton and Thomas (1984: 236) defined the 'progress function', expressing it in the following functional form:

$$\gamma = \gamma(1) x^{-b} \qquad (2.1)$$

where γ is the unit cost of production; $\gamma(1)$ is the unit cost to produce the first unit; x is the xth unit; and b is an exponent that represents learning and which varies across industries. This exponent tends to have a value between 1 and 3 depending on the levels of learning. In general, this value indicates that each doubling of cumulative output leads to a 20 per cent reduction in unit cost (Dutton and Thomas, 1984; Huberman, 1996). The ability to transfer knowledge is also proposed to have an important impact on the rate of learning in these studies (e.g. Argote, 1999). Various studies have suggested that productivity gains are due to experience gains and learning effects (for an overview see Argote, 1999), but some of the productivity gains may also be attributed to other factors such as gains in economies of scale or technology and process innovation. Building on early studies by among others Hirsch (1952) and Arrow (1962), Dutton and Thomas (1984: 235) refer to the gains which are due to learning as 'the progress principle' and state 'a firm can expect continuous improvement in its input-output productivity ratios as a consequence of a growing stock of knowledge'. This principle is confirmed by, for instance, Argote and Epple (1990), who find that the number of labour hours spent on each aircraft reduces substantially as output increases. As different studies find that firms vary considerably in the rate at which they learn (e.g. Hayes and Clark, 1986; Argote and Epple, 1990), OL theory tries to understand why some firms learn rapidly while others fail to grasp these advantages.

Learning can be defined as the process that, through repetition and experimentation, enables tasks to be performed in a more effective and efficient manner that results in new opportunities for the firm (Levitt and March, 1988). As such, it relates to the development of insights and knowledge representing the associations between past actions, the effectiveness of those actions and possible future actions (Fiol and Lyles, 1985). Some have referred to this as the 'knowledge evolution cycle' or the 'knowledge transformation cycle' (Zollo and Winter, 2002; Carlile and Rebentisch, 2003), which is an amendment of the classical evolution cycle (i.e. variation, retention and selection; see Nelson and Winter, 1982; Zollo and Winter, 2002). The logic underlying all of these models is that collective understanding can be nurtured and adjusted by acquiring, storing and retrieving knowledge (Hargadon and Sutton, 1997). For instance, by sharing (or 'acquiring') knowledge among different units or department, the people within that unit may find it helpful to better fulfil their practices as a consequence of which they may decide to adjust their practices and 'store' it in the organizational memory (Walsh and Ungson, 1991). Once the practice needs to be performed again, they may decide to 'retrieve' the newly acquired knowledge.[9] In general, learning allows a firm to improve its ability to anticipate and respond to contingencies that cannot be prescribed (Anand and Khanna, 2000). Organizational learning theory proposes that trial and error lie at the very root of organizational learning, which is done by 'adopting those routines, procedures, or strategies that lead to favorable outcomes' (Levitt and March, 1988: 322). Consequently, *how* firms learn is a central question for organization learning theory, which is referred to as a field of descriptive research describing the process of change (Vera and Crossan, 2003). Building on the 'learning curve notion', various scholars have posed that it is precisely these routines that allow firms to improve their ability to perform certain tasks as experience accumulates (Amburgey and Miner, 1992; Ingram and Baum, 1997), because knowledge gained from experience becomes embedded in a firm's routines (Coriat and Dosi, 1999; Argote and Darr, 2000). This is highly related to the argument of 'absorptive capacity' put forward by Cohen and Levinthal (1989, 1990), who suggest that a firm's ability to learn is itself a capability and it is related to its ability to assimilate new knowledge. Moreover, they stress that absorptive capacity can be invested in and is cumulative, which implies that it probably is a function of related current knowledge. Hence, firms tend to rely on knowledge gained through earlier endeavours to learn. In this way, OL theory can be thought of as the catalyst of capability development in firms (Sanchez and Heene, 1997).[10]

Organizational learning theory has contributed to alliance research along two lines: inter-firm learning and intra-firm learning (Grant and Baden-Fuller, 2002; Zeng and Hennart, 2002). Although these two types of research are related, studies focusing on inter-firm learning emphasize knowledge acquisition, whereas studies that investigate intra-firm learning analyse knowledge internalization (Hamel, 1991). The former group of studies is dominant and has paid attention to the role of the partners' ability to learn (or 'partner-specific absorptive capacities') to understand the dynamics in the alliance process (see e.g. Hamel et al., 1989; Kumar, 1995; Inkpen, 1998a, b, c; Kumar and Nti, 1998; for an overview see Mowery et al., 2002). The latter group focuses on intra-firm learning, thereby specifically underscoring the need to internalize specific or alliance-related knowledge (Simonin, 1997). It stresses the advantages of leveraging prior experience by transferring it to others within the firm and integrating it into organizational processes (Doz and Hamel, 1998; Reuer et al., 2002a). Organizational learning theory is relevant to this study as it underscores the need to understand how firms learn from prior experiences and how they internalize alliance-related knowledge in order to improve alliance performance.

Despite the fact that some scholars have relied on single theories (e.g. Das and Teng, 2000a), the vast majority has relied on a multitude of theories to investigate antecedents of alliance performance (see Table 2.1).

More importantly, given the complexity of researching alliance capability development, studies have implicitly or explicitly referred to different theories to ensure a sound description and embeddedness of the concepts used (Dosi et al., 2000b). A recent example is a study by Helfat and Peteraf (2003), who propose 'a dynamic resource-based view', which bundles elements from theories such as EE, the KBV, DCV and the RBV. As Coriat (2000: 213) stresses, for the process of capability development to be well understood, analyses should include a firm's routines as well as its intra-firm mechanisms since these concepts are critical to a firm's capabilities. Thus, applying a combination of different theories has allowed scholars to thoroughly define and better analyse the concepts of central concern (for an overview see Bogaert et al., 1994).

As can be concluded from the descriptions of the six theories, their concepts and contributions are highly related (see Tables 2.2 and 2.3). Table 2.2 gives an overview of the theories discussed and summarizes the key concepts and contribution to alliance research. Table 2.3 describes the relationship between the term 'capability', which terminology-wise stems from the DCV (Chandler et al., 1999; Rindova and Kotha, 2001), and the concepts and terminologies related to the remaining five theories. It also mentions the authors that either conceptually or empirically suggested that a certain concept is linked to the term 'capability'. Obviously, this list could be extended to include other relationships as well, but this table suffices to show that the concepts used by the six theories tend to overlap and are highly interrelated (Helfat, 1997; Hagström and Chandler, 1999; Dosi et al., 2000b; Sanchez, 2001a; Barney, 2002).[11]

So, despite contributive in vary distinct ways (Sanchez and Heene, 1997), the theories depicted in Figure 2.3 are also interrelated and act synergistically with respect to alliance capability research (see e.g. Larsson et al., 1998; Coriat and Dosi, 1999; Coriat, 2000; Zollo and Winter, 2002). In this way, these theories have cross-fertilized one another. It is this cross-fertilization that has so far led to an interesting array of studies of alliance capabilities (see Table 2.1). In general, as already shortly mentioned, there are a number of reasons why recent studies rely on a multitude of theories to analyse antecedents of alliance performance. First, using different theories allows scholars to make novel and potentially more accurate representations of alliance practices in firms.

The complementary nature and overlapping characteristics of different theories stimulates discussion of their converging and diverging aspects, but also seems to increase simultaneous application of theories (Mahoney and Pandian, 1992). As a consequence, different scholars have started to describe and operationalize concepts that stem from

Table 2.2 Contributions of theories applied to alliance research

	Key concepts	References	Contribution
Resource-based view (RBV)	Causal ambiguity Resource picking Isolating mechanisms	Penrose, 1959; Pfeffer and Salancik, 1978; Wernerfelt, 1984; Barney, 1986, 1991; Dierickx and Cool, 1989; Peteraf, 1993; Foss and Robertson, 2000; Barney et al., 2001.	Underscores that idiosyncratic resources are needed to create sustainable competitive advantage in alliance management.
Dynamic capability view (DCV)	Capabilities Resource deployment Capability development Internal mechanisms	Dickson, 1996; Teece et al., 1997; Eisenhardt and Martin, 2000; Rindova and Kotha, 2001; King and Tucci, 2002; Oxtoby et al., 2002.	Emphasizes the need to develop organizational processes in order to develop alliance capabilities.
Competence-based view (CBV)	Core competences Competence development	Prahalad and Hamel, 1990, 1993; Hamel, 1991, 1994; Hamel and Heene, 1994; Sanchez et al., 1996a; Heene and Sanchez, 1997.	Emphasizes the need to integrate resources and capabilities to grasp complexity of performance antecedents and the role of a meta-capability to develop a firm's capabilities over time.
Knowledge-based view (KBV)	Knowledge Knowledge sharing/ internalization Knowledge evolution or transformation cycle	Nonaka, 1988, 1990, 1991, 1994; Grant, 1991, 1996; Kogut and Zander, 1992; Conner and Prahalad, 1996; Lei et al., 1997; Larsson et al. 1998; Von Krogh et al., 1998; Nonaka and Takeuchi, 1999; McEvily and Chakravarthy, 2002; Zollo and Winter, 2002; Carlile and Rebentisch, 2003.	Emphasizes the creation, integration and sharing of knowledge and the mechanisms needed for this as a basis for capability development and competitive advantage.
Evolutionary economics (EE)	Routines Organizational memory Selection, retention, replication cycle	Cyert and March, 1963; Campbell, 1969; Nelson and Winter, 1982; Aldrich, 1999; Lewin and Volberda, 1999; Williamson, 1999; Karim and Mitchell, 2000.	Highlights the process involved in leveraging experiences through routines and describes routines as a source of inertia.
Organizational learning theory (OL)	Absorptive capacity Learning barriers Experience internalization	Fiol and Lyles, 1985; Stata, 1989; Cohen and Levinthal, 1990; Senge, 1990a, b; Huber, 1991; March, 1991; Levinthal and March, 1993; Leonard-Barton, 1995; Lei et al., 1997; Lane and Lubatkin, 1998; Crossan et al., 1999; Dyer and Nobeoka, 2000; Pisano et al., 2001.	Emphasizes the need to internalize knowledge gained through experience and directs attention to learning barriers.

Table 2.3 Overlap in concepts and terminology used in different theories

	Resource (RBV)	Competence (CBV)	Knowledge (KBV)	Routines (EE)	Absorptive capacity (OL)
Capability (DCV)	Barney, 1986, 1991; Amit and Schoemaker, 1993; Mahoney and Pandian, 1992; Fujimoto, 1999; Das and Teng, 2000a; Eisenhardt and Martin, 2000; Makadok, 2001.	Prahalad and Hamel, 1990; Markides and Williamson, 1994; Sanchez et al., 1996b; Henderson and Cockburn, 2000; Pisano, 2000; Lambe et al., 2002.	Kogut and Zander, 1993; Grant, 1996b; Probst et al., 1998.	Campbell, 1969; Nelson and Winter, 1982; Teece et al., 1997; Aldrich, 1999; Williamson, 1999; Anand and Vassolo, 2002; Zollo et al., 2002.	Cohen and Levinthal, 1990; Kumar and Nti, 1998; Lane and Lubatkin, 1998; Lane and Levinthal, 2000; Lane et al., 2001.

different theories (see e.g. Dyer, 2000). Other studies follow the lines of the CBV by integrating various levels of analysis. For instance, Sivadas and Dwyer (2000) introduce the term 'cooperative competence' to represent a firm's capability to perform in a new product development setting. Cooperative competence includes various inter-firm or alliance-based antecedents (such as trust and mutual dependence) as well as intra-firm or internal antecedents (administrative mechanisms and institutional support) of alliance performance.

Second, and more general, simultaneously applying different theories helps overcome conventional theoretical demarcations and limitations of individual theories (Hagström and Chandler, 1999; Helfat, 2003). While traditionally strategy (business administration) and organization (microeconomics) were considered to provide distinct theoretical underpinnings, more and more scholars acknowledge the difficulty to maintain this distinction (Hagström and Chandler, 1999; Mahoney and Pandian, 1992). Increasingly, scholars use a number of theories to support their investigations (Chandler et al., 1999; Helfat, 2003). Scholars contributing to alliance research follow these trends by using various theories to embody their analyses. The deterministic or proverbial 'black box' view of the firm seems to collide more with voluntaristic views of strategic choice (De Wit and Meyer, 1994). In this way, organizational economics (containing theories such as transaction cost economics, EE and industrial organization theory) becomes more intertwined with theories such as the RBV, DCV, OL theory and the KBV of the firm (e.g. Coriat and Dosi, 1999). For instance, Dyer and Nobeoka (2000) suggest the DCV and KBV to be highly related when it comes to organizational learning. Furthermore, Mahoney and Pandian (1992), referring to Barney and Ouchi (1986), argue that the RBV and DCV are highly related to organizational economics. Another example is the KBV of the firm that can be considered an outgrowth of the RBV and DCV, as organizational knowledge creation can be seen as a firm-level capability to create and apply knowledge (Grant, 1996a; Sanchez, 2001b). Moreover, given the recently emerging consensus on the specific contributions of the DCV (Zott, 2003) and the ability of certain theories such as the RBV to bring together different strands of research (Rugman and Verbeke, 2002), different theories seem to become more clearly established. This, on the one hand, increases the identity and applicability of individual theories, while at the same time it allows scholars to simultaneously use various theories in order to come to a better understanding of complex strategic realities.

3
Describing the Phenomenon: Alliance Capabilities

3.1 Introduction

The number of publications based on (a mix of) the six theories discussed in Chapter 2 has grown exponentially over the past years (Foss, 2000; Helfat, 2000). Two main streams of research have emerged from this (Hamel, 1991; Ranft and Lord, 2002): a body of research which has been referred to as external sources of capabilities and another body of research which centres on internal sources of capabilities (Grant, 1998), also referred to respectively as knowledge acquisition and knowledge internalization (Hamel, 1991), inter-firm and intra-firm learning (Grant and Baden-Fuller, 2002), internal and external learning (Bierly and Chakrabarti, 1996), learning outside and inside the firm (Leonard-Barton, 1995), or vicarious and experiential learning (Huber, 1991). This book builds on the concepts underlying the second stream of research. The second stream of literature focuses on processes within the individual firm that foster knowledge dissemination and integration (e.g. Henderson and Clark, 1990; King and Zeithaml, 2001). In fact, the second stream fills the void left open by the first stream, which essentially answers questions like: how can firms learn from their collaborative experience? How can firms transfer and internalize knowledge (Inkpen and Crossan, 1995; Tsang, 2002a)? And can firms cultivate the development of alliance capabilities (Reuer et al., 2002a)? In this stream of research, the building blocks of alliance capabilities are the main topic of research (Simonin, 1997; Gulati, 1998). Hence, studies of this kind suggest that firm-specific resources, capabilities, routines and competences explain competitive heterogeneity as well as firm dynamics (e.g. Hitt and Ireland, 1985). Notwithstanding the significant contribution of both streams, limited attention has so far been paid to explain how experience can be translated into a capability (Kale et al., 2002; Tsang, 2002a). As most studies have pursued a macro-focus, firms are left in the dark about the adequate actions that can be taken at the micro-level. As a consequence, a growing debate is surrounding academic strategy research with respect to its practical relevance (see e.g. Johnson et al., 2003). This critic also counts for alliance research, as contributions aimed at enlightening the process underlying the development of capabilities and the potential mechanisms to be used have been limited in number and have so far lacked micro-level evidence and detail (Grant, 1996b; Williamson, 1999; Eisenhardt and Martin, 2000; Thomke and Kuemmerle, 2002; Zollo and Winter, 2002). Hence, there is an evident need to understand *how* firms can internalize their acquired experience in order to develop alliance capabilities. Despite recent attention for the need for firms to develop alliance capabilities, research into mechanisms and routines that are purposefully designed to accumulate, store and integrate alliance-related knowledge is practically non-existent (Fiol and Lyles, 1985; Anand and Khanna, 2000; Lehtonen, 2003).

The aim of this chapter is twofold. First, it intends to discuss the context from which the key concepts are derived and on basis of which they are defined. These key concepts are related to the six theories used in the theoretical framework. We provide a description of the central concepts involved in the development of alliance capabilities. Second, we discuss how these concepts (i.e. experience, capabilities, performance) are related. In this way, the current understanding of the underlying process of experience leveraging through the creation of organizational capabilities is extended (Helfat, 2000; Sanchez, 2001a). Having done so, the basis is laid for an empirical investigation of the role of intra-firm mechanisms in capability development and the relationships between the critical concepts (see Chapters 4 and 5).

3.2 Deriving and defining alliance capabilities

Although the number of publications on concepts such as resources, capabilities and competences has grown significantly over the recent years, their terminology has been subject to a lot of confusion (Williamson, 1999; Dosi et al., 2000b; Priem and Butler, 2000; Sanchez, 2001a, b; Rugman and Verbeke, 2002). Various scholars have used different definitions of concepts such as knowledge, mechanisms, resources, assets, capabilities and competences (for an overview see Bogaert et al., 1994). In order to gain insight into what the critical internal factors are which explain competitive heterogeneity when it comes to alliance management, it is important to have clear definitions of the different concepts as well as to understand where these concepts originate from. Therefore, to understand how concepts such as experience, knowledge, mechanisms, routines and capabilities are linked, the next section pays attention to this topic. More importantly, this section will discuss how firms can make experience their 'best teacher' (Kleiner and Roth, 1987: 137) according to both a scholarly and a practitioner's perspective.

To understand how alliance capabilities can be developed, it is important to on the hand review prior research and on the other hand analyse how organizations in practice have tried to develop these capabilities. In order to uncover what 'organizational gear or equipment' firms use to develop alliance capabilities, it is essential to seek for information and evidence that hints what activities or mechanisms firms engage in or use to develop alliance capabilities. To comprehend why intra-firm mechanisms are important to alliance capability development, two groups of studies are relevant to consider: theory-based or academic studies and more practical or case-based studies. The first group involves studies describing and investigating contributions made by theories key to this study (see Figure 2.3). The second group refers to studies that have sought to create particular insights from practical experiences and backgrounds. These can be related to the way in which firms deal with alliances or what activities they undertake to cultivate alliance capabilities.

The first group of studies has raised our understanding of alliance capability development via the analysis of different theories. As extensively discussed in Chapter 2, the six theories that are included in the theoretical framework underlying this study each contributes different concepts and logics that are again linked. Miller (2003), in his analysis of the capability development process among twenty-three international firms, at various occasions explicitly outlines the critical role mechanisms, such as project teams, local managers, cross-functional committees and communities of practice, play in developing capabilities. Miller (2003: 969) goes on noting that these mechanisms not only help 'share knowledge across different parts of the organization ... [but also contain] routines [which] institutionalize knowledge'. Nelson and Winter (1982) further enlighten our understanding of the capability development process as they underline that routinization of activities encapsulates the most important form of knowledge storage in a firm. Knott (2003: 941), operationalizing routines on basis of among others trainings, on-site (management) assistance and manuals, finds support for the fact that routines are a valuable resource. Her study shows that these routines or mechanisms help explain at least part of the observed performance heterogeneity among firms. 'Remember by doing' then becomes an obvious term to refer to an organization's basis for the development of its capabilities. Similarly, Aldrich (1999: 127) extensively talks about so-called 'communities of practice', which are defined as patterned social interactions between organizational members that sustain organizational knowledge and routines. Another important notion put forward by Aldrich (1999: 133) is the use of mechanisms such as reward and bonuses and control systems. In line with Van de Ven et al. (1984), he argues that personnel instability can seriously disrupt the development of organizational knowledge. Moreover, stability will engender continuity, commitment and increase the opportunity to learn from mistakes. In short, personnel instability is a serious detriment to the sustainability of organizational memory (Nelson and Winter, 1982). In the same vein, Boone (1997) investigates large multinational firms (i.e. Canon, Unilever and ITT) to analyse the way in which these firms transfer knowledge internally. He concludes that these firms use a sophisticated set of mechanisms consisting of management tools and supporting management systems (e.g. performance metrics, global network infrastructure or intranet) in order to support institutionalization of knowledge and experiences.

Although little research has so far been done on the specific intrafirm mechanisms used to manage portfolios of alliances, a recent special issue on building effective networks (*Academy of Management Executive*, 2003, 17(4)) pays attention to a number of these mechanisms. More closely related to the topic of this book, this issue extensively discusses ways in which firms can manage portfolios of alliances. In this issue, Parise and Casher (2003) for instance list a number of tools and techniques such as communities of practice, formal and informal communication channels among alliance managers, trainings and workshops. More and more, they observe, are firms installing alliance directors, vice-presidents of alliances, or alliance departments in order to optimize a firm's alliance portfolio performance. Successful firms, they reckon, use these mechanisms in order to ensure that alliance managers for instance are aware of each other's activities in order to not duplicate partnering efforts with certain partners. Moreover, these mechanisms are installed to ensure that managers not only focus on their own objectives, but also use other people's experiences to optimize performance in their alliances. Ultimately, they reckon that these mechanisms have a direct effect on performance and learning outcomes (Parise and Casher, 2003: 35). In a similar vein, Borker et al. (2004) argue that alliance offices or departments are a critical ingredient to institutionalize alliance-related knowledge and can function as a monitor to support organizational processes, tools and work practices. They reckon that successful firms develop an alliance competence to capture lessons learned in prior alliances and ensure that these are dispersed throughout the firm. A study by Lambe et al. (2002) confirms this, as they find empirical support for the fact that a firm's alliance competence positively influences alliance success.

Boddy et al. (2001) identify various institutional mechanisms on basis of a three-year study of seven firms active in supply-chain partnering. These mechanisms supported interaction between the partner firms investigated. They looked at such mechanisms as weekly scheduled review meeting and monthly commercial review meetings, which served as a forum to openly discuss and solve relevant issues. Similarly, Bakker and Helmink (2000) argue that for organizations to successfully cooperate or integrate their businesses, certain mechanisms will serve to facilitate learning from prior experiences in that process. Moreover, they mention that employees should exchange, integrate and institutionalize knowledge in order to become effective in managing alliances. Mechanisms such as training courses or intranet can be seen as processes through which firms disseminate knowledge. Similarly, Salk and Simonin (2003: 260) mention that 'the mechanisms through which learning is realized and potentially converted into performance, often indirectly inferred rather than directly observed, imply structures and processes at the organizational and sub-organizational levels'. This line explicitly refers to organizational processes and structures through which learning occurs and it clearly indicates that these mechanisms are hard to directly observe. However, they can be deduced from the processes and structures a firm has in place.

The second group of studies is grounded in and confers to practice when it comes to alliance capability development. As 'they [theorists] cannot aim to tell the whole truth' (Nelson and Winter, 1982: 134), it is important to also look at practice in order to derive how organizations develop alliance capabilities. *Forbes* Magazine and Accenture presented a list called 'The Forbes Magnetic 40', which contains forty companies considered to be so-called 'partners of choice' in their sector (*Forbes Magazine*, 2001). This list of partners of choice gives practical insight into how firms from different industries have developed their ability to manage alliances. Frequently, the use of mechanisms such as alliance managers, use of best practices, cultural trainings or alliance departments are said to be critical to the firm's ability to successfully manage alliances. Harbison and Pekar (1998a: 135) confirm that firms which are successful in managing alliances evolve their capabilities over time. They reckon that firms develop their ability to manage alliances using a mixture of mechanisms. They refer to such mechanisms as alliance specialist, sharing best practices, alliance repositories and installing an alliance office or department. They also found that several companies using these intra-firm mechanisms to institutionalize prior experiences have been able to raise their alliance success rate up to 90 per cent (1998a: 129). In a comparable study, the Corporate Strategy Board (2000) finds that alliance capability development, which is apparently, as they observe, nurtured via internal mechanisms, is critical in order to enhance alliance success rates. Various examples are given of how firms successful in managing alliances, such as Corning and Dow Chemical, have developed alliance capabilities applying a variety of mechanisms.

Other studies, which are also written from a more practical standpoint, have also been advocating the use of mechanisms to institutionalize capability development over the last years. Bamford and Ernst (2003) extensively discuss the different elements firms can use to create an advanced alliance infrastructure. This infrastructure consists of staff, tools, organization structure and information systems or databases. They posit that, following different stages, these elements can help firms develop alliance capabilities. Likewise, Freidheim (1998) extensively describes the internal mechanisms through which a firm can leverage alliance experiences. For instance, in line with Dyer (2000) who analyses how among others Chrysler manages its alliance practices, Freidheim refers to first-rate communication systems as a critical means to have employees be up-to-date on advances in alliances in which they participate or to disseminate best practices. Moreover, Freidheim (1998) continues to meticulously analyse how firms from different industries, for example, Motorola, Hewlett Packard, BellSouth and Nortel, have prepared their organizations to be successful in managing alliances. He describes how these firms proceeded in following a well-defined and structured process to institutionalize the ability to manage alliances successfully. These firms relied on mechanisms such as workshops, trainings, exchange of experiences and a supportive internal infrastructure. Gomes-Casseres in a recent article in the *Financial Times* (2000) reckons that firms who tend to be successful in their alliances have 'integrated alliances into a coherent strategy and manage them over time [which] allowed it [the firm] to get the most from partnerships'. The reference to integrating alliances clearly refers to acknowledging the interdependence between the alliances formed by one firm and the need to consciously pay attention to the design and management of its alliance portfolio (Gomes-Casseres, 1996; De Man et al., 2001; Lemmens, 2003; Beerkens, 2004; Sarkar et al., 2004). These authors all hint to or make explicit reference of internal mechanisms influencing the ability of the firm to manage its alliances.

So far, various firms that are known for having substantially increased their alliance performance over the years, such as Chrysler, Eli Lilly, Hewlett Packard, Xerox and Unisys, made use of intra-firm mechanisms to enhance alliance performance (Alliance Analyst, 1994; Dyer, 2000; Sims et al., 2003). These firms are cited to have developed an 'alliance capability'. A distinct organizational feature these firms have installed is an internal infrastructure that consists of processes to support the management of the firm's alliance portfolio (Kanter, 1994; Corporate Strategy Board, 2000; *Financial Times*, 2000). In general, although the internal infrastructure can take different organizational forms, it tends to be founded within either a separate department or fall within the responsibility of an assigned business unit manager (Corporate Strategy Board, 2000; Bamford et al., 2003).

Consequently, practical insights suggest that certain intra-firm mechanisms may play a critical role for firms to enhance the performance of their alliance portfolio. However, empirical evidence with respect to what extent different (groups of) mechanisms influence alliance performance is to the best of our knowledge practically non-existent. Although a recent investigation by the Corporate Strategy Board (2000) suggests that the management of alliance skill transfer only has a moderately positive influence on the most important reasons for failure, to date no study has come up with clear evidence of the impact of individual or groups of intra-firm mechanisms and the extent to which these contribute to a firm's ability to successfully manage their alliance portfolio.

Having looked at how critical concepts are related to alliance capabilities in theory and practice, it is equally important to clearly define these concepts. Various scholars have committed to the daunting task of identifying sound distinctions, thereby proposing different approaches (e.g. Dosi et al., 2000a; Merali, 2001; Sanchez, 2001a, c; Stein and Ridderstrale, 2001). This book does not aim to provide an extensive overview of all definitions available of critical concepts in the alliance capability development process.[1] However, given the need for clarity in this emergent field of study (Foss, 1997b), it is important to define the most important concepts, thereby underlining that these may be not universally applicable but are primarily defined so as to be suitable and appropriate to the study at hand. Following Sanchez (2001b: 6), we refer to organizational knowledge which 'exists when individuals in an organization share sets of beliefs about causal relationships that enable them to work together in doing something'. Knowledge then allows people inside the organization to either be able to use (know-how) or to understand and create (know-why) (Glazer, 1991; Kogut and Zander, 1992; Bohn, 1994; Zander and Kogut, 1995).[2] Von Hippel (1984) adds that know-how is the accumulated practical skill or expertise that allows one to perform effectively and efficiently. The pivotal term 'accumulated' stresses that know-how must be learned and acquired through experience (Kogut and Zander, 1992). The notion that knowledge is a relatively static phenomenon as suggested by the positivist view, that is, knowledge as 'justified true belief' (Nonaka and Takeuchi, 1995), should be complemented by a dynamic aspect (Nonaka et al., 2001: 14). As Polanyi (1967) underlines, 'knowledge is an activity, which could be better described as a process of knowing' (in Vera and Crossan, 2003: 125). Many scholars also differentiate between explicit and tacit knowledge. Explicit knowledge is expressed in formal and systematic language and includes data, facts, symbols, scientific formulas and manuals as a consequence of which it is easily transferable (Szulanski, 1996; Kogut and Zander, 1997). Tacit knowledge is defined as sticky, difficult to codify, highly personalized and hard to formalize and tends to be deeply rooted in actions, ideals, routines, procedures and values (Winter, 1987; Cohen and Bacdayan, 1994; Nonaka et al., 2001). Grant (1995, 1996a) and Kusunoki et al. (1998) add that organizational capabilities can be viewed as the outcome of knowledge integration. Likewise, Lei et al. (1996) suggest that the management of knowledge is a firm's ultimate dynamic capability and driver of all capabilities. In the same vein, Collis (1991) and Zollo and Winter (2002) argue that organizational capabilities are developed via the use of dynamic routines, which facilitate innovation, foster collective learning and transfer information and skills throughout the organization. In line with this logic, this study also maintains that experience accumulation lies at the basis of alliance capability development.

'Resources' are defined as the stock of available factors (tangible or intangible assets) owned or controlled by the firm (Wernerfelt, 1984; Amit and Schoemaker, 1993). Resources, however, are distinct from capabilities. A 'capability' refers to the capacity to deploy resources (Mahoney and Pandian, 1992; Makadok, 2001) or 'the ability of a firm to perform a coordinated set of tasks using organizational resources for the purpose of achieving a particular end result' (Helfat and Peteraf,

2003: 999). In general, a firm possesses a 'routine' or a 'capability' when it has learned to perform some activity or function with sufficient distinction in comparison with a control group (Cyert and March, 1963; Nelson and Winter, 1982). Sanchez (2001c: 7) defines capabilities as 'repeatable patterns of action that a firm can use to get things done'. One could say, as Helfat and Peteraf (2003) suggest, that a capability refers to the firm's skilfulness with regard to performing a certain task. Hence, whereas resources are assets that are either owned or controlled by the firm, capabilities pertain to its ability to exploit and combine resources through organizational routines (Amit and Schoemaker, 1993, in Spanos and Lioukas, 2001: 909). Hunt and Morgan (1996) refer to lower- and higher-order resources. Similarly, Henderson and Cockburn (1994) differentiate between component and architectural competence. Consequently, higher-order resources are referred to as 'capabilities' (Amit and Schoemaker, 1993) and determine the way in which firms manage their resources (Teece et al., 1997). Makadok (2001) defined a capability as a special type of resource that is organizationally embedded and non-transferable and improves the productivity of other resources possessed by the firm. This definition explicitly suggests capabilities should be built to enable resources to be efficiently deployed. A 'competence' is different from a capability in that it enables the firm to sustain the way in which it deploys its resources (Sanchez et al., 1996b). This refers to a meta-capability or evolutionary capability, which represents a firm's ability to develop its capability (Fujimoto, 1999, 2000). Still others distinguish between zero-level or ordinary capabilities and dynamic capabilities (Winter, 2003), operational and dynamic capabilities (Teece et al., 1997; Helfat and Peteraf, 2003) or first- and second-order dynamic capabilities (Collis, 1994). In evolutionary economic terms, this distinction would be referred to as operating and search routines (Nelson and Winter, 1982; Zollo and Winter, 2002). Lyles (1988: 86–87), relying on organizational learning theory, similarly distinguishes between lower- and higher-level learning, where the former is a result of repetition and routine-like activities and the latter creates new frames of reference, novel skills to resolve recurring issues and new values.

As is obvious from the overlap in definitions of, for instance, 'capabilities' and 'routines', it is noteworthy and important to stress that different theories tend to use different terminologies to refer to the same issues. Depending on the theoretical tradition, scholars adopt different terminologies when it comes to business processes firms develop to get something done or to outperform others: those adopting an evolutionary economics perspective would refer to 'routines', organization economics scholars would refer to 'activities' and scholars adopting a resource-based or dynamic cpapbility view would refer to 'capabilities' (Ray et al., 2004: 24). Following the logic of Hunt and Morgan (1996), Makadok (2001) and Thomke and Kuemmerle (2002), an alliance capability can be seen as a higher-order resource which is difficult to obtain or imitate, has the potential to enhance the performance of other resources owned by the firm and which are committed to its alliances. This higher-order resource consists of or is captured by mechanisms (Grant, 1995; Tsang, 2002b), which can increase a firm's ability to perform repeatable patterns of action with respect to, for instance, identifying partners, initiating relationships or restructuring individual alliances as well as alliance portfolios (Simonin, 1997; Spekman et al., 1999; Dyer et al., 2001). What is critical in this respect is that these mechanisms can act as organizing principles or higher-order routines to facilitate the transfer of and adaptation of knowledge and practices to a wider circle of individuals (Kogut and Zander, 1997: 314; Winter, 2003: 191). This capability supports the firm in raising and maintaining the alliance performance of their entire alliance portfolio by sharing, internalizing and adjusting alliance-related knowledge and stimulating the adoption of repeatable actions.

For the purpose of this study, we refer to Eisenhardt and Martin (2000), Harbison et al. (2000), Kale et al. (2002) and Helfat and Peteraf (2003) and define an alliance capability as the firm's ability to capture, share, disseminate, internalize and apply alliance management know-how and know-why. If the firm has developed an alliance capability, it is likely to have repeatable patterns of action with respect to managing alliances. Hence, the ability of the firm refers to the extent to which the firm can ensure this know-how and know-why (i.e. knowledge) become embedded in repeatable patterns of action (Sanchez et al., 1996b; Teece, 1997) and refers to identifiable and specific routines (Eisenhardt and Martin, 2000). However, this definition does not *necessarily* include the 'dynamic' aspect (or higher-order capability or routine) to which the dynamic capability and competence-based views and evolutionary economics refer. Grant (1995: 18) specifies two types of mechanisms that stimulate knowledge integration: direction (knowledge integration through rules, guidelines and directives) and routines (knowledge integration through patterns of interactions among specialists). In line with Nelson and Winter (1982), Helfat and Peteraf (2003: 999) state that capabilities include two types of routines: those to perform individual tasks and those that coordinate and potentially amend the individual tasks. As a result, a firm's capabilities are embedded in organizational routines, which are repetitive activities a firm develops in using its resources (Nelson and Winter, 1982, in Sanchez, 2001a: 150). These routines allow for the transfer, copying and recombination of knowledge by managers within the firm (e.g. Szulanski, 1996). A concept related to the term 'routine' is practice, which refers to the organization's routine use of knowledge (Szulanski, 1996: 28). This concept is often said to have a tacit component as its origins are embedded in individual skills (Nelson and Winter, 1982). Various studies have looked at the transfer of best practices with firms (see e.g. Szulanski, 1996; Zollo, 1997; Maritan and Brush, 2003). Winter (1995) adds that the transfer of best practices can be thought of as replication of organizational routines.

In every day practice, firms have accumulated experience and started to invest in mechanisms that support dissemination of experience with alliances throughout the firm in order to overcome performance disturbances (e.g. Alliance Analyst, 1994, 1996a; Corporate Strategy Board, 2000; Gueth, 2001; Accenture Consulting, 2002; Tsang, 2002b; *Financial Times*, 2004a). This has resulted in among others a rise in the number of firms that have installed internal infrastructures or so-called dedicated alliance groups to support the dissemination of alliance knowledge (Kale and Singh, 1999; Dyer, 2000). These mechanisms help develop alliance capabilities as they formalize and provide a structure for alliance management processes (Harbison et al., 2000; Bamford and Ernst, 2003; Sims et al., 2003). Intrigued by these developments, different scholars have identified different levels of alliance experience and capabilities (Harbison and Pekar, 1998b; Anand and Khanna, 2000; Draulans et al., 2003). As mentioned earlier, experience is often seen as a critical input for alliance capability development as it helps build alliance-related know-how (e.g. Simonin, 1997; Kale and Singh, 1999). In the same vein, Helfat and Peteraf (2003) in their recent article introduce the concept of capability lifecycles. The different stages of the lifecycle reflect different levels of capabilities that represent the skilfulness of the organization in executing a particular activity. In line with this logic, the Alliance Analyst (1996a) and Draulans et al. (1999, 2003) have defined three levels of alliance experience on the basis of the number of alliances formed by a firm. The argumentation of these studies is based on the logic that the more firms are engaged in alliances, the more successful they will become. As mentioned earlier, proxying alliance experience by the number of prior alliances is an established way of measuring (see e.g. Gulati, 1998; Kale et al., 2002). Moreover, they suggest that, at different experience levels, different mechanisms can be used to enhance alliance performance. These different levels in some way resemble the levels of knowledge transfer identified by Inkpen and Crossan (1995) and Crossan et al. (1999), who differentiate between individual-level (interpreting and sensemaking), group-level (integrating) and organization-level (institutionalizing) learning. Table 3.1 summarizes the main issues regarding the different levels of alliance experience and potential mechanisms that can be used.

Identifying different levels of alliance capabilities, different studies come up with an extensive number of important suggestions (Alliance Analyst, 1996a; Draulans et al., 1999, 2003). Studies by Harbison and Pekar (1998a) and Draulans et al. (1999, 2003) distinguish between three levels of alliance capabilities. At the first level, firms are in a situation where one or several alliances demand corporate attention. The firm has limited experience in preparing for inter-firm activities as well as the actual implementation of an alliance. Therefore, in-house knowledge consists mainly of general, non-specific contractual, organizational know-how. At this level, firms tend to favour learning-by-doing over a structural approach to accumulate alliance-related knowledge (Harbison and Pekar, 1998b). Although the learning curve is likely to be steep at this level of alliance experience (see e.g. Deeds and Hill, 1996), most firms will have limited success with their strategic cooperative movements.

In order to prevent firms from unsatisfactory results at this level, research has maintained that firms can use a number of mechanisms

Table 3.1 Levels of alliance experience

	Level 1	Level 2	Level 3
Number of alliances	Small	Reasonable	Large
Importance	Operational	High for certain units or divisions	Strategic for the entire company
Geographical reach	Regional/national	Starting with internationalization	International
Management tools (Cumulative examples per level)	Legal knowledge Checklists for partner selection and monitoring Evaluation of individual alliances	Best practices Alliance specialist Cultural trainings	Partner program Alliance department Alliance knowledge dispersed via trainings Alliance database

Source: (adapted from) Alliance Analyst, 1996a; Draulans et al., 1999.

(Draulans et al., 1999). First of all, tools such as alliance evaluation and a partner selection approach are easy ways to increase awareness and decrease ad-hoc decision-making in alliances. Second, culture programs or external alliance trainings may help firms increase alliance know-how (Spekman et al., 1999). The mechanisms should be aimed at gaining a proper understanding of the most relevant principles in alliances for the particular firm so as to avoid common pitfalls (Dyer et al., 2001).

At the second level, a firm's experience increases as its alliance portfolio starts to comprise more inter-firm activities. Firms start to create standard procedures to manage alliances and often experience leads to greater success in their alliances. Standardization of alliance procedures helps converge tacit into explicit or codified knowledge, which facilitates intra-firm learning (Nonaka and Takeuchi, 1995). Though mostly restricted to top management, it is at this level that firms actually start to build specific alliance knowledge. This partly generalized knowledge, however, resides in the minds of a small number of specialists who are active in the firm. A primordial and detrimental drawback of this position is that it may prohibit the dissemination of alliance knowledge to the employees in need. As the importance of alliances for the firm has increased at this level, resources should be allocated to the development of alliance capabilities by committing to group-level knowledge sharing (Inkpen and Crossan, 1995). This will disperse critical knowledge and practices among employees, as a consequence of which more employees will be able to apply these practices.

At this level, various mechanisms can help develop a firm's alliance capability. First, firms can gather best practices based on their own experiences and those of other firms and evaluate their alliances. This demands the same procedure as for firms at level one, which means that knowledge which resides in habits should be transformed so as to allow firms to learn in a more efficient manner (Nonaka, 1994; Spender, 1996). Moreover, explication of alliance-related knowledge will increase the collective store of knowledge. This again is likely to enhance the ability to exchange and integrate, which can potentially improve alliance management (Inkpen and Dinur, 1998). Second, to stimulate sharing of these lessons, alliance trainings and use of external specialists may help extend and disseminate specific knowledge. As Aldrich (1999: 93) argues, knowledge from experts can substitute for direct experience. Third, firms can use alliance metrics and reward and bonus systems to motivate business unit managers to increase success rates. Fourth, firms can assign an alliance specialist (Draulans et al., 1999), manager or gatekeeper at this level. These can be used to monitor the environment and translate information into applicable knowledge (Cohen and Levinthal, 1990; Leonard-Barton, 1995; Doz and Hamel, 1998). The prohibition of unnecessary knowledge leaks (Lei et al., 1997) and protection of intellectual property (e.g. Grindley and Teece, 1997) can prove a useful means to decrease conflict situations. It is therefore critical for firms to prevent the use of a weak liaison involved in its alliances (Kanter, 1983; Doz and Hamel, 1998). At this level, these mechanisms may help extend the body of knowledge in order to achieve a higher level of alliance capability (Simonin, 1997).

At the third level, alliances have become a top management priority. This phase requires alliances to be thoroughly embedded in business strategy, reflecting the highest level of alliance capability attainable. The essential characteristic of this stage is that the firm is consciously building and dispersing its alliance experience and knowledge throughout the firm in a deliberate and structural way. No longer does alliance knowledge reside in a few professionals, but dedicated investments are made to disperse knowledge throughout the firm in order to institutionalize it at the firm level. To this end, top management is dedicated to build and maintain a distinct set of mechanisms to optimize alliance performance (Dyer, 2000). Thus, alliances are not merely of operational or business unit concern, but instead are given attention at the strategic or corporate level (Draulans et al., 1999).

Several mechanisms can support firms to develop capabilities at the third level. First, central coordination becomes important as a means to facilitate knowledge sharing on a structural basis (Kale and Singh, 1999; Dyer et al., 2001). For instance, an alliance department or function can act as a central coordination mechanism to increase coordinative capacity (Harbison and Pekar, 1998a; Kale and Singh, 1999; Kale et al., 2002). In the same vein, this mechanism may positively influence the absorptive capacity of the firm and help overcome the factors that impede learning, such as fragmentation of knowledge, conflicts, tacitness, memory or too small sample sizes (see e.g. March et al., 1991; Zollo and Winter, 2002). Using an alliance department together with a gatekeeper, alliance manager or vice-president combines external and internal coordinative capabilities at the same time. In alliances, internal and external coordination should both be appreciated and consistently applied (Teece and Pisano, 1994; Takeishi, 2001). Second, an alliance database can help accumulate and assemble experience in such a way that it is easily transferable (Khanna et al., 1998). A database then serves as an organizational attribute to gather and institutionalize alliance knowledge.

In general, mechanisms such as those referred to at different experience levels help to disperse knowledge gained through experience throughout the organization. Therefore, intra-firm mechanisms in general can be conducive to the ability of the firm to manage alliances and to the development of repeatable alliance management practices. Consequently, they can increase a firm's ability to learn (Spekman et al., 1999). In the end, various scholars posit that a firm can develop an alliance capability by internalizing alliance knowledge using intra-firm mechanisms (e.g. Simonin, 1997, 2002; Bamford and Ernst, 2003).

In the literature on alliance research, recent investigations started paying attention to these developments in practice and tried to unravel the underpinnings of structural fixed-firm alliance performance differences. However, the precise interplay between the constructs experience, mechanisms, routines, capabilities and performance has remained obscure (King and Zeithaml, 2001; Shafer et al., 2001). In order to increase our understanding of this topic, the next section will discuss the relationships between these concepts and their role in the alliance capability development process.

3.3 Alliance capability development process

Improvements in the functioning of a firm's alliance capability, as Helfat and Peteraf (2003: 1002) argue, 'derive from a complex set of factors that include learning-by-doing of individual team members and of the team as a whole, deliberate attempts at process improvements and problem-solving, as well as investment over time'. Using experience as a single means to explain performance limits our understanding of how firms can leverage their experience and how firms can develop their alliance capability, because it neglects the importance of knowledge transfer and seems to be an overly simplistic representation of reality (Argote and Ingram, 2000). Although alliance experience is likely to have a direct and positive influence on alliance performance (Deeds and Hill, 1996), we argue there is a more subtle process underlying the development of alliance capabilities. Therefore, a number of other variables besides experience are expected to be involved in the development of an alliance capability (Kale et al., 2002). Lenox and King (2004: 342), for instance, find that information provision has a significant and positive effect on the extent of the adoption of a certain practice or routine. This suggests that the availability of sources that provide access to information can play a critical role in the institutionalization of certain activities. Similarly, they find that information systems, functioning as 'knowledge institutionalizers', cannot fully replace prior experience when it comes to the adoption of certain practices. Therefore, experience continues to play a critical role in institutionalizing certain practices, but certain mechanisms can be highly useful to have employees adopt certain practices or routines. In the same vein, Zollo and Winter (2002: 340) propose that learning mechanisms, dynamic capabilities and routines are inherently linked.

In line with Simonin (1997), Gittell (2002), Kale et al. (2002) and Zollo and Winter (2002), we suggest that alliance capabilities mediate between alliance experience and alliance performance (Asher, 1976; Lehmann et al., 1998). This implies that the effect experience has on alliance performance is explained via a firm's alliance capability (Eisenhardt and Martin, 2000). In line with organizational learning theory logic, we expect the process to be subject to iterations because learning is an inherently interactive and volatile process (Argyris, 1977; Lyles, 1988; Vicari and Troilo, 1998). Learning often results in the adoption of new processes or insights that are expected to yield better outcomes. Subsequently, the adoption of new processes or insights may hamper the experimentation with new or better processes. However, this also gives rise to a tension, which may jeopardize the continuing thrust for improved alliance capabilities as a consequence of the inertia that results from prior experience (March, 1991, in Sampson, 2002: 2).[3] As mentioned earlier, in evolutionary economics terminology, the process is called the evolution cycle (i.e. variation, selection, retention), whereas the knowledge-based view and organizational learning theory refer to the knowledge evolution or transformation cycle (i.e. variation, selection, replication, retention or storage, retrieval, transformation) (Aldrich, 1999; Zollo and Winter, 2002; Carlile and Rebentisch, 2003). Independent of the theoretical tradition, the logic is that firms that effectively integrate knowledge by internally creating variation in the way in which they handle new challenges, subsequently select those practices which have the greatest potential and thereafter routinize these, are most likely to outperform competitors (Grant, 1996a). In Helfat and Peteraf's (2003: 1002) words: '[the] development of a new capability may proceed via an iterative process'. More specifically, the codification of experience makes it easier to apply the lessons learned and accelerates the development of the firm's capabilities and routines (Zander and Kogut, 1995; Argote, 1999). Intra-firm mechanisms help transfer and disseminate knowledge throughout the firm (Grant, 1995), which induces the creation of organizational routines (Nelson and Winter, 1982). Following Grant (1995), mechanisms, such as a vice-president of alliances or an alliance department, are expected to accelerate the learning process as they help institutionalize alliance knowledge throughout the firm. Hence, an alliance capability is an important variable explaining why alliance experience positively influences alliance performance, since it can induce the development of repeatable practices (Eisenhardt and Martin, 2000) via the transfer and replication of experiences and knowledge (Florida and Kenney, 2000) using knowledge-sharing routines (Helleloid and Simonin, 1994; Dyer, 2000; Dyer and Singh, 1998).

4
Towards a Micro-level Understanding of Alliance Capabilities

4.1 Introduction

Recently, scholars suggested that an alliance capability could be viewed as a rare, valuable and difficult-to-imitate resource at the firm level in order to explain the differences in alliance performance between firms (Dyer et al., 2001). In line with earlier studies, we define an alliance capability as a firm's ability to capture, share, disseminate and apply alliance management knowledge (see Chapter 3). This chapter analyses the role (groups of) mechanisms play in enhancing alliance performance. To do so, four groups of mechanisms are identified after which an explication is given of the reasons why that particular group is important for alliance capability development. In order to analyse if indeed these intra-firm mechanisms play an important role in enhancing alliance performance, a comparison is made between low- and high-performing firms using data from a survey of 192 firms worldwide.

4.2 Groups of mechanisms

Intra-firm mechanisms can play an important role as alliance performance antecedents as has been discussed in Chapter 3. They can be divided into four categories. (See Figure 4.1 for an overview of the thirty mechanisms investigated.) The first group consists of 'functions', referring to individual positions or units that manage a number of critical tasks for a firm with respect to its alliances (e.g. a vice-president of alliances or an alliance department). These functions support alliance management in a number of ways. First of all, functions can aid in accumulating and assembling experience in such a way that it is easily transferable to new situations (Cohen and Bacdayan, 1994; Kale et al., 2002). This is sometimes referred to as 'assimilation' (Zahra and George, 2002). Firms may not enter into a new alliance every month nor does it speak for itself that knowledge is not fragmented within the organization. This makes it more relevant to ensure that prior experiences are well stored so that knowledge on, for example, the stages of the process remains up to date (Singh, 2003). Functions can for instance develop codified knowledge about how the various stages of alliances evolve by creating accessible documents. The intention driving this process surpasses mere knowledge transfer and is geared towards supporting the knowledge evolution process of the firm (Zollo and Winter, 2002). Moreover, an alliance department or alliance manager may for instance support day-to-day alliance activities and delineate the critical aspects in a particular stage of a firm's alliance. In this way, earlier experiences can be more easily disseminated throughout the firm and are more likely to create value in the firm's entire alliance portfolio, thereby stimulating alliance performance over the longer run.

Second, functions can help *structurally* coordinate alliance knowledge in the firm (Kale et al., 2002). This means knowledge is shared on a structural basis (Kale and Singh, 1999), which allows individuals to communicate in a more effective manner (Dyer, 2000). For instance, whereas alliance trainings would stimulate knowledge transfer in a restricted period of time, an alliance department provides a structural mechanism to leverage knowledge. In this way, it can act as a central coordination mechanism (Harbison and Pekar, 1998a) or coordinative capacity (Kale and Singh, 1999) to institutionalize alliance knowledge. The ability to integrate and institutionalize knowledge that resides either inside or outside the firm is a distinctive part of an alliance capability (Prahalad and Hamel, 1990; Lorenzoni and Lipparini, 1999). Several studies claim that 'a learning capability' is stimulated by separate organizational units, which are given the responsibility to accumulate, store, integrate and disperse specific knowledge (e.g. Clark and Fujimoto, 1991). For instance, Dyer and Nobeoka (2000) argue that Toyota's Operations Management Consulting Division has developed such a learning capability as a consequence of an organizational unit dedicated to gathering and diffusing valuable production knowledge throughout Toyota and its network of partners.

In similar vein, functions also relate to the concept of absorptive capacity (Cohen and Levinthal, 1990; Lane and Lubatkin, 1998; Zahra and George, 2002). A prerequisite for learning is the existence of a certain knowledge set or body of knowledge in a firm (Oliver, 2001). Nti and Kumar (2001: 121) argue that 'knowledge appropriated by a firm depends on its absorptive capacity and the volume of alliance knowledge created'. The absorptive capacity of the firm is therefore constituted by its prior related knowledge, enabling it to recognize the value of new information and to assimilate and apply it to commercial ends (Cohen and Levinthal, 1990). Although some name experience 'a poor teacher' (Levinthal and March, 1993: 96), it certainly aids in extending a firm's body of prior related knowledge in order to develop an alliance capability (Simonin, 1997).

In general, functions can enhance a firm's ability to learn (Spekman et al., 1999). For instance, assigning an alliance specialist may improve the stock of knowledge related to critical alliance management issues such as what criteria should be applied to future partners. These mechanisms can positively influence the transferability factor in two ways (Khanna et al., 1998). First, these functions determine the extent to which the scope of the alliance overlaps with current firm activities. Second, it can increase the firm's skills to accomplish the transfer of learning. In this case, external coordination of alliances is supported by internal coordination (Takeishi, 2001). Coordination in the alliance itself, in addition to coordination at the firm level, is important (Teece and Pisano, 1994; Nault and Tyagi, 2001) and can be facilitated by the use of for instance an alliance manager or vice-president of alliances.

Moreover, the creation of any of these functions may increase external visibility and give a firm-wide sign that alliances are deemed important (Kale et al., 2002). In this way, it rejects the notion of the 'not-invented here' syndrome (Leonard-Barton, 1995) and can reflect management commitment to both internal and external knowledge exchange (Inkpen, 1998a, b). For instance, an alliance department can help ensure that resources are allocated in an appropriate manner over the firm's alliance portfolio, thereby reducing the chances that alliances fail because of a lack of commitment or poor coordination (Kale et al., 2002).

The second group of mechanisms consists of 'tools'. Tools are practical mechanisms that aid in dealing with day-to-day alliance management issues by increasing know-how of particular stages of the alliance lifecycle or by raising alliance know-how throughout the firm. Tools tend to support functions as they help disseminate knowledge by either codification (e.g. best practices or alliance database) or verbalization (e.g. alliance training). Tools can support management in various ways. First of all, they support alliance management by their potential to ease conflict situations and aid in joint problem solving activities (Mohr and Spekman, 1994; Kale et al., 2000). For example, a firm's ability to find the right partner is critical to its ability to generate sufficient pay-off in the end (Dyer and Singh, 1998). In a similar vein, by sharing their knowledge and expectations in a joint business planning session, partners will become aware of the future direction of the alliance (Spekman et al., 1999).

Second, tools can stimulate sharing of individual experiences and knowledge in general, which in the end fosters the collective competence of the firm (Zollo and Winter, 2002). For instance, the use of an alliance database can prove a structural means through which information on alliance progress is dispersed throughout the firm and codification can be stimulated (Harbison and Pekar, 1998a). Even cultural sensitivity, which can be fostered by cultural trainings, can enhance alliance performance (Johnson et al., 1996).

Third, management of the alliance itself can be supported using tools. The use of evaluation techniques can aid in realizing the alliance objectives. In similar vein, self-assessment and evaluation by partners can instil experiences into alliance managers (Harbison and Pekar, 1998b). Moreover, they can be used to review the health of an alliance and, as a result, help to react in time in case the alliance needs improvement (Callahan and MacKenzie, 1999).

Control and management processes make up the third group of managerial mechanisms. These mechanisms are geared towards support of specific aspects of alliance management; that is control (e.g. alliance metrics), formal use and sharing of particular knowledge (e.g. formally structured knowledge exchange) and accountability (e.g. responsibility level for alliances or reward and bonuses). A number of advantages can result from these mechanisms. First of all, they allow firms to ensure that learning occurs at the firm level, the alliance level as well as on the individual level, thereby optimizing the advantages associated with cooperation (Spekman et al., 1999). At the firm level, control and management processes stimulate learning as they allow different people inside the firm to benefit from knowledge of others, for instance through formally structured knowledge exchanges between alliance managers. At the alliance level, alliance metrics and reward and bonuses that are linked to alliance performance stimulate those involved to perform well but also to remember the lessons learned so as to avoid the same mistakes in future projects. At the individual level, people inside the organization will be more motivated to learn if they know that success is rewarded, potentially leading to more conscious behaviour by the individual. Value creation in alliances will only become effective if knowledge is both transferred and integrated (Almeida et al., 2002). In this context, it is critical to acknowledge that acquired knowledge is only valuable after its diffusion (Hamel et al., 1989) and that the most effective manner to exchange knowledge is from peer to peer (Alliance Analyst, 1999a). For instance, knowledge exchange between alliance managers can be an effective means to formalize communication channels through which valuable knowledge can be transmitted. In many instances, tacit knowledge is shared via informal organizational structures. Formalizing this mechanism may enhance knowledge to not only flow via the informal but also via the formal communication channels. Without underestimating the importance of informal knowledge flows, formalization of knowledge exchange structures helps overcome the incidental nature of informal knowledge exchanges. It may increase the firm-wide awareness of the importance of consistent rather than occasional knowledge exchange between alliance managers.

Second, as is the case for functions, control and management processes can help increase coordination. Since firms are most effective in sharing and transferring knowledge between individuals and units (Kogut and Zander, 1992), they should exploit this ability by establishing both tacit and explicit rules for coordination (Kogut and Zander, 1996). Complexity, being a feature of coordination and integration, will reduce the effectiveness of knowledge exchange (Cyert and March, 1963) and will increase the need to establish clear rules for alliance management. For instance, formalizing knowledge exchange between alliance managers can be a useful mechanism to ensure effective knowledge transfer. Moreover, using sophisticated incentive systems not only stimulates employees to share knowledge in an alliance, but it can also increase employee involvement. Alliance metrics and rewards and bonuses can prove to be useful means to this end. Appropriately rewarding employees positively influences the continuity among personnel, which in turn greatly affects the success of knowledge absorption in the firm (Leonard-Barton, 1995). For instance, when employees involved in a successful alliance are given bonuses or other (financial) rewards, they will be more inclined to stay with the company which prevents the outflow of potentially important insights.

The fourth set of mechanisms that can be used to support alliance management consists of external parties. Firms can use different third parties, such as consultants, lawyers, mediators or financial experts to complement their own knowledge. In other words, third parties can preempt a firm's own lack of knowledge regarding, for instance, contractual arrangements by lawyers or due diligence and valuation by financial experts. Especially companies initiating cooperation with other firms or small firms may find it more useful to build alliance experience via external parties (Alliance Analyst, 1994). External parties can be beneficial for a number of reasons. First, the potential value a third party can contribute resides not only in practical problem solving or in developing alliance-specific know-how; it can also assist in conflict resolution (Conlon and Sullivan, 1999; Margulis and Pekar, 2001). Second, it can underscore the partners' commitment to the alliance as an external party tends to be more objective, to increase neutrality and bring an increased level of equality in the planning process (Alliance Analyst, 1996b). Third, it may enhance the commitment to deliver and ensure the goals set are reached (Alliance Analyst, 1996b).

This section of the study has categorized the intra-firm mechanisms that may play an important role in developing alliance capabilities. As mentioned, these mechanisms are important for a great variety of reasons. Not only do different mechanisms engender the ability to share knowledge inside the firm, they also help in day-to-day management practices and coordination and control of responsibilities. Moreover, taking a broader perspective, they allow for a better understanding of capability development in general, which has recently been identified as a central research theme in strategic management (e.g. Gittell, 2002; Montealegre, 2002; Ranft and Lord, 2002). Given its relative youth, this field has only advanced the topic via a restricted number of studies that contribute to enhancing our understanding of the critical mechanisms involved in capability development (Dosi et al., 2000b). We expect the various groups of intra-firm mechanisms to play a central role in the development of alliance capabilities. Therefore, we formulate the following research question: *what is the influence of (groups of) intra-firm mechanisms on alliance performance?*

4.3 Analysis and results

In this section, we look at the following two issues: (1) the influence of individual or item-level analysis of the intra-firm mechanisms and (2) the influence of groups of intra-firm mechanisms or scale-level analysis to explain the role of these mechanisms in developing alliance capabilities.

Item-based testing of mechanisms

For the purpose of this section of the study, low-performing firms were separated from high-performing firms. Low-performing firms were defined as having an alliance performance level between 0 per cent and 40 per cent and high-performing firms between 61 per cent and 100 per cent. Firms having a performance level between 41 per cent and 60 per cent were left out of this particular analysis. We chose to exclude this category because prior studies suggest that on average success rates of alliances vary from 40 per cent to 60 per cent (for an overview see Duysters et al., 1999a). Differentiating between low- and high-performing firms allows for a comparison of these groups and to what extent they use different kinds of mechanisms. Having specified the mechanisms that firms can use to develop alliance capabilities, Figure 4.1 shows the top ten mechanisms that are most often used. First, a striking 87 per cent of the respondents confirms the use of partner programmess to manage their alliances. A partner programme is defined as a tool that describes different types of alliances and accompanies alliance management processes. Second, 69 per cent of the respondents makes use of an alliance specialist, someone who knows much about alliance management and supports alliance managers in their day-to-day activities. Third, 65 per cent of the respondents evaluates its alliances separately. Fourth, 64 per cent of the respondents uses an alliance database containing information about the firm's alliance experiences so far. Fifth, joint business planning,

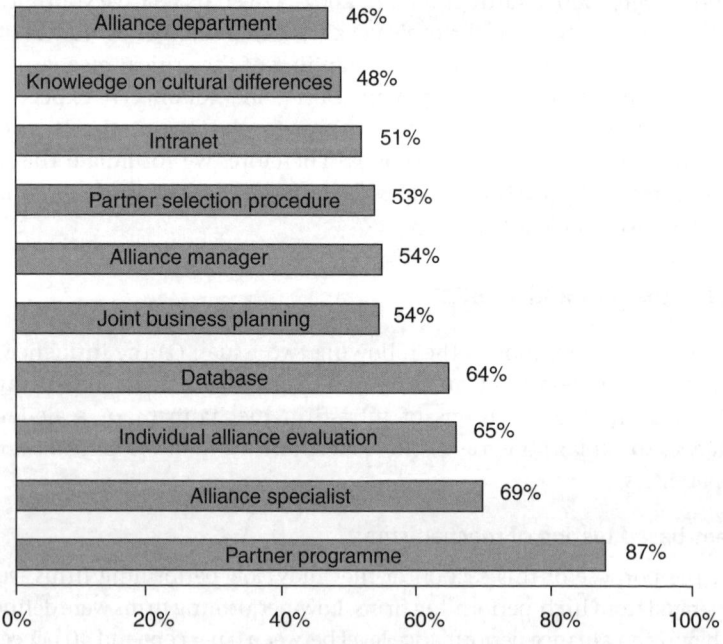

Figure 4.1 Use of alliance mechanisms in percentages

which has been defined as a standardized approach to define a business plan together with partners, is used by 54 per cent of the respondents. Sixth, an alliance manager is in place in 54 per cent of the respondent firms. Seventh, a standard partner selection approach is used by 53 per cent of the respondents, while 51 per cent uses intranet to disperse alliance-related information. Ninth, 48 per cent of the firms in our dataset makes use of specific knowledge to manage country differences in alliances. Last, 46 per cent uses an alliance department or alliance function to internally organize and structure alliance management.

For the analysis of differences or similarities among low- and high-performing alliance firms, this study – in line with Duysters and Hagedoorn (2001) – uses discriminant analysis. Various analyses were supported by the SPSS 10.0 version. Discriminant analysis is a statistical method that enables us to identify differences between classes or groups, where group membership is determined a priori (McLachlan, 1992; Tabachnick and Fidell, 2001).[1] Huberty and Barton (1989) and Huberty (1984) distinguish between descriptive discriminant analysis (equality of group means) and predictive discriminant analysis (prediction of group membership). Discriminant analysis has been widely applied in the social sciences, where it has proved to be a powerful technique to uncover differences between groups with respect to various variables simultaneously. Over the years, it has allowed scholars from a wide variety of research backgrounds to articulate statistical solutions to an array of predictive problems (Klecka, 1980). In this study, by making use of various dummy variables that represent the different mechanisms, discriminant analysis can help analyse if high-performing firms use certain mechanisms more often than low-performing firms. It may allow us to verify which mechanisms are most important in enhancing alliance performance.

In contrast to regression analysis, where the dependent variable is continuous, discriminant function analysis can be used to deal with categorical dependent variables (Klecka, 1980; Hair et al., 1998). This allows for a differentiation among the various categories of alliance performance by means of a discriminant function, which derives the maximum discrimination between the two groups using alliance performance group membership as a categorical, dependent variable. The weights of the discriminant function are estimated in order to obtain the largest discriminating power between the categories. A test of equality of group means is used to generate additional information that can be used to determine if the groups differ significantly on the various variables. In total, thirty mechanisms were identified that could enhance a firm's alliance performance. If significant differences were found between low- and high-performing firms, this would support the view that the mechanisms investigated can be used to develop alliance capabilities. This would indicate that these intra-firm factors play a critical role in enhancing a firm's alliance performance.

To reveal patterns of the effect of alliance capabilities on alliance performance, discriminant function analysis was applied using the dummy for alliance performance as a categorical, dependent variable. The starting point for this analysis is the evaluation of the mean scores on the individual variables of firms from the two main success categories. A test was performed to measure whether group means of independent variables differ significantly (see Appendix 6).[2] The results indicate that the mean values of fifteen variables differ significantly between the two groups. The 'goodness' of the discriminant functions is also considered and the results are reflected in various indicators presented in Tables 4.1 and 4.2.[3] The first indicator is the eigenvalue which represents the relationship of the between group and the within group sum of squares. Higher eigenvalues can be associated with more discriminating functions. In this case, the function seems to have moderate to strong discriminating power. Other important statistics include the canonical correlation, which represents the proportion of total variance that is accounted for by differences among low- and high-performing firms. A chi-square value of 39.959 and a corresponding significance of .085 imply that the hypothesis, that the mean scores on the various variables for the different groups are equal, can be rejected at the 10 per cent level. The effectiveness of the discriminant functions is measured by classifying all cases according to their scores on the combined discriminant functions.

Table 4.1 Eigenvalues

Function	Eigenvalue	% of variance	Cumulative %	Can. correlation
1	.386*	100.0	100.0	.528

* First 1 canonical discriminant functions were used in the analysis.

Table 4.2 Wilks' lambda

Test of function(s)	Wilks' lambda	Chi-square	df	Sig.
1	.722	39.959	29	.085*

* $p < .10$

Whereas the prior probability of classification is 50 per cent in case of equally sized groups, the actual classification procedure results in a correct classification of 74.8 per cent of the cases. This points to a relatively large degree of divergence among firms from the two success categories. To ensure that the results of the model tested were indeed robust, we performed a number of additional tests (i.e. the Box's M test, the hit ratio and Pearson correlation matrix, variance matrix and nominal regression; see Appendix 10 for the results of these tests). These tests all confirmed that our results are robust and are not influenced by violation of assumptions.

In order to get additional insight into the importance of the predictors, it is interesting to investigate structure coefficients. Although some scholars also suggest analysing standardized coefficients to verify the relative impact of the predictors, we did not perform this analysis since the results can be skewed dependent upon the overlap in discriminating information (Klecka, 1980).[4] The next table (Table 4.3) shows the structure matrix, which shows the structure coefficients for our predictors. The predictors are listed from high loadings to low loadings. These coefficients help determine the relative similarity between a certain variable and a discriminating function (Klecka, 1980). They represent full correlations (loadings) and tell us how closely a certain variable and the discriminating function are related. The greater the absolute magnitude nears + 1.0 or –1.0, the more a coefficient carries the same information as the function. In this way, these coefficients provide us with another means to determine what variables are most useful in discriminating between low- and high-performing firms. There is no consensus with respect to what level represents a good cut-off point (Tabachnick and Fidell, 2001). However, in general loadings of .30 and higher denote a significant contribution of the predictor to the discriminant function. We reckon that eleven predictors have sufficiently large loadings to identify these as discriminating factors between low- and high-performing firms. Consequently, the following variables are considered important on basis of the structure matrix: alliance database, vice-president of alliances, use of intranet, use of own knowledge of prior experiences, alliance manager, partner selection programmes, formal exchange of alliance knowledge, joint alliance evaluation, individual alliance evaluation, alliance metrics and alliance department. Of these eleven variables, all eleven show a significant p-value (< 5%) in Appendix 6. Consequently, we deem these predictors relevant in order to distinguish between low- and high-performing firms.

Table 4.3 Structure matrix

Mechanisms	Function 1
Alliance database	−.546
Vice-President of alliances	.441
Use of intranet to disperse alliance knowledge	.418
Use of own (international) alliance knowledge	.379
Alliance manager	.379
Partner selection programmes	.367
Formally structured knowledge exchange between alliance managers	.340
Joint alliance evaluation	.332
Individual alliance evaluation	.331
Alliance metrics	.314
Alliance department	.295
Mediators	.268
Alliance best practices	.259
External alliance training	.255
Local alliance manager	.247
Rewards and bonuses for alliance managers	.219
Rewards and bonuses for business managers	.214
Consultants	.194
International alliance training	.169
Alliance specialist	−.168
Financial experts	.154
Gatekeepers	.147
Internal alliance training	.135
Country-specific alliance policies	.132
Partner programmes	−.125
Comparison of alliance evaluations	.076
Legal experts	−.058
Joint business planning	.039
Culture programmes	.008

Scale-based testing of mechanisms

In addition to the analyses reflecting the significance of individual mechanisms, it is also important to analyse whether underlying dimensions exist which link individual mechanisms (see e.g. Gorsuch, 1983). To investigate whether any underlying dimensions exist in our variable set, we apply exploratory factor analysis (EFA) for dichotomous independents (see e.g. Muthen, 1978; Muthen and Christoffersson, 1981). The goal of EFA is to derive the smallest number of interpretable factors so as to adequately explain the apparent correlations among the variables used. The basic principle underlying factor analysis is that measures that are highly correlated are likely to be influenced by the same factors, while those that are relatively uncorrelated are likely to be influenced by different factors (Kim and Mueller, 1978; DeCoster, 2003). Therefore, in contrast to other data reduction techniques such as principal component analysis, factor analysis only carriers out the common variance in the factor matrix, thereby excluding the specific and error variance. Whereas EFA allows each observed variable to be related to a latent variable contained in the analysis, confirmatory factor analysis (CFA) does not (see for an overview Suhr, 2004). In other words, factors in an exploratory setting do not correspond to the constructs represented by each factor, but each factor is defined as a weighted sum of all observed variables (Gerbing and Anderson, 1988: 189). Therefore, EFA is preferred to CFA as, to the best of our knowledge, no classification of intra-firm mechanisms involved in the development of alliance capabilities has to date been specified. Having performed EFA, it is essential to embed these interpretations into the theoretical underpinnings of the study. Hence, EFA was used to uncover dimensions underlying groups of mechanisms deployed by firms in our database. Using such a data reduction technique, this analysis helps us identify latent dimensions underlying groups of mechanisms (Hair et al., 1998). Given the nature of this technique, the exploratory factor analytic model used can be written as (see Bollen, 1989; Muthen, 2004):

$$y_i = \upsilon + \Lambda\eta + \varepsilon_i \tag{4.1}$$

where y_i is the p-dimensional latent response variable vector, η is the m-dimensional vector of latent variables (constructs or factors), ε_i is a p-dimensional vector of residual or measurement errors which is uncorrelated with other variables; and υ and $\wedge$ are parameter arrays with υ being the p-dimensional parameter vector of measurement intercepts and $\wedge$ the $p \times m$ parameter matrix of measurement slopes or factor loadings. This model has restricted computational conditions that are particular to the EFA model in Mplus. These restrictions are imposed to ease computational ways of reaching viable statistical solutions (see Muthen (2004) for a complete overview of the technical appendices and assumptions underlying Mplus).

In line with a comparable recent study by Davies and Walters (2004), we made use of EFA to construct our scales and verify the validity of our constructs. We used the original dataset to construct a 30 × 192 matrix containing the 30 mechanisms for our 192 respondents. The matrix consists of mechanisms that are all dichotomous (see earlier discussion on measurement). Given that applying the familiar factor analysis procedures with dichotomous items often produces uninterpretable results (Bernstein and Teng, 1989), a statistical package called Mplus was used to perform the factor analysis.[5] Given the categorical nature of the data, Mplus instead of more conventional packages were used since this program is able to perform factor analyses with binary variables (Muthen, 1978; Bartholomew, 1987; Agresti, 1990). Mplus 2.14 Muthen & Muthen was used to perform the analysis (for an overview and comparison of the programs used for factor analyses, we refer to Bartholomew (1987) and Uebersax (2000)). In Mplus, factor indicators for EFA may be continuous, categorical or a combination of continuous and categorical. Consequently, Mplus diverges mostly from other Structural Equation Modelling software packages because of its ability to fit latent variables to databases which consist of dichotomous outcome variables (see also Muthen, 1983, 1984; Xie, 1989). In these factor analyses, a rotational method called oblique or PROMAX rather than an orthogonal method or VARIMAX was used, as the latter assumes there is no intercorrelation between the independents (Lawley and Maxwell, 1971; Tucker and MacCallum, 1997). Since we do expect the mechanisms to be correlated, PROMAX was chosen. In other words, oblique rotation more accurately reflects the underlying structure and nature of the data. As the mechanisms have been measured as nominal variables, the factor analysis made use of dichotomous variables (Muthen and Christoffersson, 1981).

On basis of an iterative process, we compared and contrasted different factor structures. The results for the multi-item measures are presented in the next table (Table 4.4). With a sample size of approximately 200 cases, the factor loadings should be .40 or higher in order to be significant at the 5 per cent level (Hair et al., 1998: 112). We also looked at the construct validity, which verifies whether the performance of the measure is consistent with the theoretically derived expectations (Lewis-Beck, 1994: 19), by calculating the Cronbach's alpha. Cronbach and Meehl (1955: 282) underline the importance of construct validity when they mention that 'construct validity must be investigated whenever no criterion or universe of content is accepted as entirely adequate to define the quality to be measured'. The coefficient alpha is calculated to measure the internal consistency of the items used in the scale as follows (Lewis-Beck, 1994; Garson, 1999):

$$\alpha = \frac{N\rho}{(1+\rho(N-1))} \quad (4.2)$$

where N equals the number of items and ρ is the mean inter-item correlation.[6] When the α is greater than .50, the variance explained by the trait is greater than that by the error components (Bagozzi, 1981). The coefficient alphas are allowed to decrease to the .70 level (Nunally and Bernstein, 1994). Whereas the second factor is slightly below the recommended level (0.63), the first factor is substantially higher (0.82). However, both factors are adopted for a number of reasons. First of all, although the Cronbach's alpha is somewhat lower for one of our measures, it may be somewhat lower and drop to the .60 level in exploratory research settings (Robinson et al., 1991). As to our knowledge no mechanisms have so far been empirically derived that distinguish between different levels of organizational learning, we reckon that it is important to develop such a measure.

Moreover, this study does not measure items that relate to a certain psychological issue, attitude or consumer behaviour typology (Oppenheim, 1966). Such scales are much more likely to show high correlations (e.g. Nunally, 1978; Peter and Olson, 2004). Second, and perhaps more importantly, these empirically derived mechanisms allow us to better understand how firms develop alliance capabilities. It is only when looking for such measures that we can get a micro-level understanding of the mechanisms that lie at the basis of alliance capability development. Third, prior conceptual research has hinted at the existence of different types of learning infrastructures (Scharmer, 2001), which aim to coordinate learning within the organization. Last, in factor analysis one should always try to balance between optimizing the Cronbach's alpha of a measure and the items contained in the measure. When very few items which correlate highly are chosen, this increases the Cronbach's alpha but is likely to reduce the explanatory power of the measure For these reasons, we decided to include the items shown in Table 4.4.

In addition to the calculation of the Cronbach's alphas for the internal consistency of the items used, two other types of scale validity are interesting: criterion-related validity and content or face validity (Nunally and Bernstein, 1994). Concurrent validity, which is a form of criterion-related validity, refers to the relationship between the dependent and independent measures (Hinkin, 1995). With respect to criterion-related validity, Nunally (1978: 87) notes that this 'is at issue when the purpose is to use an instrument to estimate some important form of behavior that is external to the measuring instrument itself'. In case of measuring alliance capabilities, this issue seems highly relevant, since the mechanisms measured are expected to represent a firm's dedication

Table 4.4 Exploratory factor analysis and reliability of factor-based scales[a]

Subordinate variables[b] (Questionnaire items)	Factor 1 Organization-level learning mechanisms	Factor 2 Group-level learning mechanisms
Cronbach's alpha	0.82	0.63
Eigenvalue	6.864	1.778
VP of alliances (1)	0.728	
Alliance manager (4)	0.885	
Local alliance manager (6)	0.784	
Internal alliance training (7)	0.463	
External alliance training (8)		0.557
International alliance training (9)		0.551
Partner selection programmes (10)	0.516	
Intranet (13)	0.541	
Alliance best practices (14)		0.938
Culture programmes (15)		0.589
Comparison of alliance evaluations (18)	0.532	
Rewards for alliance managers tied to alliance performance (21)	0.960	
Formally structured knowledge exchange between alliance managers (23)	0.591	
Alliance metrics (25)		0.688
Country-specific alliance policies (26)	0.521	

[a] Factor analysis and Cronbach's alpha were performed for the entire sample ($N = 192$)
[b] All variables used are measured as dichotomous items (0 = mechanism is not used; 1 = mechanism is used)

and intention to share alliance-related knowledge and institutionalize it. Concurrent validity is assessed by correlating a measure Y (i.e. alliance performance) and the criterion X (i.e. mechanisms) at the same point in time (Lewis-Beck, 1994). As Y is continuous and X is dichotomous (of the 0–1 type), we can use Pearson correlation (Tabachnick and Fidell, 2001). Appendix 7 shows that eighteen out of the thirty variables measured have a correlation between .10 and .30 (of which nine are significant at the 5% level). We reckon that even though these are modest correlations they represent an important aspect of the internal drivers of a firm's alliance capability development.[7]

Content or face validity, as Nunally (1978: 11) notes, 'concerns judgments about an instrument after it is constructed'. Consequently, it examines the extent to which it 'looks like' it measures what it intends to measure (Lewis-Beck, 1994). All twelve experts considered the questionnaire items relating to alliance capability (i.e. the thirty mechanisms) to be highly important or important to the firm's ability to develop an alliance capability. Moreover, very recent studies by Gittell (2002), Kale et al. (2002) and Sarkar et al. (2004), which can be seen as recent exceptions as they make new contributions to measuring capabilities, have also used mechanisms as a proxy for a firm's capability. This establishes the content or face validity of this study (Cronbach and Meehl, 1955). Concluding, we reckon that, despite the relative absence of operationalizations in the field of capability development, the results of the reliability and validity statistics suggest that this study has found a sound fashion for grasping the essence of alliance capabilities and potentially organizational capabilities in general.

Finally, besides internal validity, external consistency can be determined by calculating by substituting indicators of one construct with those of another construct (Gerbing and Anderson, 1988). Calculating this figure by exchanging indicators among our constructs substantially decreased the coefficient alphas. These results confirm the internal and external consistency of our scales (Gerbing and Anderson, 1988: 186). On the basis of these results, unidimensionality is also ensured for both scales, since the alpha coefficient suggests that the measures used refer to the existence of a single trait (Churchill, 1979; McDonald, 1981).

Table 4.4 also shows the eigenvalues of the factors, which is a criterion for the number of factors to extract from the analysis. As the values of the latent root or eigenvalues are all greater than 1, they are all above the cut-off level of 1 (Hair et al., 1998: 103). This indicates that these factors explain more than the variance of a single variable and hence they can be included. The root mean square residual is 0.0707, which is an acceptable level (Hair et al., 1998). The factor correlation is 0.551, which is a moderate level of intercorrelation, suggesting that the factors overlap to some degree but also represent conceptually distinct measures.

Having derived two factors using exploratory factor analysis, a summated scale, which consists of the sum of the individual variables, is formed on basis of a composite measure (Spector, 1991; Hair et al., 1998). Our summated scale or alliance capability development construct (ACDC) then looks as follows:

$$\text{ACDC} = \text{organization-level learning mechanisms} + \text{group-level learning mechanisms} \quad (4.3)$$

where organization-level learning mechanisms represent the sum of the items listed in the second column and group-level learning mechanisms represent the sum of items listed in the third column. In this way, we have created a summated scale for alliance capability development. Using a summated scale has several benefits. First of all, in our case a summated scale helps correct for non-normality. As all of our independent variables are binary, creating a summated scale turns non-metric data into metric data. Second, measurement error that is inherent in any measured variable is reduced. As a consequence of the summated scale, several indicators are used to represent a certain phenomenon. Third, combining various mechanisms in a summated scale for alliance capability development allows us to better capture the many facets of such a complex concept. Therefore, as EFA has allowed us to eliminate some less relevant mechanisms, we have created a richer and more developed description of the concept. And finally, and perhaps most important, using a summated scale substantially reduces the amount of independent variables used in our analysis. This will support the trustworthiness of our results in the next chapter as we have a very high ratio of cases to variables (i.e. 1:96), which is more than sufficient to generate reliable results (Schwab, 1980; Hosmer and Lemeshow, 2000; Tabachnick and Fidell, 2001).

To reveal patterns of the effect of these two factors on alliance performance, we test if these two factors make a difference when it comes to developing alliance capabilities. Therefore, we make again use of a categorical dependent variable to compare high- (61%–100%) and low-performing firms (0%–40%). In line with Duysters and Hagedoorn (2001), discriminant analysis is again used to compare these two groups and the extent to which these two factors are critical to enhance alliance performance. As the 41–60 per cent-performance group is left out of the analysis and due to missing cases, for this analysis $N = 117$. As control variables, we include firm size (calculated as the number of employees), alliance experience (calculated as the number of alliances formed) and two control variables for the ICT and service sector respectively. The results are presented in the next table (Table 4.5). It shows that the mean values of the two 'factor' variables differ significantly and that both factors discriminate between the two groups. Moreover, of the four control variables included two are significant. While neither of the two industry controls, ICT and service sector, are significant, both alliance experience and firm size play respectively a very important to moderately important role in explaining alliance performance differences. The Wilks' lambda reports on the group variance in relation to the total variance. Higher ratios reflect equality of group means, whereas lower values are associated with greater differences of group means. Moreover, for each factor the *F*-value is calculated, which verifies whether all group means are equal. The results show that the hypotheses that group means are equal can be rejected at the 5 per cent level for the organization-level mechanisms while it can be rejected at the 1 per cent level for the group-level mechanisms. This suggests that both factors discriminate between low- and high-performing firms and implies that high-performing firms make substantially more use of the mechanisms underlying these two factors than low-performing firms.

After the test of equality of groups means, additional statistics were analysed to assess the discriminatory power of the total set of variables. The goodness of fit of the overall function is presented in the next two tables (Tables 4.6 and 4.7).

Table 4.5 Test of equality of group means

	Wilks' lambda	F-value	df	Sig.
Organization-level learning mechanisms	.947	6.386	129	.013*
Group-level learning mechanisms	.944	6.847	129	.010**
Alliance experience	.890	14.259	129	.000***
Firm size	.973	3.146	129	.079+
ICT sector	.999	0.120	129	.729
Service sector	.997	0.391	129	.533

*** $p < 0.001$; ** $p < 0.01$; * $p < 0.05$; + $p < 0.10$

Table 4.6 Eigenvalues

Function	Eigenvalue	% of variance	Cumulative %	Can. correlation
1	.204*	100.0	100.0	.412

* First 1 canonical discriminant functions were used in the analysis.

Table 4.7 Wilks' lambda

Test of function(s)	Wilks' lambda	Chi-square	Df	Sig.
1	.831	20.791	6	.002***

*** $p < .001$; ** $p < .01$; * $p < .05$; + $p < .10$

The tables report on various indicators such as the eigenvalue, canonical correlation, Wilks' lambda and the chi-square statistic. The eigenvalue represents the relationship of the between group and the within group sum of squares. Higher eigenvalues can be associated with more discriminating functions. In this case, the functions seem to have moderate discriminating power. Other important statistics include the canonical correlation, which represents the proportion of total variance that is accounted for by differences among low- and high-performing firms. A chi-square value of 20.791 and a corresponding significance of .002 implies that the hypothesis, that the mean scores on the various variables for different performance groups are equal, can be rejected at the 0.1 per cent level.[8]

Moreover, the effectiveness of the discriminant functions can be measured by classifying all cases according to their scores on the combined discriminant functions. Whereas the prior probability of classification is 50 per cent in case of equally sized groups, the actual classification procedure results in a correct classification of 68.4 per cent of the cases. This points to a relatively large degree of divergence among firms from the two success categories.

The next table (Table 4.8) shows another interesting measure that was also used in the former analysis: the structure matrix. This matrix is highly relevant as it reflects the relative similarity between a certain variable and a discriminating function (Klecka, 1980). They represent full correlations (loadings) and tell us how closely a certain variable and discriminating function are related. The greater the absolute magnitude nears +1.0 or −1.0, the more a coefficient carries the same information as the function. In this way, these coefficients provide us with another means to determine what variables are most useful in discriminating between low- and high-performing firms. As mentioned earlier, there is no consensus with respect to what level represents a good cut-off point

Table 4.8 Structure matrix

	Function 1
Organization-level learning mechanisms	.522
Group-level learning mechanisms	.540
Firm size	.366
Alliance experience	.780
ICT sector	.072
Service sector	.129

(Tabachnick and Fidell, 2001). However, any loading exceeding the .30 level is deemed substantial. From the table, it is apparent that both factors have high to very high loadings. Hence, both factors can be identified as discriminating factors between low- and high-performing firms. Furthermore, on basis of these statistics the control variables representing firm size and alliance experience also discriminate between successful and unsuccessful firms.

4.4 Interpretation and discussion

In line with recent research on alliance capability development, this chapter has confirmed the positive relationship between alliance capabilities and alliance performance (e.g. Powell et al., 1996; Anand and Khanna, 2000; Sivadas and Dwyer, 2000; Kale et al., 2002; Lambe et al., 2002). In doing so, the attempt was to fill the empirical lack of micro-level evidence by analysing the influence of intra-firm mechanisms on alliance performance. This chapter therefore investigates the specific mechanisms or building blocks underlying a firm's ability to develop an alliance capability at two levels: item-level and scale-level.

Item-level analysis

With respect to the item-level analysis, we find that successful alliance firms employ certain alliance functions, tools and alliance control and management processes to a greater extent than unsuccessful firms. Of course, this is to a certain degree dependent on the number of alliances a firm engages in. Moreover, the duration of a firm's alliances may also influence its ability to develop an alliance capability. However, the latter issue is not taken into account in this study. These results are also in line with other studies related to capability development, which have recently been performed in various broader settings and confirm the influence of mechanisms on performance (see e.g. Coriat, 2000; Fujimoto, 2000; Gittell, 2002). The results of our empirical analysis enable us to reveal some important findings about the use and performance effect of various mechanisms. Because of their potential to enhance learning in alliances, a number of functions were expected to significantly contribute to alliance performance. The analyses demonstrated that high-performing alliance firms had a significantly higher number of important functions in place than low-performing firms. In particular, the use of vice-presidents of alliances, alliance departments and alliance managers proved to be a key factor to obtain enhanced alliance performance for many firms in our sample. These functions are likely to facilitate and direct the dissemination of alliance knowledge within their firm. Furthermore, they act as human-embodied repositories of alliance knowledge within the firm. In many instances, they also take on an active role in coordinating and managing alliance activity within a firm.

The second group of mechanisms under study was referred to as 'tools'. Tools are needed to support management in making the right alliance decisions and in dealing with critical choices, such as partner selection and alliance evaluation issues. In this respect, the use of partner selection programmes proved to be a critical tool for many high-performing alliance firms. Moreover, the application of knowledge dissemination tools, such as alliance databases and intranet environments, proved to be of significant importance. Their role is to stimulate the sharing of individual and collectively acquired know-how among members of the organization. Finally, making use of specific tools can support the operational phase of alliance management. From the results, it was evident that successful alliance firms employed significantly more alliance evaluation tools than their low-performing counterparts.

Control and management processes make up our third group of mechanisms. Evidence indicated that successful firms use alliance metrics to measure their performance in alliances. Furthermore, two mechanisms, which are aimed at sharing and transferring knowledge between individuals and units, seemed to be of particular importance: formal exchange of experience among alliance managers and the use and distribution of knowledge about national culture differences in international alliances. Strikingly, the only external party supporting alliance management that proved to play a moderately significant role in determining alliance success was an alliance mediator ($p < .10$). The results of our study indicate that high-performing alliance firms seem to be confident and capable enough to do without the intervention of other external parties such as financial experts, consultants or legal experts. Another explanation is that these functions are already available internally.

This study also looked at mean differences of important factors such as firm size (measured in terms of sales revenues), alliance experience (measured as the number of prior alliances) and industries (for ICT and service sectors). Alliance experience and to a lesser degree firm size were found to play a significant role. Within our database, large firms tend to perform better than their smaller counterparts. In line with earlier studies, alliance experience is suggested to be an important determinant of a firm's alliance performance (e.g. Westney, 1988; Lei and Slocum, 1992;

Simonin, 1997; Kale et al., 2002; Reuer et al., 2002b). The next chapter will more extensively deal with the role of alliance experience and its relationship with alliance capabilities.

Scale-level analysis

In addition to the item-level analysis results, we have also analysed the role of mechanisms at a higher level of abstraction. Given the absence of a sound construct in the area of alliance capability development, it is important to develop a reliable and valid construct. We used exploratory factor analysis to derive different groups of mechanisms and determine what mechanisms were to be included in our measurement scale (Rummel, 1970; Comrey and Lee, 1992; DeCoster, 2003; Suhr, 2004).

Having created a summated scale that defines two factors critical to developing alliance capabilities, it becomes interesting to interpret their precise meaning. Interpreting the dimensions that result from the factor analysis, we reckon that there is evidence that these two factors represent the mechanisms through which firms integrate (group-level learning – Factor 2) and institutionalize (organization-level learning – Factor 1) alliance-related knowledge (Crossan et al., 1999). Whereas group-level learning mechanisms help firms disperse knowledge on alliances among employees, organization-level learning mechanisms help firms to embed practices and routines on alliances inside the firm. One of the obvious advantages of embedding knowledge is that it becomes engrained in the organization's memory (e.g. Cohen and Bacdayan, 1994). However, when becoming 'sticky', it also creates organizational inertia (Szulanski, 1996; Tripsas and Gavetti, 2000). Similarly, Brown and Duguid (2001) describe the difficulty of balancing 'unstructured creative practices' and 'explicit and structure processes'. Crossan et al. (1999: 525) suggest that 'integrating' knowledge aims to create shared understanding in order to engender coherent and collective action through shared practices at the group. 'Institutionalizing', however, refers to the extent to which a firm has embedded knowledge in systems, structures, information systems, routines and prescribed practices. Whereas the integration of knowledge mainly takes place at the group level, institutionalization mainly takes mainly place at the organization or corporate level. Similarly, group-level learning refers to the degree to which a firm has installed an internal learning infrastructure which builds on action and reflection between group members, while organization-level learning involves the creation of shared action, reflection, will, and or routines among all people inside the organization (Kanter, 1994; Dyer, 2000; Scharmer, 2001). The main characteristic of organizational learning therefore is that lessons learned are accepted and seen as guiding principles firm-wide. From a positivist viewpoint, they become 'justified true beliefs'. At the same time, for learning to occur over time different levels are dependent on one another. For instance, by developing new manuals and training material for group-level learning, an organization is likely to adapt new routines over time. Similarly, an alliance department may call upon external trainings or development of best practices to ensure employees are given new information on alliance management. In this way, group-level learning can be an impetus to renew or an input to adjust organization-level learning practices.

While the dimensions identified are related to different levels of learning, there is an interesting difference between group and organization-level learning with respect to the purpose served. Taking a closer look at the five mechanisms of group-level learning (see Table 4.4), we see that these mechanisms largely help transfer knowledge which fosters the firm's ability to manage individual alliances. For instance, external alliance trainings and sharing best practices is likely to facilitate the sharing of generalized lessons from past experiences or other firms. These mechanisms are likely to mainly transfer generic or instrumental knowledge. They are likely to involve tools and instruments that provide insight into the 'basics of alliance management'. Hence, the mechanisms used for group-level learning are most likely to enhance a firm's ability to manage individual alliances more successfully. The mechanisms used for organization-level learning (see again Table 4.4) are of different bread. While the group-level learning mechanisms were specifically useful to transfer knowledge with regard to successful dyadic alliance management issues, the organization-level learning mechanisms are more appropriate to enhance alliance management practices with respect to the firm's alliance portfolio. For instance, mechanisms such as an alliance manager, a vice-president of alliances and rewards for alliance managers become especially useful in case a firm has to manage multiple alliances simultaneously. In this way, coordinative efforts and responsibility assignment ease the difficulty to manage a set of alliances. Other mechanisms such as an internal training and comparison of alliance evaluations can be used to compare lessons from different alliances the firm is engaged in. This reasoning is in line with a study by Draulans et al. (2003), who find that comparison of alliance evaluations enhances alliance performance for firms with extensive alliance experience; it does not substantially impact the performance of inexperienced firms. Hence, organization-level learning mechanisms help share knowledge that is contextual and specific rather than generic. In this way, as Sarkar et al. (2004: 3) posit, 'coordinating knowledge and resource flows across the different constituent elements of a firm's alliance portfolio may be a value creating mechanism in itself'.

In practice, firms have also shown to make use of a mixture of learning mechanisms to reap the benefits of their learning experiences. Ghoshal and Bartlett (1999) pay extensive attention to how successful firms, such as IBM, 3M and McKinsey manage to internalize their experiences. They suggest that *individual* experiences and the ability to leverage these experiences via transfer and learning mechanisms in these firms are key drivers of their success. Success at, for instance, McKinsey depends heavily on investments in the expertise of personnel, the use of tools, processes and internal information systems such as workshops and trainings. These aspects have enabled McKinsey to capitalize on individual knowledge and embed these in organizational routines. In short, they enhanced McKinsey's ability to learn and develop shared practices (Ghoshal and Bartlett, 1999: 77). Similarly, Kleiner and Roth (1987) demonstrate the relevance and necessity for firms to capture and disseminate prior lessons learned. When it comes to alliance management, Dyer (2000) describes a number of successful firms and what actions they undertook to develop their alliance capabilities. His book clearly delineates the internal process and commitment that is needed to make this happen. It requires prolonged dedicated efforts to learn from experiences and to consciously disperse and embed these lessons in routines to foster sustainable competitive advantages.

In line with the logic that firms can develop their own capabilities, the concept of capability lifecycles or stages has only very recently been introduced. In these studies, different cycles or stages are suggested to require different mechanisms in order to develop alliance capabilities. Draulans et al. (2003) and Helfat and Peteraf (2003) posit that firms can go through different 'development paths', deploying different types of mechanisms along the way. Different mechanisms and routines are therefore suggested to be of particular use at different stages. Helfat and Peteraf (2003) contend that the capability lifecycle consists of a number of stages. There is an optimum or maturity in the level of capability each stage can bring, but it requires a complex interplay of various factors to get to the next stage of the lifecycle. This logic is in line with recent organizational learning literature, which suggests that learning cycles – like 4I framework by Crossan et al. (1999)[9] or the knowledge transformation cycle by Carlile and Rebentisch (2003) – lie at the basis of institutionalization. These studies also suggest that firms learn via

84 *Developing Alliance Capabilities*

internal mechanisms (see e.g. Argote, 1999; Hansen et al., 1999; Mankins, 2004). The next figure (Figure 4.2) represents the organizational learning process that lies at the basis of capability cycles.

The figure attempts to enhance our understanding of what role intra-firm learning mechanisms play in advancing alliance capabilities. It depicts three capability curves that represent different stages of capability development (see also Table 3.1 and the accompanying discussion). Each capability curve is related to an experience level. Each stage is linked to a level at which learning is most likely to be predominantly observable. Therefore, whereas the first stage is related to individual level learning, the second stage is linked to group-level learning and the third stage is linked to organization-level learning. Comparing the means of the low, medium and high experience groups in our study, the F-tests clearly indicate that the use of both organization-level mechanisms ($F = 32.388$, $p < .001$) and group-level mechanisms ($F = 3.120$, $p < .05$) significantly differ between experience levels (see Appendix 11 for results). These figures suggest that, when firms are said to have difficulty in advancing their alliance capabilities, learning mechanisms can help them overcome the limitations of each capability cycle. Hence,

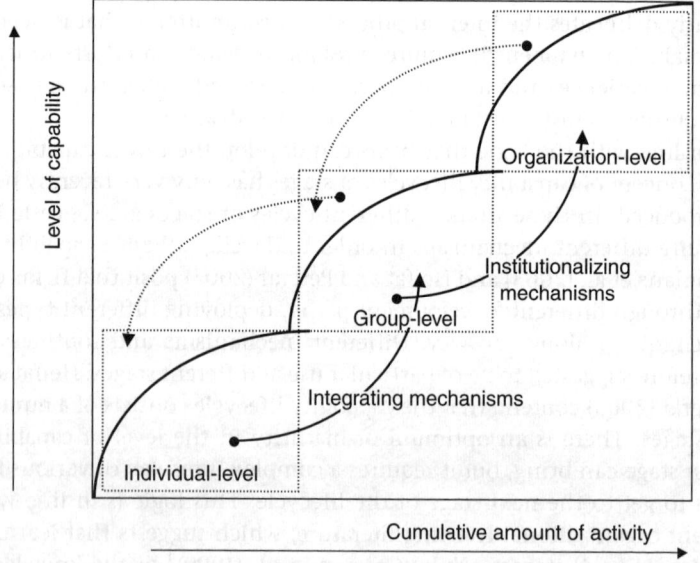

Figure 4.2 Role of mechanisms in alliance capability development
Source: (adapted from) Crossan et al., 1999; Draulans et al., 2003; Helfat and Peteraf, 2003.

we argue that mechanisms can be seen as drivers of alliance capability development.

The fact that firms tend to follow a certain development path when it comes to developing alliance capabilities was confirmed during the expert interviews. An expert from practice summarized the development path of the company he works for by stating that initially they primarily gained experience by managing one major alliance. However, over the years, as more alliances were formed and alliances gained in importance in terms of sales revenues and positioning, the knowledge accumulated was spread around to line managers using internal alliance trainings. The contents of these trainings was put together with the use of a leading management consultancy, which supported his firm in distilling and structuring the knowledge to be shared in these trainings. Using this material, internal alliance managers then instructed other employees and provided them with critical knowledge on alliance management. At this point in time, various functions have been installed which ensures that knowledge becomes deeply rooted inside the organization's system. Moreover, this expert added, managers continue to frequently share specific and experience-based knowledge in meetings. When reflecting on the usefulness of the mechanisms investigated, he added that in an early stage group-level mechanisms could help share generic knowledge distilled from prior alliances; afterwards organization-level mechanisms become more important as these help embed knowledge and allow for sharing of more specific knowledge. More specifically, he continued, established functions such as a vice-president of alliances can call upon group-level mechanisms to help disperse newly derived generic lesson throughout the organization. This way, practices can be amended via the spreading of new insights.

Another expert stressed, [that] 'They [the mechanisms] are building blocks and can almost be called artifacts.... I don't think you can learn very well if you don't have them.... Some of these mechanisms are resources and some are processes. Some refer to a higher level of capability, some to more static or operational level of capability development'. Another expert added, 'One can jumpstart successful alliance management by for instance gathering best practices and going to external trainings'. A recent article by Leonard and Swap (2004) hints at the limited contribution of certain learning mechanisms, or as they call them 'transfer mechanisms'. They summarize their article by stating, 'Your best employees' deepest knowledge can't be transferred onto a series of PowerPoint slides or downloaded into a data repository. It has to be passed on in person – slowly, patiently, and systematically' (Leonard and Swap, 2004: 88). Therefore, only by surpassing the limitations of mechanisms that help transfer explicit and non-specific knowledge can a firm optimize its capability. In other words, there are limitations to the extent to which certain mechanisms can develop a firm's alliance capability. The insight that tacit knowledge sharing is perceived to be more valuable than explicit knowledge is a recurring finding is various studies (Nonaka and Takeuchi, 1995; Dyer, 2000). It is summarized by Boisot (1995: 493), who states, 'Codified knowledge is inherently more diffusible than uncodified knowledge. That is to say, as it gains in utility it loses in scarcity.'

The group-level mechanisms can help firms move from the inherent disadvantages of the first to the second level of capability. When starting to form their first alliances, firms typically hold top management responsible for their management. However, when the alliance portfolio starts to grow, middle management tends to become involved. Relying on individual-level learning, or intuiting and interpreting (Vera and Crossan, 2004), is unlikely to ensure immediate success in a complex matter as alliance management is. In this setting, group-level learning mechanisms facilitate the sharing and dispersal of practices. In this way, experiences and the lessons learned are shared between those involved. One of the experts interviewed said:

> Initially, alliances were managed individually. At that point, we primarily relied on exchanging best practices. However, as we reckoned alliances were a major contributor to the business development of our firm, we started building alliance competences; consolidating our knowledge did this. This way, we anticipated, we could develop the discipline called alliance management.... We set up an alliance department through which institutional learning could take shape, in which knowledge could be developed and processes could be adopted more easily.

As this expert also implied, organization-level mechanisms primarily capture the aspects that allow firms to move beyond mere group-based practices. These become essential when a firm's alliance portfolio is such that it generates a substantial percentage of a firm's revenues. These mechanisms can actually help institutionalize certain routines and practices that are necessary to help advance a firm's alliance capability to the third capability level. Another expert stressed that there is a difference between mechanisms aimed at exchanging knowledge of dyadic and day-to-day management issues and those aimed at managing portfolios of alliances, such as a vice-president of alliances who is responsible for managing a group of alliances. Consequently, he added, there is a sort of hierarchy in the mechanisms investigated. On the one hand, group-level mechanisms involve tool-based learning, which is based on instruments that mainly makes use of generalized knowledge. It provides for the basics of successful alliance management. On the other hand, organization-level mechanisms allow for the institutionalization of specific knowledge. For instance, partner selection programmes are useful to firms that rely on information from their network and seek to select the right partner that has a reliable reputation. Using formally structured knowledge exchange meetings between alliance managers is another example of a mechanism that is highly useful to exchange knowledge that refers to specific or contextual experiences in prior alliances. Hence, only when experiences and lessons learned are integrated and institutionalized can firms really develop their alliance capabilities (Winter, 2003). These capabilities can be renewed or made dynamic using intra-firm mechanisms.

Although it is relevant to distinguish between different levels of learning (i.e. individual, group and organization level), it is also important to mention that they are interrelated. In practice, firms have shown to use different ways to transfer knowledge (Kleiner and Roth, 1987; *Financial Times*, 2004b). Whereas some prefer using mainly information technology tools, others prefer to rely on informal knowledge sharing. Despite the fact that different firms use different practices, the usefulness and the cost of utilization differ strongly between group- and organization-level learning. As knowledge becomes embedded in for instance routines, it becomes more difficult to transfer (Szulanski, 2000). Hence, it is insightful to distinguish between group-level and organization-level learning because they serve different purposes (i.e. group-level learning mainly pertains to train individuals whereas organization-level learning involves developing institutionalizing routines). The results of the expert interviews confirm the possibility in overlap between the dimensions identified. Various experts indicated that it is likely that some variables will be used at different stages of the alliance capability development process. However, all experts recognized the differences in usability and contribution of the group- and organization-level mechanisms: they confirmed that the former group of mechanisms mainly serves to transfer knowledge on dyadic issues at the group level, whereas the latter group can help institutionalize and routinize knowledge on issues related to a firm's alliance portfolio.

An important nuancing was brought forward by an expert, who stressed that it is important to take into account differences in sectors and firm history. He argued:

> Many firms in the IT sector view alliances as a part of their sales process. Similarly, pharmaceuticals tend to manage alliances mainly as part of their research trajectory or pipeline.... At our firm, businesses are run independently.... We organically developed our alliance capabilities distilling best practices from individual alliances and use this input to feed network-sharing sessions and our intranet.... Only after multiple people formed a group, this knowledge was consciously institutionalized and shared processes evolved.... It was a bottom-up process. Currently, we share our knowledge in workshops that are co-developed and taught by an external party. However, as our firm has many alliances (we have 8 separate businesses with each approximately 100 partnerships) and mainly relies on businesses to form their own joint ventures, we do not manage alliances centrally.

When he was asked whether his firm had an alliance department or any other corporate or organization-level mechanism to manage alliances, he responded: 'No, we don't, although this would surely help create institutionalized learning. This simply doesn't fit our organization and culture.' This example demonstrates that there is not one best way to develop alliance capabilities. Whether or not alliances are managed centrally also depends on historical and sectoral contingencies. However, a remarkable observation is that all experts indicated their firms, which are all considered leading in terms of alliance capability development, either deliberately or organically followed a certain development path. First, knowledge from individual alliances was gathered. Second, this knowledge was transferred via training and information systems, often using outside help. And third, this knowledge was institutionalized to develop shared practices and routines either at the corporate level or within a separate business of the firm. Although some of the individual intra-firm mechanisms deployed to develop alliance capabilities may differ between firms, they all confirmed following identical steps. Hence, successful firms share an important common feature: they all follow a comparable development path when it comes to developing alliance capabilities.

4.5 Conclusions

The findings presented in this section clearly show that both individual and groups of mechanisms play an important role in developing alliance capabilities. With respect to item-level analysis of the mechanisms, we found that indeed eleven of the tested mechanisms discriminate between low- and high-performing firms (at the 5% level). Thereafter, an exploratory factor analysis was run to identify latent dimensions that influence alliance capability development. When these were then tested on low- and high-performing firms, it became apparent that two factors represent mechanisms needed at different levels of alliance capability development. Following the logic of Crossan et al. (1999), the first factor helps firms increase their performance by institutionalizing an alliance capability (at the organizational level), while the second factor helps firms to integrate critical knowledge (at the group level). These interpretations were supported by the insights generated via expert interviews. The different stages of capability development were clearly recognized and explicitly defined by the experts. All experts confirmed that their firm used a process where at first lessons were derived from individual alliances. Thereafter, these lessons were shared among a selected group of people, to, in a third stage, they said, initiate a process of institutionalization which entailed the instalment of a department or use of alliance managers to manage the firm's alliance portfolio and develop routines in alliance management among a broader range of people within the firm.

These findings are highly relevant for two reasons. First of all, because we have found micro-level evidence of how firms develop alliance capabilities. Different mechanisms were found to be critical for firms in order to improve internal practices related to alliance management. Second, we found evidence of different mechanisms stimulating different types of learning when it comes to alliance management. This implies that different mechanisms are useful at different stages of the capability development process.

Of course, the findings of this study should not be dealt with in isolation. Distinctive competitive advantage cannot be distilled from the mere possession of a certain mechanism. This requires the development of managerial capabilities as well as the difficult-to-imitate combinations of organizational, functional and technological skills (Teece et al., 1997; Montealegre, 2002). However, although the ability to make use of a mechanism is obvious, Knott (2003: 942) in a similar study underlines that the isolating mechanism is to some extent related to the resource or the mechanism itself; it is on the one hand a function of the management holding the mechanism, but on the other hand the isolating principle is 'self-imposed by the would-be imitators'. In practical terms, this implies that firms should make use of the mechanisms investigated to transfer knowledge and develop certain managerial attributes to support the use of these mechanisms (see Dent, 1999; Spekman et al., 1999). However, in line with our findings, she also indicates that the mere fact that a firm uses certain mechanisms already allows it to develop capabilities that generate superior rents. Hence, simply using these mechanisms can create competitive advantages. The reason for the very existence of this book is to go beyond conventional understanding and find out what role mechanisms play in developing alliance capabilities. In order to find out how alliance experience and capabilities relate to one another, additional analyses are required. These analyses will be performed in the next chapter.

5
An Analysis of the Alliance Capability Development Process[1]

5.1 Introduction

Having empirically examined the impact of intra-firm mechanisms on alliance performance in Chapter 4, we found evidence for the fact that mechanisms help develop alliance capabilities as they positively influence the ability to manage alliances. This enhances our micro-level understanding of the impact of these mechanisms. Moreover, the results of the expert interviews clearly show that successful firms follow a certain path when it comes to developing alliance capabilities. This, however, has not been substantiated empirically. To fill this gap, this chapter empirically analyses the relationships between the key concepts involved in the alliance capability development process. It analyses the interactions between experience, alliance capabilities and performance. Examining the relationships between these concepts may facilitate a better understanding of the intra-firm process underlying alliance capability development.

Applying the theories described in the theoretical framework (see Figure 2.3), various researchers have investigated issues such as alliance experience, learning in alliances, investments in specialized resources and alliance performance (Draulans et al., 1999; Kale and Singh, 1999; De Man, 2001; Dyer et al., 2001; Inkpen, 2002; Kale et al., 2002; Reuer et al., 2002b). Experience can be critical for firms to better anticipate and respond to contingencies (Spekman et al., 1999; Anand and Khanna, 2000; Pisano et al., 2001). From this perspective, earlier trials and tribulations in alliances have been suggested to enhance a firm's alliance capability. Some scholars have suggested a positive relationship between learning mechanisms in organizations related to alliances and alliance performance (Kale and Singh, 1999). Other studies found that experience levels and alliance capabilities differ between firms (Anand and Khanna, 2000). In addition to experience, scholars have suggested that organizational routines (Nelson and Winter, 1982) and absorptive capacity (Cohen and Levinthal, 1990; Lane and Lubatkin, 1998) can foster differentiated learning effects (Larsson et al., 1998; Nti and Kumar, 2001) and create unobserved heterogeneity (Das and Teng, 2000a). In the end, past learning behaviour is proposed to influence future learning abilities, making learning in alliances a path-dependent phenomenon (Anand and Khanna, 2000). Firms indeed differ in their ability to derive value from alliances (Khanna et al., 1998; Madhok and Tallman, 1998; Anand and Khanna, 2000) and some firms simply seem to be more effective in applying their knowledge to other alliances (Spekman et al., 1999). Given these intriguing findings, researchers have increasingly paid attention to internal organization features, such as managerial processes, routines and values as a basis for firm-specific capabilities and competencies that are difficult for other firms to buy or imitate (Leonard-Barton, 1992; Henderson and Cockburn, 1994; Teece and Pisano, 1994; Eisenhardt and Martin, 2000). While recently scholarly attention has been directed at alliance capability development, most studies derive the existence of a firm's alliance capability from the number of alliances it has formed over time. However, suggesting a direct relationship between experience and performance seems to ignore the intriguing question of how these capabilities come into being. In fact, these studies do not pay attention to the role intra-firm mechanisms play in developing alliance capabilities. Notwithstanding their extensive contributions to the field of study, the transition from experience to capability has remained obscure (Kale et al., 2002). Furthermore, except for a number of very recent publications on the broader issue of capability development such as Helfat (1997) and Gittell (2002), an in-depth investigation of the various mechanisms used in practice and their impact on alliance performance is missing. The aim of this chapter is to fill this void by empirically investigating the relationships between the critical concepts needed to understand the alliance capability development process.

5.2 Hypotheses

In reference to the theoretical framework presented in Chapter 2 (see Figure 2.3), the conceptual contributions of these theories (see Table 2.2) and critical issues related to prior studies such as alliance experience (e.g. Kale and Singh, 1999), mechanisms (e.g. Kale et al., 2002) and routines

(Zollo et al., 2002), this section elaborates on these issues and their role in the alliance capability development process. The critical issues will be discussed in greater detail and be presented in relation to their theoretical underpinnings.

Experience

The impact of 'experience' on firm performance has been investigated in various empirical settings (e.g. Ingram and Baum, 1997; Simonin, 1997; King and Tucci, 2002). Borrowing mainly from evolutionary economics and organizational learning theory, various studies have linked experience and learning curves to productivity gains and rent generation (Dutton and Thomas, 1984). The majority of these studies finds a positive relationship between experience and performance, suggesting experience to be the predominant explanatory variable for capability development (Teece et al., 1997; King and Tucci, 2002). Lack of experience and ignorance are said to be a critical cause for alliance failure (Lei and Slocum, 1992). Furthermore, as firms gain experience, they can afford to devote less attention to solving a particular problem (Bereiter and Scardamalia, 1993, in: Koka and Prescott, 2002: 800), providing the firm with standardized solutions. More specifically, gaining experience allows firms to become more effective at managing particular processes in comparison to less experienced firms (Das and Teng, 2002b).

Still other studies have investigated organizational learning and firm differences in learning curves (e.g. Levin, 2000; Lapré and Van Wassenhove, 2001). These studies generally refer to the need of using prior experiences to enhance a firm's learning curve (Stata, 1989). Experience is often suggested to be an essential input when it comes to knowledge sharing (Harrigan, 1985; Lei and Slocum, 1992; Pennings et al., 1994; Grant, 1995; Abramson and Ai, 1999; Argote and Ingram, 2000). Mukherjee et al. (1998) make a distinction between operational and conceptual learning, thereby referring to respectively input-output understanding or know-how and the acquisition of cause-and-effect relationships or know-why. In a similar vein, King and Tucci (2002: 172) refer to these two types as static and transformational experience. Differentiating between these different types of experience or ways of learning enables us to understand that on the one hand experience fosters inertia and routinization (Lorenzoni and Lipparini, 1999), while on the other hand it enables a firm to adapt and create and adjust routines that enable organizational change (Katz and Allen, 1982; Amburgey et al., 1993).

In line with previous research, we define alliance experience as the lessons learned, as well as the know-how generated through a firm's former alliances (e.g. Gulati, 1995; Kale and Singh, 1999; Hoang, 2001; Hoang et al., 2002; Kale et al., 2002; Reuer et al., 2002b; Vanhaverbeke et al., 2002). These lessons and know-how are likely to become embedded in the minds of the individuals involved. This provides a basis for an organizational routine with respect to performing a certain task or activity (Nelson and Winter, 1982, in Kale and Singh, 1999: 7). Certain mechanisms for learning, such as an alliance database or gathering best practices, may enhance the firm's ability to implement and embed the lessons and know-how in existing practices (Hamel, 1991; Inkpen and Dinur, 1998; Khanna et al., 1998; Inkpen, 2000).

Various researchers have investigated the role of alliance experience as an antecedent of alliance performance. Although the majority of these studies finds positive linear relationships (Anand and Khanna, 2000), other studies suggest curvilinearity (Draulans et al., 2003). They come up with an inverted U-shaped relationship between experience and alliance performance (Deeds and Hill, 1996; Hoang et al., 2002). Overall, these studies seem to suggest a positive relationship between experience and performance. A number of reasons account for this positive relationship. First of all, previous research suggests that experience enables firms to better understand the critical processes and issues in alliance management. Not only does it allow firms to select more appropriate partners and enables more effective management of the alliance process (Simonin, 1997), but also increases their ability to ease conflict situations (Mohr and Spekman, 1994).

Second, shared experience engenders the development of 'common perspectives' (Nonaka, 1994: 24), enabling a firm to absorb new knowledge more effectively (Grant, 1996b). In this context, various studies have analysed the role of absorptive capacity to understand differences in rates of learning in alliances (Hamel et al., 1989; Kumar and Nti, 1998; Shenkar and Li, 1999; Lane et al., 2001; Nti and Kumar, 2001). Obviously, absorptive capacity is a key determinant of the input provided through 'experience', as it permits the assimilation and exploitation of new knowledge (Cohen and Levinthal, 1990: 135). Stressing the need to thoroughly embed knowledge in the organization's routines and practices to be optimally leveraged (Merali, 1997), prior experience is often suggested to shape future firm capabilities (Helfat, 2000). Overall, these arguments suggest that alliance experience fosters a firm's ability to consciously foresee and act upon earlier trials and tribulations. On basis of these arguments, alliance experience is posited to engender more positive outcomes of a firm's alliance performance.

H1: Prior alliance experience has a positive impact on alliance performance.

Capabilities

A large body of research has been conducted in the area of resources, capabilities and competences over the past years (e.g. Dosi et al., 2000a; Helfat, 2000). Relying on different theories such as the resource-based view (Pfeffer and Salancik, 1978; Barney, 1991), the dynamic capability view (Teece et al., 1997; Eisenhardt and Martin, 2000) and the competence-based view (Prahalad and Hamel, 1990; Hamel and Heene, 1994; Sanchez et al., 1996a)[2], various scholars have proposed different constructs to underline distinct differences between resources and capabilities, which contribute to our understanding of capability development in general. Building on Penrose (1959), who separated management *of* resources from management *as* a resource per se, scholars have described the differences between resources and capabilities as lower and higher order resources (Hunt and Morgan, 1996) and component and architectural competence (Henderson and Cockburn, 1994) (see also Section 3.2).

Although experience seems to play an important role in increasing our understanding of the antecedents of capability development in alliances, experience per se may not be sufficient (Levinthal and March, 1993; Simonin, 1997; Kale et al., 2002). Tsang (2002a) suggests that learning myopia is likely to be a key factor influencing the quality of experiences. Therefore, firms should actively manage their learning processes. In a similar vein, Simonin (1997) concludes that experiences have little impact on alliance performance if lessons are not internalized and transferred into know-how.

As already extensively described in Chapter 3, building on Eisenhardt and Martin (2000), Harbison et al. (2000) and Kale et al. (2002), in this book an alliance capability is defined as the firm's ability to capture, share, disseminate and apply alliance management knowledge. The very existence of such a capability and the extent to which a firm can develop it depends on the use of intra-firm mechanisms that can help firms engage in a stable and repetitive activity pattern to capture, share, disseminate and apply alliance management knowledge (or know-how and know-why). In line with the previously mentioned distinction between picking and deploying resources (Makadok, 2001), this definition adds an 'application' element to the 'creation, sharing and disseminating' elements of Kale et al.'s (2002) definition. Creating repeatable patterns of action or developing alliance capabilities requires firms to make use of intra-firm mechanisms and routines (Sanchez, 2001c). Intra-firm mechanisms then are the ingredients required to develop alliance capabilities (Dosi et al., 2000b; Gittell, 2002). As a result, in order to ameliorate our understanding of the antecedents of capability development, it becomes essential to investigate the mechanisms that firms employ to accumulate and disseminate knowledge.

Micro-mechanisms can represent 'an intent to learn' (Hamel, 1991; Doz and Hamel, 1998), thereby referring to a firm's dedication to develop an alliance capability. This also implies that investment in these mechanisms, which aid knowledge articulation and codification, seems to reflect a firm's commitment to deliberate learning (Zollo and Winter, 2002; Van der Bij et al., 2003). Nonaka (1994: 17) argues that 'Commitment is one of the most important components for promoting the formation of new knowledge within an organization'. Thus, for instance, having an alliance department might imply that a firm is consciously paying attention to the integration, internalization or dispersion of alliance-related knowledge. It is likely that a firm would not install such a mechanism if it had not defined clear reasons and ambitions for its existence. We thus presume the firm to be self-reflective in this way. This reasoning was confirmed during the expert interviews (see Section 4.4).

We define an alliance mechanism as an internal organizational attribute that aids firms in managing their alliance portfolio by capturing, sharing, disseminating or applying alliance management knowledge. Mechanisms can be represented by functions (e.g. alliance department), tools (e.g. alliance training), control and management processes (e.g. alliance metrics) and external parties (e.g. use of external consultants). An overview of these groups and the mechanisms belonging to each group is presented in Appendix 4, Table App. 4.2.

Mechanisms are expected to be critical in the capability development process for a number of reasons (for a more extended overview of the contributions per group of mechanisms, we refer to Appendix 4). First, they allow firms to internalize generated experiences. More specifically, mechanisms allow the firm to embed experiences into stable patterns of behaviour by accumulating, articulating and codifying knowledge (Zollo and Winter, 2002). By their ability to embed knowledge in the organization's routines and practices, mechanisms form the basis of organizational routines (Merali, 1997). Fujimoto (2000: 276) refers to an 'internal evolutionary mechanism', which ensures the evolutionary process of organization routines. Employees themselves guide this process by creating short-term solutions to a variety of problems that arise, thereby creating dynamic rather than static routines and capabilities. However, using these mechanisms enables a firm to standardize or repeat (creating operational effectiveness and efficiency) as well as to diffuse new routines (creating optimal learning potential). Ultimately, the synthesis of these concepts enables a firm to develop capabilities, providing the firm with a distinct problem-solving competence (Fujimoto, 2000: 277). In this context, various scholars have recently referred to a meta-capability to change routines (Amburgey et al., 1993; King and Tucci, 2002).

Certain routines can be critical for the evolutionary process of the firm (Fujimoto, 1999). Given the path-dependent and organization-embodied nature of knowledge, organizational routines can store and reproduce problem-solving skills via certain structural mechanisms that then serve as carriers (Coriat and Dosi, 1999: 123). Tsang (2002b), for instance, argues that sharing experience among alliance managers is an efficient way to disperse knowledge. In similar vein, Zahra and Nielsen (2002) suggest that formal coordination mechanisms such as using specialized task forces to promote active involvement can be an important way to improve a firm's technology commercialization.

Second, mechanisms help firms to structurally coordinate alliance knowledge within the firm (Kale et al., 2002). Mechanisms facilitate learning and leveraging of lessons by providing feedback throughout the firm (Kale and Singh, 1999; Van der Bij et al., 2003), not only by stipulating the need to convert tacit into explicit knowledge and vice versa (Nonaka, 1994), but also by providing a platform for the transfer of experience (Brown and Duguid, 1991). For instance, the use of alliance database enables a firm to explicate its experiences and thereafter disperse them throughout the firm. In doing so, a larger number of people have access to the lessons learned in earlier alliances. The same holds for formally structured knowledge exchange platforms for alliance managers, which provide a structurally recurring occasion for experiences to be shared. These processes can have a substantial impact on performance and a firm's learning curve, since by exchanging experiences and lessons managers may become increasingly sensitive to and aware of potential pitfalls in alliance management. In this way, these processes can stimulate the amendment of routines.

Third, day-to-day alliance activities are supported by various mechanisms. Using a partner programme or partner selection programme routinizes and therefore eases the partner selection process. Moreover, conflict situations can, to a certain extent, be avoided if a firm makes use of joint business sessions in order to define goals and share expectations (Mohr and Spekman, 1994).

Fourth, mechanisms help spreading a message or signal that alliances are deemed important by the firm. The fact that a firm decides to employ a certain set of mechanisms represents a certain degree of commitment to not only the performance of its alliance portfolio, but also to internal knowledge exchange (Inkpen, 1998a). This commitment or dedication to alliances can be an important driver to create an alliance capability (Spekman et al., 1999), as employees are more likely to recognize the value of alliances and adopt the proposed routines. Furthermore, it also sends a message to potential partners that a firm is committed, which may positively influence a firm's reputation as a dedicated partner.

As mentioned before, routines play an important role in developing alliance capabilities.[3] As routines are largely 'tacit' and vary between firms, they contribute to our understanding of the persistent differences in firm performance (Coriat, 2000). Routines are suggested to be critical in the capability development process, because they support the interaction between individuals in the absence of rules. They are often seen as the equivalent of individual skills (Nelson and Winter, 1982: 73). Moreover since routines and mechanisms are highly interrelated (Gittell, 2002), they both allow the firm to successfully apply the knowledge gained.

In the context of this study and in line with Dyer and Singh (1998) and Winter (2000, 2003), we define routines as the higher-organizing principles through which knowledge is captured, shared, disseminated and applied, providing the basis for repetitive patterns of actions in alliance management practices. There are a number of reasons why routines are important in the process of capability development. First of all, our definition of routines contains both a problem-solving or learning-oriented aspect and a control-oriented aspect (Coriat, 2000). The problem-solving or learning aspect is evident from the fact that for firms to learn from their experiences, lessons need to be drawn. In order to do so, capturing, sharing and disseminating these lessons is essential. For instance, only if firms succeed in creating a successful platform for sharing experiences among alliance managers can alliance-related knowledge be shared and disseminated. The control-oriented aspect refers to the application of knowledge, since firms should control for the effectiveness of the way in which employees use alliance-related knowledge. This can be done by, for instance, using alliance metrics to verify progress in the individual alliance to see whether the lessons learned are successfully applied.

A theme which is related to the dual nature of routines as defined by Coriat (2000) and central to strategic management literature is the way in which firms optimize exploitation via routines (which are sticky by nature) while at the same time realizing optimal exploration by remaining strategically flexible through learning (which is by nature a dynamic process) (March, 1991; Levinthal and March, 1993; Koza and Lewin, 1998). Various scholars have argued that routines cause organizational inertia (Hannan and Freeman, 1984), leaving firms resistant to change (Thompson, 1967). Moreover, experience is said to restrict adaptive behaviour and reinforces existing practices by its continued reliance on conventional wisdom. With respect to alliances, Eisenhardt and Martin (2000) argue that repeated practices lead to enhanced alliance capabilities as firms learn from their experiences by translating these experiences into processes and routines.

Second, routines compose an essential building block of capabilities (Dosi et al., 2000b: 4). They capture the lessons learned from prior experiences, thereby stimulating a process of adoption and replication without reinventing the wheel (Levitt and March, 1988). More specifically, individual experiences and skills can be thought of as building blocks of organizational routines. They consist of an essential part of the organizational memory and are comprised of a set of repetitive activities ensuring a smooth functioning of the organizational operations (Coriat, 2000). Routines include both technical and social skills (March, 1994).

On basis of these arguments and prior findings, we hypothesize that the level of a firm's alliance performance depends on the extent to which firms use mechanisms to integrate alliance-related knowledge and establish routines for managing alliances.

H2: A firm's alliance capability is positively related to a firm's alliance performance.

Interaction between experience and capabilities

With respect to the alliance capability development process, one last interaction needs to be addressed. Capabilities must be built through experience, since they are an outcome of the firm's ability to integrate knowledge (Grant, 1996b) and are not easily available in the spot market (Teece et al., 1997). Earlier on, we have argued that mechanisms are expected to play an important role in two ways. First, it was suggested that mechanisms allow firms to leverage their alliance experience. Second, a description was given of the related notion of how firms can develop alliance capabilities by proposing that experience provides an essential input to intra-firm mechanisms.

Therefore, it is expected that alliance experience and mechanisms reinforce a firm's ability to improve its alliance performance. This implies that alliance experience is expected to positively influence alliance performance via its positive impact on alliance capability building (thus alliance capability is a mediating variable) (Sharma et al., 1981; Gittell, 2002). However, we may also expect that firms that have extensive experience with alliances *and* have developed an alliance capability are more likely to be successful in managing alliances. In this case, we test whether alliance capability moderates the effect of alliance experience on alliance performance (Lehmann et al., 1998; Heath, 2001; Irwin and McClelland, 2001). Therefore, we posit:

H3A: Alliance capability mediates between alliance experience and alliance performance.
H3B: Alliance capability moderates between alliance experience and alliance performance.

5.3 Data collection and methodology

This chapter uses the same data gathered via a survey method as the former chapter (Chapter 4). A survey questionnaire was sent to 650 vice-presidents and alliance managers worldwide, which after data screening resulted in a dataset containing information of 192 firms. In addition to the survey, twelve experts in the field of alliances and capability development were interviewed. Both the survey and the results of the interviews should provide us with insightful material to understand how firms develop alliance capabilities.

In line with Anand and Vassolo (2002), this study uses the alliance portfolio as a unit of analysis. Given the objective of this study, this is considered to be an appropriate unit of analysis as this study seeks to investigate the influence of a firm's experience and alliance capability on its alliance performance. The dependent variable (alliance portfolio performance) was measured along a 5-point interval scale (with performance intervals of 20%) and was thereafter, for the purpose of this specific analysis, recalculated into a dichotomous variable. A low- (0%–40%) and a high-performing (61%–100%) firm categories were defined. The respondents having an alliance performance lying between 41% and 60% were left out as most research suggests this is the average level of performance in alliances (see Park and Ungson, 2001). Consequently, the outcome variable is measured as a discrete (nonmetric) ordinal scale. In line with previous studies, alliance performance is defined as the percentage of alliances in which the original goals were realized (Hamel et al., 1989; Hamel, 1991).

Three main independent variables were included in this study: experience, capabilities and their interaction effect. First, in line with earlier studies (Kale and Singh, 1999; Kale et al., 2002; Li and Rowley, 2002; Tsang, 2002b; Zollo et al., 2002), the number of alliances that a firm has formed was used (in our case over the last five years) as a proxy for alliance experience. A scale was defined for different categories representing a firm's number of alliances (see Appendix 4 for questionnaire format). Despite the omnipresence of the term 'alliance experience' in research on alliance capabilities, criticism has also surrounded the operationalizations used for it. While most studies use the firm's number of alliances as a proxy for its alliance experience, others have considered this an imperfect measure. However, only very recently have alternative approaches been simultaneously proposed and applied by using a multi-dimensional construct for measuring a firm's alliance experience. The contribution of this multi-dimensionality resides mainly in its ability to more fully reflect the various dimensions in which firms can gain experience. For instance, Reuer et al. (2002b) used technological experience (accumulated expertise in a certain technological domain), partner experience (prior agreements with same partner) and collaborative experience (i.e. number of firm's prior agreements) in a study on post-formation dynamics of strategic alliances. Despite the recent trend to incorporate various dimensions to measure a firm's alliance experience, this study relies on a single measure. The reasons mainly refer to the fact that additional dimensions would refer to situational factors such as length or type of the alliance. Although these dimensions could enrich our database, they are more difficult to capture since our unit of analysis is the firm's alliance portfolio. It would be highly complex for a database using this type of analysis to incorporate duration and type of alliance for each of the firm's alliances. This would be more accurate in case the dyad was used as level of analysis. Hence, this study – as have the vast majority of prior studies – relies on a unidimensional construct to capture a firm's alliance experience.

Second, in spite of the difficulty of measuring 'capabilities' (Dosi et al., 2000b) and the relative infancy of studies investigating capability development, we posit that the alliance mechanisms investigated compose a valid representation of a firm's alliance capability.[4] Despite the fact that capabilities consist of intra-firm mechanisms and routines, they are difficult to separate at an operational level. Consequently, mechanisms and routines are highly related and difficult to separate (Levitt and March, 1988; Gittell, 2002). Therefore, we use the summated scale (F1 + F2) defined in Chapter 4 to operationalize a firm's alliance capability (see Table 4.4 and Equation 4.3). This construct allows a firm to obtain a score that lies between 0 and 15, depending on the number of mechanisms in use. The individual mechanisms then add up to the firm's score representing its score for alliance capability. This is a method used more often in psychometric theory to quantify the extent to which someone has a certain orientation or interest (see e.g. Rotter, 1966; Lambin, 1993, 2000).

In order to objectively measure whether a firm makes use of intra-firm mechanisms, all mechanisms are represented by a dichotomous variable (functions, tools, control or management processes or external parties). Whereas some earlier studies use alliance experience as a proxy for alliance capabilities and routines (Zollo et al., 2002) or measure one mechanism such as an alliance department (Kale et al., 2002), measuring alliance capability using a composite measure of mechanisms allows for a more complete picture of the different facets involved in developing alliance capabilities. Various scholars have suggested that capabilities involve a complex interaction between a firm's resources and organizational processes (e.g. Karnoe, 1995; Simonin, 1997; Rindova and Kotha, 2001; Montealegre, 2002; Ranft and Lord, 2002; Helfat and Peteraf, 2003). Moreover, given the inherent complexity of managing alliances, it is expected that measuring alliance capabilities using multiple items which are aimed at different aspects of alliance management (e.g. Dyer et al., 2001; Das and Teng, 2002b) is more likely to give a solid representation of a firm's ability to fully master all aspects involved in managing alliances.

5.4 Analysis and results

An ordinal logistic regression model was used to test the hypotheses. In general, logistic regression is a technique that is more flexible than other techniques such as multiple regression analysis. Moreover, the dependent variable may be continuous, discrete or dichotomous (Tabachnick and Fidell, 2001). For our analysis, ordinal logistic regression was chosen in order to be able to clearly distinguish between groups in our analysis (Hosmer and Lemeshow, 2000). As mentioned earlier, the outcome variable used is ordinal, because there is a rank or degree involved when comparing low and high performance group. In such instances, ordinal regression is to be preferred over binary or multinomial logistic regression. The (ordinal) logistic regression model, for a model with for instance two independents, is generally represented as (Tabachnick and Fidell, 2001):

$$Y_i = \frac{\varepsilon^{A+B_1X_1+B_2X_2}}{1+\varepsilon^{A+B_1X_1+B_2X_2}} \tag{5.1}$$

where Y_i is the dependent variable and the linear part of the equation (i.e. $A + B_1X_1 + B_2X_2$) is the logit. In our model, the ordinal outcome variable Y_i can take on the value 0 or 1. In contrast to linear regression, in logistic regression the logit is used to find the odds of being in one of the categories of the dependent variable.[5] The odds ratio represents the increase (in case $\varepsilon^A > 1$) or decrease (in case $\varepsilon^A < 1$) in odds of being in one category of the dependent in case the value of the dependent increases by one unit (Tabachnick and Fidell, 2001). The coefficients are then given by the natural logs of the odds ratio.

A first analysis of the data showed that the independent variables seemed to be highly correlated with the interaction term. This is a recurring problem in extended models containing mediating variables (Mason and Perreault, 1991). In order to solve this problem, the data was mean centred in order to overcome the problems associated with multicollinearity (see e.g. Aiken and West, 1991). Applying this method allows us on the one hand to reduce the correlation between the variables and on the other hand to render meaningful results (Aiken and West, 1991; Long, 1997). Table 5.1 shows the unstandardized descriptive statistics and the correlation matrix. Table 5.2 lists the results of the regression analyses. In Table 5.2, we also mention the Nagelkerke pseudo R-square and the log likelihood ratio test.[6] Whereas the former test is also known as 'coefficient

Table 5.1 Descriptive statistics and correlation matrix

	Mean[a]	S.D.	EXP	MECH	EXP*MECH
Alliance performance[b]	3.2216	1.3057	.248**	.185*	−.007
EXP	2.3177	1.2399	1		
MECH[c]	5.0990	3.7814	.474***	1	
EXP*MECH	12.0104	13.3405	.417***	.494***	1

*** $p < .001$; ** $p < .01$; * $p < .05$; + $p < .10$

[a] Mean and standard deviation are uncentred, while correlations are given for centred variables
[b] Categorical variable representing alliance success
[c] MECH = organization level mechanisms + group level mechanisms (F1 + F2)

Table 5.2 Results of ordinal regression analysis

	Model I	Model II	Model III	Model IV
Alliance experience	1.003**	0.846*	0.894*	0.340+
	(0.298)	(0.313)	(0.318)	(0.194)
Alliance capability –mechanisms		0.102+	0.118+	0.135*
		(0.064)	(0.066)	(0.065)
Interaction effect			−0.107	−0.084
			(0.082)	(0.054)
Service-related sectors (control)				0.643
				(0.402)
ICT-related sectors (control)				0.285
				(0.386)
Firm size–sales (control)				0.204
				(0.168)
Chi-square	14.485***	17.616***	18.778***	20.077**
-2 Log likelihood	16.638	72.207	70.590	156.542
Nagelkerke R^2	0.157	0.184	0.200	0.183
df	1	2	3	6
Number of observations	117	117	117	117

SE in parentheses; *** $p < .001$; ** $p < .01$; * $p < .05$; + $p < .10$

Note that N = 117 due to leaving out the 41%–60% performance group and missing data.

of determination', the latter is known as 'deviance' (McCullagh and Nelder, 1989; Hair et al., 1998). However, both statistics indicate the amount of variance explained by the predictors, verifying whether inclusion of a variable adds to explaining shifts in the dependent variable. The likelihood ratio test in logistic regression analysis is similar to the residual sum of squares in linear regression. It provides a convenient way to understand what the contribution of a certain variable is to the function, thereby comparing observed and predicted values.

Whereas in linear regression, unknown parameters are estimated using ordinary least squares, logistic regression models are generally fitted on basis of the maximum likelihood principle. Hence, in linear regression observed and predicted values are compared in order to determine the square of the distance between the two using the following function:

$$SSE = \sum_{i=1}^{n} (\gamma_i - \hat{\gamma}_i)^2 \qquad (5.2)$$

where y_i denotes the observed value and $\hat{y}_i$ refers to the predicted value for the ith individual in the model. In logistic regression, on the other hand, the likelihood function is a product of the terms in the expression (Hosmer and Lemeshow, 2000):

$$L(\beta) = \sum_{i=1}^{n} \pi(x_i)^{y_i}[1-\pi(x_i)]^{1-y_i} \quad (5.3)$$

where $\pi(x_i)^{y_1}$ expresses the conditional mean; π denotes the outcome variable and x denotes a value of the independent variable. It follows that $1 - \pi(x)$ gives the conditional probability that the outcome variable is equal to zero given x. For the log likelihood expression, the natural logarithm is taken (Hosmer and Lemeshow, 2000; Tabachnick and Fidell, 2001):

$$L(\beta) = \sum_{i=1}^{n} y_i \ln[\pi(x_i)] + y_{1i} \ln[\pi(x_i)] + ... y_{ki} \ln[\pi(x_i)] \quad (5.4)$$

Hence, the sum of these products indicates the contribution of the independent variable. It provides a check to verify the significance of the addition of new independents to our model. In logistic regression analysis, the overall measure of model fit or likelihood ratio test is obtained by multiplying the difference between the log likelihood results of the different models by –2. This is done to obtain a number whose distribution is interpretable and useful for hypothesis testing purposes.

In order to test this study's hypotheses, different models were analysed. First of all, a model containing experience as independent variable was tested to verify if experience positively influences alliance performance (H1). The results show that this variable is significant at the 1 per cent level and has a coefficient of 1.003. Second, we tested whether alliance capability mediates between experience and alliance performance (H3A). Following a procedure suggested by Baron and Kenny (1986)[7], we found that indeed alliance capability is a mediating variable for two reasons. First, we found that experience is a significant variable explaining alliance capability. Second, the results of Model II show that the coefficient of experience as well as its significance decreases if mechanisms are included in the analysis.[8] Moreover, both the log likelihood ratio and the chi-square statistic increase substantially if we include the new covariate. And third, the residual variance represented by R^2 decreases, as is represented by an increase in the Nagelkerke R^2 (Baron and Kenny, 1986; Cote, 2001). These results indicate that alliance capability is a mediating variable between alliance experience and performance.

Thereafter, Model III was defined containing all three independent variables (experience, alliance capability and their interaction effects; Heath, 2001). The results indicate that alliance experience and alliance capabilities are significant predictors of alliance performance. The third predictor, the interaction effect of alliance experience and alliance capabilities, is not significant and has a negative coefficient. The interaction term was included to test H3B, which seeks to verify whether alliance capability moderates between alliance experience and performance (Heath, 2001; Irwin and McClelland, 2001).[9] Consequently, H3B is rejected. Again, the log both likelihood ratio and the Nagelkerke R^2 increase, which underlines the necessity to include these variables in our model.

In order to verify the validity of these results, Model IV controlled for a number of variables: two industry-related control variables (using an ICT-related and service-related sector control) and a firm size variable (using sales revenues). ICT-related sectors consist of ICT and ICT-service sectors (43% of the total sample); service-related sectors were defined as ICT-services, financial services, other services and public sectors (65% of the sample). With respect to firm size, sales revenues were defined as the total worldwide sales of the parent firm in the year 2000. Again, an ordinal logistic regression was used to test the model. The results indicate that all three predictors related to alliance capability development are significant, while none of the control variables proves of substantial importance.

In addition to the survey, the expert interviews allowed us to verify the findings and to nurture a better understanding of the complex nature of alliance management in general. A number of relevant contributions were made with respect to the different hypotheses. First, the results of the expert interviews demonstrate that alliance experience was considered to be a synonym for learning-by-doing. More specifically, various experts underlined the fact that experience allows firms to improve their understanding of the alliance process, such as partner selection, execution and evaluation. In addition, some experts underlined the need to disperse experience using intra-firm mechanisms in order to be optimally leveraged.

Second, all experts indicated they considered the alliance mechanisms as adequate and highly useful representation of a firm's alliance capability, which confirmed the validity of the construct used. As mentioned earlier, one expert indicated that these mechanisms represent 'physical artifacts' of a capability, implicitly representing and referring to an essential element of organizational memory and routines as defined by Moorman and Miner (1997), not only because they represent a firm's intent to learn, but also because they comprise an essential element to foster a firm's alliance capability development (Doz and Hamel, 1998). Although the literature provides various examples of firms developing alliance capabilities in very different ways (e.g. Alliance Analyst, 1994; Hill and Hellriegel, 1994; Takeishi, 2001), various experts emphasized the fact that *all* of the pre-defined mechanisms were important to develop alliance capabilities. All experts confirmed that the specific contribution of mechanisms was evident from their ability to contribute to the dissemination of experience throughout the firm. This process, they confirmed, induces a potential basis for the creation of repeatable patterns of actions.

5.5 Discussion and conclusions

This chapter was devoted to empirically examine the relationship between critical concepts in the alliance capability development process. The relationship between experience, alliance capability and their interaction on alliance performance was tested using data from 117 firms worldwide. Considering the asymmetries in firm's capability acquisition in alliances (Mowery, 1988) and rates of organizational learning (Pisano et al., 2001), a novel manner for measuring a firm's alliance capability was proposed. So far, alliance experience (measured as the number of a firm's prior alliances) has often been used as a proxy for a firm's alliance capability (Kale et al., 2002: 754). However, as firms make use of various mechanisms (e.g. alliance manager, database, training) to enhance their alliance performance, the aim was to gain a more detailed understanding of the antecedents of alliance performance and their interaction. By using a firm's alliance portfolio performance as the dependent variable and by measuring alliance capabilities as a composite variable of its alliance mechanisms, direct attention was paid to the micro-level process of capability development (Grant, 1996b). Moreover, in this way it was possible to differentiate between a firm's experience and a firm's alliance capability as a consequence of its intra-firm mechanisms. To this end, we used the summated scale, which resulted from an exploratory factor analysis (see Table 4.4).

The results of our study show that both experience and alliance capabilities are important antecedents of alliance performance. In line with earlier studies (Anand and Khanna, 2000; Hoang et al., 2002), experience is found to be indeed an important antecedent of alliance performance. While the large majority of previous studies focused on individual alliance performance, this study confirms that experience also is an important antecedent of a firm's entire alliance portfolio.

Hypothesis 2, which states that alliance capability is an important antecedent of alliance performance, is also supported. Model II shows that alliance capability is a significant predictor of alliance performance. Also when controlling for a firm's sales, number of employees and industry, it remains a significant variable. Although one may argue that a positive relationship between a capability and performance is straightforward, the operationalization used provides critical insight into the building blocks of alliance capabilities and hence into *how* firms can develop alliance capabilities. Thus, this study's results provide convincing support for Simonin's (1997) and Kale and Singh's (1999) argument which entails that processes supporting the accumulating, codification and sharing of knowledge are an important determinant of fixed-firm differences in alliance performance.

Following Cote (2001) and Baron and Kenny (1986), we also found moderate support (i.e. at the 10% level) for the fact that alliance capability is a mediating variable in explaining alliance performance. This is in line with Simonin (1997)[10] and Gittell (2002: 1423), who find that coordinating mechanisms and routines improve performance by facilitating interaction among employees in the work process. Being one of the first to empirically test the role of routines and mechanisms (Gittell, 2002: 1423), she finds that mechanisms and routines play a mediating role in the structure, process, outcome model. The results provide moderate support for H3A and confirm the importance for firms to cultivate alliance capabilities (Bamford and Ernst, 2003). Although alliance capabilities partly take away the effect when introduced into the analysis, alliance experience remains an important explanatory variable. In contrast to Simonin (1997), the results of our study indicate that alliance experience can also lead to alliance performance increases directly. However, this finding is in line with the suggestion of Aldrich (1999) and the findings of Kale et al. (2002) and Lenox and King (2004): alliance experience may substitute for the dissemination of knowledge via intra-firm mechanisms.

The moderating effect, as defined in H3B and operationalized by the interaction term, was not supported. Both experience-based learning or learning-by-doing and capabilities play an important role when firms seek to improve their alliance performance. This means that the relationship between a firm's alliance experience and performance is not moderated but mediated by a firm's alliance capability. As argued by Lenox and King (2004: 342–343), we expect that this result points to a differentiated effect of intra-firm mechanisms: their effect will be greatest when the knowledge disseminated is new and has only a minor overlap with the recipient's knowledge, while there will be no effect if the knowledge shared is similar.

The importance of intra-firm mechanisms for developing alliance capabilities is supported by the results of the expert interviews. All of the experts interviewed considered the mechanisms to be of substantial importance to developing a firm's alliance capabilities. Various experts however reckoned that merely having these mechanisms in place does not suffice; the use and application of these mechanisms is of prime importance to realize improved alliance performance. One of the experts added that it would be very difficult for firms to learn without these mechanisms in place. Overall, we find that mechanisms are not only an important means for firms to develop alliance capabilities, but also reflect a serious ambition by the firm to capture, share and disseminate alliance management know-how. However, management of the mechanisms is also an issue which should be kept in mind and which we expect – but cannot empirically confirm – to contribute to consistent performance differences between firms.

The results point to a number of important insights on the complex issue of alliance capability development. First, as far as we are aware, this is one of the first studies to provide micro-level evidence for intra-firm learning with respect to alliance management. Leaving exceptions such as Kale et al. (2002), Knott (2003) and Sarkar et al. (2004) aside, most prior studies (e.g. Anand and Khanna, 2000; Zollo et al., 2002) derive the existence of learning from alliances on the firm's level of alliance experience, which is often referred to as an imperfect proxy for a firm's ability to learn and develop its alliance capability (Kale et al., 2002; Sarkar et al., 2004).

Second, this study, as opposed to prior empirical analyses, empirically validates the sequential relationship between experience, alliance capability and a firm's alliance portfolio performance. We find that alliance capabilities act as a mediator. In this way, insight is enhanced concerning the internal process underlying the development of an alliance capability, which adds to prior studies as these left any potential latent variables mediating between experience and performance undiscussed. Given the fact that we find evidence that mechanisms play a mediating role in the alliance capability development process, there is an obvious need for firms to pay attention to internal knowledge transfer and integration. This also provides empirical evidence for the role intra-firm mechanisms and routines play in alliance practices. Although a recent study by Zollo et al. (2002) hints at the positive influence of inter-firm routines on alliance performance, the positive impact of intra-firm routines on alliance performance has to the best of our knowledge so far not been validated. Therefore, these results suggest that intra-firm knowledge sharing in many instances is essential to make optimal use of prior experiences.

6
Conclusions, Implications, Limitations and Future Research

6.1 Conclusions

This book has analysed the effect of firm-specific alliance capabilities on strategic alliance performance. We have used the term 'strategic' to refer to alliances that are particularly geared towards realizing an improved product market combination for any of the firms involved (Duysters and Hagedoorn, 2000) as well as to shared goals and objectives or mutual benefits (Spekman et al., 1999). In this book, strategic alliances (also referred to as 'alliances') have been defined as temporary cooperative agreements in which two or more firms share reciprocal inputs to realize improved competitive positions for the partners involved, while maintaining their own corporate identities (Contractor and Lorange, 1988; Parkhe, 1993; Vanhaverbeke et al., 2002).[1] Typically, in line with Contractor and Lorange (1998), a definition of alliances excludes both spot market arrangements and mergers and acquisitions, which are entirely integrative agreements. However, for agreements to be called 'strategic', they need to pertain to agreements such as strategic sourcing transactions, co-sourcing agreements, strategic R&D partnerships or be equity-based (see e.g. Yoshino and Rangan, 1995; Rule, 1999).

Studies analysing factors explaining alliance performance have been manifold and can be categorized in two groups, which centred on the contributions of different streams of literature: inter-firm antecedents literature and intra-firm antecedents literature. Essentially, the former of these two streams examines capability development *between* firms, while the latter centres on capability development *within* firms (Grant and Baden-Fuller, 2002). Referring to different theoretical backgrounds, the contributions of the studies analysing inter-firm antecedents of alliance performance centre on critical success factors for managing alliances (e.g. Killing, 1983; Harrigan, 1986; Pekar and Allio, 1994; Dussauge and Garrette, 1995; Douma, 1997; Whipple and Frankel, 2000). In general, studies of this type suggest a set of success factors that considerably influence the performance of the dyadic relationship. For instance, trust and commitment are essential to make strategic alliances succeed (Morgan and Hunt, 1994; Aulakh et al., 1996; Arino et al., 1997, 2001; Holm et al., 1999; Dyer and Chu, 2000). Although contributive to our understanding of the complexity involved in managing alliances, these studies concentrate on dyadic issues, which tend to be case-specific and remain anecdotal (see e.g. Killing, 1983; Doz, 1996; Jap, 2001; Young-Ybarra and Wiersema, 1999). Consequently, although evidence confirms that these dyadic factors can create relation-specific rents (Khanna et al., 1998; Madhok and Tallman, 1998; Kale et al., 2000), this evidence can at best partially explain the differences in individual firms' alliance performance (Park and Ungson, 2001).

Being more recent, the contributions of the second stream of literature are primarily related to uncovering the role of intra-firm antecedents of alliance performance. In this light, experience and mechanisms are suggested to be critical antecedents of alliance performance (e.g. Simonin, 1997; Hoang et al., 2002; Kale et al., 2002). These two concepts seem to explain the considerable fixed-firm effects in individual firm's alliance performance (e.g. Kale and Singh, 1999). More specifically, this stream of literature underlined the need for firms to develop an alliance capability as critical antecedent of alliance performance. Different scholars have suggested an alliance capability to be a rare, valuable and difficult-to-imitate resource at the firm level (e.g. Gulati, 1998; Kale and Singh, 1999). These studies posit that a firm's alliance capability provides a candidate explanation for the fixed-firm differences in alliance performance. Alliance capabilities are seen as a key resource, which originates from a firm's ability to leverage its prior experiences. The ability to do so would enable a firm to integrate and institutionalize the lessons learned. Despite the relative youth of the second stream of studies, it seems to provide a suitable complement to the first stream as it emphasizes the role of internal organizational features rather than relational issues as antecedents of alliance performance. The issue that remained unsolved so far is how firms should develop alliance capabilities to enhance their performance in alliances. Therefore, in order to understand how firms can outperform competitors in alliances and how the significant differences in the individual firm's alliance performance come about, this book's central question was defined as: *How do firms develop alliance capabilities?*

The objective of the underlying study is to examine the impact of intra-firm mechanisms on alliance performance and engender a proper understanding of the alliance capability development process. Three sub-questions, which are derived from the central research question, help reach this study's objective. First, what are alliance capabilities (Chapter 3)? Second, what is the influence of (groups of) intra-firm mechanisms on alliance performance (Chapter 4)? Third, what is the relationship between the critical concepts in the alliance capability development process (Chapter 5)? In order to answer these questions, this study consists of six chapters.

After the introduction, Chapters 2 and 3 constitute the qualitative analysis, which consisted of a literature review on alliance research and the examination of the critical concepts when it comes to developing alliance capabilities. The contents of these two chapters help answer the first sub-question. Moreover, Chapter 2 provided a review of alliance research and presented the theoretical framework in which the different theories underlying this study were put into perspective in order to provide for a sound framework to investigate alliance capability development. This ensured a sound embeddedness in strategic management literature. On the basis of the theoretical underpinnings presented in Figure 2.3, experience, mechanisms, routines and capabilities (consisting of mechanisms and routines) were considered to be essential in understanding the internal or intra-firm process underlying the development of an alliance capability. Experiences are the lessons learned and the knowledge that can be distilled from them. The virtue of experience resides in its provision of knowledge of critical issues in alliance management. As such, it can be seen as a key resource for firms involved in managing alliances. Mechanisms are the internal organizational attributes that help transfer a firm's prior experience (e.g. alliance training or database). They directly or indirectly help firms capture, share, disseminate or apply alliance management knowledge. As the lessons learned are transferred throughout the firm, organizational routines or repeatable patterns of actions can result as a consequence (Sanchez et al., 1996b; Teece, 1997: 106). These concepts form the basis for the development of a firm's alliance capability.

The role of intra-firm mechanisms in developing alliance capabilities

As the strategic importance of alliances continues to grow, many firms may yield superior rents from the ability to successfully manage alliances. However, few firms seem to be blessed with a superior capability to manage alliances. Even fewer firms seem to be able to *consistently* derive above-average rents from their alliances. In order to get a better understanding of the way in which firms can develop alliance capabilities, we analysed 192 firms, which have a total alliance portfolio of approximately 2973 alliances, and interviewed twelve experts. The results of expert interviews were used to verify the empirical results and extend and validate argumentations for our findings.

The first issue that needs to be investigated to get a micro-level understanding of alliance capability development is to study the intra-firm mechanisms successful firms use in comparison to unsuccessful firms. To this end, Chapter 4 compared low- and high-performing firms and found that the following eleven mechanisms were especially conducive to enhance a firm's alliance performance: alliance database, vice-president of alliances, use of intranet, use of own knowledge from prior experiences, alliance manager, partner selection programme, formal exchange of alliance knowledge, joint alliance evaluation, individual alliance evaluation, alliance metrics and alliance department. These findings provide evidence for the substantial role intra-firm mechanisms play when it comes to developing alliance capabilities. The intra-firm mechanisms foster the internalization of certain experiences and therefore enhance the development of a firm's alliance capability. Leaving some notable exceptions aside (e.g. Beugelsdijk et al., 2002; Draulans et al., 2003; Aulakh et al., 2004), the majority of prior related studies only analyses the impact of one mechanism on alliance performance, such as for instance an alliance department or function (Kale et al., 2002). Our findings confirm and extend these results as they point to a notable and substantial impact of different intra-firm mechanisms on alliance performance. These findings are highly relevant as they provide thorough understanding of the micro-level elements or building blocks of alliance capabilities.

To further engender our understanding of how groups of intra-firm mechanisms contribute to alliance capability development, we performed a factor analysis to uncover latent dimensions underlying the intra-firm mechanisms investigated. We found that groups of mechanisms are related to respectively knowledge transfer on dyadic management issues and knowledge transfer concerning alliance portfolio management. Moreover, the results of the expert interviews clearly showed that the firms interviewed have followed similar development paths. Experts from successful and world-renowned firms such KLM, Dow Chemical, GlaxoSmithKline, Oracle and Philips confirmed that at first instance alliance capabilities were developed using group-level learning mechanisms. All experts from practice indicated their firms at first derived lessons from individual alliances, after which these were dispersed throughout the firm using for instance trainings and workshops. While the initial empirical results only found external parties to have a moderately significant and positive impact on alliance performance (for alliance mediators $p < .10$, see Section 4.3), we have to qualify these initial findings as a great number of the interviewees indicated that they made use of external parties to codify and consolidate this expertise into transferable knowledge. Although the empirical analysis in Section 4.3 shows that the overall impact of external parties on enhancing alliance performance is limited, the expert interview results indicate many of the experts from practice make use of external parties to develop alliance capabilities in the earlier stages, that is, when it comes to 'integrating knowledge' by for instance external alliance trainings or distilling best practices (see Appendix 11). When firms start to share knowledge at the group level, mechanisms such as alliance best practices, alliance metrics and external alliance trainings prove to play an important role. Undertaking these steps helped firms to disseminate mainly generic and instrumental knowledge at a group level by for instance sharing best practices. Deploying these mechanisms, employees got acquainted with critical issues relevant when managing alliances. Once more people inside the organization were aware of such issues, almost all the experts indicated they turned to other mechanisms, which aimed to derive value from coordinating knowledge and resources of the firm's alliance portfolio. A group or department was installed to manage the firm's alliance portfolio and stimulate the development of routines and standard practices. Hence, only at second instance were organization-level learning mechanisms deployed to institutionalize alliance experiences. Although there is a relatively clear distinction between group- and organization-level learning mechanisms, the experts also indicated their firms continued to rely on group mechanisms once organization-level mechanisms were deployed. Therefore, new lessons continued to be derived from individual alliances, which could then be dispersed throughout the organization to enhance adoption of new practices and routines. These findings were confirmed when comparing the use of group and organization level mechanisms among different experience levels in our database: firms with little experience mainly use group-level mechanisms, while firms with much experience favour organization-level mechanisms. More importantly, the latter groups performs significantly better (see Appendix 11), confirming our earlier findings.

Hence, the empirical findings in Chapter 4 indicate that successful firms follow a clear development path when it comes to developing alliance capabilities. Initially, group-level learning mechanisms are used to disseminate knowledge derived from individual alliances. Thereafter, they use organization-level learning mechanisms to institutionalize their experiences. The intra-firm mechanisms investigated therefore play an elementary role when it comes to advancing a firm's alliance capabilities. These insights substantially advance current understanding in this field of study. Whereas the concept of alliance capability development and (learning) curves has only recently been introduced (e.g. Anand and Khanna, 2000; Draulans et al., 2003; Helfat and Peteraf, 2003), this study deepens our understanding as it unravels how firms develop alliance capabilities and what role intra-firm mechanisms play in this respect. More specifically, the results of this study reveal that, if firms consciously commit to integrate and institutionalize prior alliance experiences, they can develop alliance capabilities and improve their alliance performance. In other words, in line with what previous studies suggested but could only marginally validate empirically (e.g. Simonin, 1997; Spekman et al., 1999; Lambe et al., 2002), firms can learn to successfully manage alliances.

Alliance capability development process

While Chapter 4 investigated the importance of mechanisms in understanding critical intra-firm antecedents of alliance performance, Chapter 5 extends the quantitative analysis by examining the relationships between critical issues in the alliance capability development process. The relationship between alliance experience, alliance capabilities and performance was analysed using the same data as in Chapter 4. The results show that both experience and alliance capabilities are key antecedents of alliance performance. In an attempt to surpass conventional understanding, which suggests experience is the prime determinant of alliance performance (e.g. Gulati, 1999; Anand and Khanna, 2000; Hoang et al., 2002; Reuer et al., 2002a, b), the results provide moderately significant support for the fact that alliance capability is a mediating variable between experience and alliance performance. This implies that indeed the lessons learned are an important input for mechanisms, which help establish firm-wide knowledge-sharing routines (Dyer and

Singh, 1998; Dyer, 2000). As both alliance experience and capabilities are significant explanatory variables, we expect the effect of intra-firm mechanisms to be greatest when the knowledge disseminated is relatively new (Lenox and King, 2004).

Relying on the novel measure for alliance capabilities derived in Chapter 4, this chapter empirically analyses the relationships between the key concepts of this study. In line with a study by Simonin (1997), we find that experiences can be transferred via intra-firm mechanisms which enhances alliance performance. However, in contrast to Simonin's (1997) findings but in line with other studies' findings (Kale et al., 2002; Lenox and King, 2004), our results also show that alliance experience may directly substitute for knowledge transfer via intra-firm mechanisms. This marks an important finding, as it underlines the need for firms to get involved in alliances: gaining experience is a first step towards improved alliance performance. However, as the results of former chapter also indicate, using intra-firm mechanisms to integrate and institutionalize these experiences is essential if firms are to develop superior alliance capabilities. So, both experience and capabilities are important for firms if they are to optimize their alliance performance. However, alliance experience is not only important because it provides input that can be dispersed via intra-firm mechanisms; it is also important because it may substitute for knowledge available inside the firm and allow it to replace existing practices.

In a broader perspective and referring to the main conclusions of this study, a number of contributions can be identified. First of all, taking into account the relative infancy of alliance research devoted to intra-firm antecedents of alliance performance, the empirical analyses of this study have sought to uncover the process underlying the development of an alliance capability. Currently, research has fallen short of clearly defining the critical components and their interrelationships that lie at the roots of alliance capability development (Simonin, 1997; Hoang, 2001). Relying on underpinnings from six theories essential to unravel the complexity of intra-firm antecedents of alliance performance, this study has found that alliance capability is a mediating variable between experience and alliance performance. These results are in line with a recent study by Gittell (2002), whose boundary spanning study confirmed that mechanisms are critical in transferring experience in the hospital sector. This study has thus been able to extend current wisdom on capability development in firms, which to date has been an emerging scientific field. More in particular, contributing to a new field in alliance research, it has examined the impact of intra-firm factors or

118 *Developing Alliance Capabilities*

internal attributes of the firm on alliance performance, by testing a set of mechanisms which can improve a firm's alliance performance.

Second, by analysing the influence of mechanisms on alliance performance, this study has contributed to understanding critical micro-level processes that have practical relevance and allow firms to take appropriate action. So far, alliance research and strategic management in general has often remained anecdotal and little specific as to how to solve the issue under investigation (Johnson et al., 2003). This study has tried to counterbalance this shortcoming by paying attention to mechanisms that are practical in origin and leave firms with the ability to take action at the micro-level. Through an empirical examination of not only thirty mechanisms which can be used to enhance and transfer proper alliance management but also the process underlying alliance capability development in general, firms are given artefacts with which they can improve their alliance management. Moreover, as trial and error is an essential process in many instances when managing alliances (Lei and Slocum, 1992), insight is given in the process that allows for the leveraging of these prior experiences.

6.2 Theoretical and managerial implications

The former section described the main results of this study. These results are of importance as they provide the basis for two kinds of implications: theoretical and managerial. With respect to theoretical implications, this study makes a number of contributions that are fundamental to the theory of organization science in general. First, in line with Gittell (2002), Knott (2003) and Sarkar et al. (2004), this study finds support for two basic assumption of the resource-based view, which holds that equilibrium can be overcome if (1) firms hold superior resources and (2) the diffusion of these resources is protected by isolating mechanisms (Rumelt, 1984; Barney, 1991; Mahoney and Pandian, 1992; Peteraf, 1993). With respect to the first assumption, the results of this study clearly show that alliance capabilities are a valuable resource. Firms deploying certain mechanisms to disperse and institutionalize critical knowledge perform better than those that do not. Approximately a sixth of the performance difference is attributable to the use of these mechanisms. We are confident that improvements in the number and characterization of alliance capabilities and routines will only enhance this figure. In this study, support for the existence of the second assumption is found in the use of the mechanisms themselves. In Knott's (2003: 942) words: 'while isolating mechanisms exist,...they aren't really controlled by the 'resource holders'. Rather the mechanisms seem to be self-imposed by the would-be imitators'. In other words, the mere usage or installment of certain mechanisms allows for the creation of superior capabilities and routines; the opposite also holds, namely that the isolating mechanism is inherent in the failure or incompetence to adopt these mechanisms. Ignorance or overconfidence and unwillingness to change render those that do not use intra-firm mechanisms unable to tap into the opportunities of superior alliance routines and capabilities.

Hence, in line with the findings by Gittell (2002) and Knott (2003), this study finds that explicit and valuable alliance routines and capabilities, which can be operationalized by mechanisms, are a source of competitive heterogeneity. Therefore, in this context, neither routines nor capabilities need to be tacit to guarantee value creation in alliances. On the contrary, deliberate attempts are needed to extract the inherent value from such mechanisms. And therefore, the isolating mechanism is held by the firm's management rather than the resource. Hence, the paradox of explicit and valuable routines dissolves. Similarly, these results also confirm the fundamental logic of the dynamic capability view: superior capabilities cause superior rents (Teece et al., 1997; Eisenhardt and Martin, 2000; King and Tucci, 2002; Zollo and Winter, 2002; Winter, 2003). More specifically, as suggested in fundamental studies by Amit and Schoemaker (1993), Makadok (2001) and Madhok (2002) and empirical studies by Madhok and Tallman (1998), Anand and Khanna (2000) and Kale et al. (2002), investment in certain resources or mechanisms (also referred to as 'resource-picking or selecting') will enable a firm to develop superior capabilities and routines (also referred to as 'resource deploying'). Hence, it may not necessarily be the 'inimitability' of resources, as many have suggested (e.g. Lippman and Rumelt, 1982; Wernerfelt, 1984; Dierickx and Cool, 1989), but perhaps the commitment to and investment in certain mechanisms which allows firms to outperform competitors when it comes to successfully managing alliances. The ability to adapt resources, capabilities and routines on the basis of new insights, lessons or experiences then turns out to be most crucial.

Second, within the literature on evolutionary economics, an ongoing debate is held on whether knowledge residing in routines is purely tacit or explicit (Nelson and Winter, 1982; Knott, 2003). This study contributes to this debate as the derived summated scale clearly shows that certain practices can also contain explicit elements such as a culture programme or partner selection programme. These mechanisms are examples of codified knowledge contained in documents that decipher the critical issues. These results are in line with recent findings by Knott (2003) and Lenox and King (2004), who also find that some intra-firm mechanisms consisting of explicit or codified material contribute to our understanding of competitive heterogeneity. These insights again confirm that the 'inimitability' element, which a valuable resource should contain, apparently not always holds.

Third, within evolutionary economics and the dynamic capability view, the conceptual basis for routines is often referred to as being inherent in the variation-selection-retention cycle (see e.g. Campbell, 1969; Bruderer and Singh, 1996; Aldrich, 1999). Although various studies have so far empirically confirmed that for instance practice transfer leads to improved performance (e.g. Szulanski et al., 2002; Maritan and Brush, 2003), far less evidence is found of the learning mechanisms underlying this cycle. This study makes a fundamental contribution as it finds evidence for the fact that alliance performance heterogeneity stems from the use of intra-firm mechanisms. The positive correlation found between alliance performance and certain (groups of) mechanisms suggests that these mechanisms also entail a dynamic aspect. The fact that these high-performing firms derive increasing amounts of their sales revenues from alliances (often over 40%) suggests that the mechanisms tested also allow for both variation and retention. This would imply that these mechanisms provide evidence of the existence of dynamic alliance capabilities. However, this is an interpretation and should therefore be considered with caution.

Fourth, with respect to organizational learning theory, this study finds micro-level evidence of how organizations learn. To date, little attention has been paid to the contribution of certain practices to organizational learning (Vera and Crossan, 2004: 226). This study extends our understanding of both the process underlying learning and the catalysts driving organizational learning. The mechanisms investigated prove to play an important role in the integration and institutionalization of alliance-related knowledge. Also, the results of Chapter 5 show that this process is critical to the development of alliance capabilities. These results mark an important finding as they extend current insight into how firms learn. Whereas often experience was proposed as a critical antecedent (Kleiner and Roth, 1987; Ingram and Baum, 1997; Carroll et al., 2003), this study embarks on the role intra-firm mechanisms play in this respect and finds convincing evidence that these mechanisms contribute to our understanding of how firms learn to manage alliances.

There are also a number of important managerial implications. Given the increasing use of alliances and their mounting stake in revenues generated, effective management becomes ever more critical. This study found evidence of the importance of alliance experience and mechanisms to alliance capability development. Hence, it has created insight into how firms can develop alliance capabilities. First of all, the results of this study suggest that certain mechanisms enhance alliance performance. In the context of the study, it was obvious that some mechanisms may even have a negative effect on the long-term success of a firm's alliances. Second, different mechanisms prove to be more appropriate at different experience levels. While some studies have looked at the impact of alliance experience, they tend to leave undiscussed differential learning effects of intra-firm mechanisms. Especially these findings are of critical importance to management, as different firms tend to have different levels of experience and hence need different mechanisms to organize learning. Third, and perhaps most important, evidence was found of the learning process underlying the development of alliance capabilities. Made aware of the necessity to pay attention to the critical role of prior experience and the need to embed these lessons learned in routines to develop alliance capabilities, firms are given critical input to nurture future alliance success. In particular, the results of the expert interviews provide valuable insight into how successful firms such as Oracle, KLM, Philips, Dow Chemical and GlaxoSmithKline have shaped their alliance capability development process: they all followed a certain path to learn and institutionalize how alliances should be managed.

6.3 Limitations and future research

Despite the contributions of this study to the emerging scientific field of alliance research by examining the process of alliance capability development, it is subject to a number of limitations. First of all, the influence of alliance mechanisms on creating routines is implicit. Although the validity of our construct of alliance capability is verified in various ways, this study assumes that mechanisms and routines are interrelated concepts and that the use of these mechanisms reflects a certain commitment and dedication to the improvement of alliance management on behalf on the firm. In this context, the use of an alliance department proved of importance for firms to enhance performance (Kale et al., 2002), this department not only enables coordination of alliance activities, but also the dispersion of certain alliance-related practices. This indicates that, at least to a certain degree, the concepts of mechanisms and routines are related. More specifically, it implies that mechanisms are likely to play an important role in changing and adapting firm routines (see e.g. Dyer and Singh, 1998). However, future research should try to extend on our analysis by empirically verifying the exact interplay between mechanisms and routines and the degree to which certain mechanisms indeed help establish certain routines.

Second, in line with arguments given by Grant (1995), Simonin (1997) and Tsang (2002a), having certain mechanisms in place does not necessarily guarantee successful dissemination of knowledge. Therefore, it becomes critical to also ensure proper measurement of the efficiency of mechanisms to integrate and transfer knowledge. As Pfeffer and Sutton (1999) legitimately argue, there is a difference between having knowledge in-house and making effective use of it. More specifically, they state that 'the fact that knowledge is acquired through experience and is often intangible and tacit produces a...problem in turning knowledge into action' (Pfeffer and Sutton, 1999: 95). They add that 'these [formal knowledge exchange] systems...capture the tacit, experiential knowledge..., such systems certainly don't capture whether or not this knowledge is actually being used'. This study does not verify the extent to which mechanisms are used and are functioning as presumed (i.e. able to indeed transfer knowledge). As mentioned in Chapter 4, this study presumes that the presence of a certain mechanism reflects a commitment to using it. This implies that the presence and use are assumed to be linked, while obviously management does not always function as it should. It would therefore be interesting to investigate the influence of an additional variable reflecting the actual usage of a certain mechanism. This is an area in which future studies can make highly relevant contributions.

Third, this study did not directly test whether different types of knowledge have a different impact on performance (see e.g. Inkpen and Dinur, 1998; Hansen, 2002) and how these relate to the different mechanisms. The majority of the mechanisms either help disseminate tacit knowledge by means of communication (e.g. alliance training), verbalization (e.g. alliance training or formalized knowledge exchange between alliance managers) or refer to explicit knowledge and are directed towards codification (e.g. partner selection programme or partner programme). However, the effectiveness of mechanisms to capture different types of knowledge they contain might be an issue for future research.

Fourth, this study analyses the alliance capability development process in a static way. We are aware of the fact that environmental changes can render obsolete a firm's set of routines, which at the same time can limit its ability to adapt (Levinthal and March, 1993). This underlines the need for firms to not only be flexible and adaptive, but also ensure that new experiences are used to feed mechanisms on a continuing basis. In this way, a firm's routines are less likely to become 'sticky'. Using cross-sectional data rather than longitudinal data does not allow us to investigate this cyclical process. Montealegre (2002: 514) argues that capability development is an iterative and gradual process that is cumulative, expansive and dependent on the combinations of a firm's resources and actions. Although this study agrees with Montealegre's argument, it has only been able to analyse the essential concepts of the alliance capability development process in a static fashion and has therefore been unable to take into account dynamic forces in this process. Since mechanisms help limit structural inertia (Eisenhardt and Martin, 2000), future research should analyse whether indeed new experiences can by means of mechanisms create dynamism in routines, which by nature are 'sticky'. Moreover, using longitudinal data may shed new light on the interrelatedness of the various concepts used in this study.

Fifth, as 'transferring knowledge is not an efficient approach to integrating knowledge' (Grant, 1996b: 114), the particular contributions of various mechanisms should be further investigated. As information capabilities of mechanisms should match information requirements of the task at hand (Galbraith, 1973), minimizing rather than maximizing knowledge transfer should be the firm's main objective. Consequently, possible redundancy or replication effects between the different mechanisms should be analysed to ensure that the appropriate set of mechanisms is used. For instance, it may suffice for a firm to install an alliance department and an alliance manager, thereby ignoring the other functions. Whereas this study was among others directed at identifying the effectiveness of individual mechanisms, future research may thus be geared towards understanding the interaction effects among different mechanisms. This remark also has another implication, which concerns the substitutability of different mechanisms. In this study, the value or contribution of each mechanism was considered to be equal. However, future research might investigate if certain mechanisms can replace others, thereby for instance limiting redundancy in knowledge transfer. Moreover, it might try to determine what set of mechanisms is useful for what occasion. For instance, the importance of different mechanisms for alliance management in different tasks and phases of the alliance lifecycle can be explored.

Sixth, this study has focused on intra-firm factors influencing alliance performance. However, as mentioned earlier, this stream of research is distinct from the stream of studies which is devoted to uncovering inter-firm antecedents of alliance performance. Studies belonging to the latter stream suggest a set of success factors that described what factors should be considered to optimize performance in the dyadic relationship. Despite the contributions of both streams, the interrelationship between these streams is a research topic that has so far been left undiscussed (Heimeriks and Schreiner, 2002a, b). Examining the relationships between alliance capability or intra-firm antecedents and success factors or inter-firm antecedents of alliance performance would be an interesting area for future research. One would expect that certain mechanisms be positively related to certain success factors. For instance, local alliance managers, country-specific alliance policies and cultural programmes can be used to bridge cultural differences in cross-national alliances. As these mechanisms are geared towards fostering awareness and sensitivity, they are likely to facilitate alliance execution by increasing understanding, enhancing trust building, and reducing conflict potential (Heimeriks and Schreiner, 2002b). Moreover, as we assumed that dyadic issues such as trust may be less of an issue in intra-firm interactions as compared to inter-firm interactions, this may be a topic where future research may shed new light on what impact these dyadic issues have on for instance intra-firm learning. Furthermore, research on the interaction effects between different inter-firm factors can reveal whether a high level of one characteristic can substitute for a low level of another. For instance, prior research suggests that formalized structures can be minimized in relationships governed by high levels of mutual trust (see e.g. Luo, 2002b; Poppo and Zenger, 2002). As a result, it would be interesting to investigate the linkages between the two streams of alliance research and to what extent they are complementary.

Last, future research should also consider the influence of, for instance, a firm's existing resource commitments and its influence on a firm's ability to develop an alliance capability. As mentioned earlier, firms can develop an alliance capability in different ways (Alliance Analyst, 1994; Hill and Hellriegel, 1994). However, the results from this study were not explicit on what mechanisms work best for what type of firm or in what type of situation. We hope future research will embark on these questions.

Appendices

Appendix 1   Alliance goals and outcomes

Various scholars have come up with many different reasons or motives why firms tend to ally (see e.g. Spekman et al., 1999). However, little research has been done to find out to what extent firms are able to realize the defined goals. In our study, five main categories were used to establish the primary motivations of firms to ally and the extent to which these particular goals are realized: (1) risk reduction, (2) economies of scale, (3) market entry, (4) co-opting or blocking competition and (5) access skills and resources. Despite the increase in importance of alliances as market value generator, our study shows that firms have great difficulty in realizing the objectives set. This appendix shows that only alliances aimed at facilitating new market entry (i.e. by entering new product or geographical markets) fully achieve their goals in 22.4 per cent of the cases. This is the only goal that showed higher success (22.4%) than failure rates (6.6%). Especially alliances aimed at co-option or blocking competition experience high failure rates: 18.0 per cent of respondents says they do not achieve these objectives at all. This figure becomes even worse if we also take into account the other categories: 53.0 per cent of the respondents indicate that they achieved only marginal co-option or blocking of competition using strategic alliances. Hence, this particular goal turns out to be the one that is most difficult to realize.

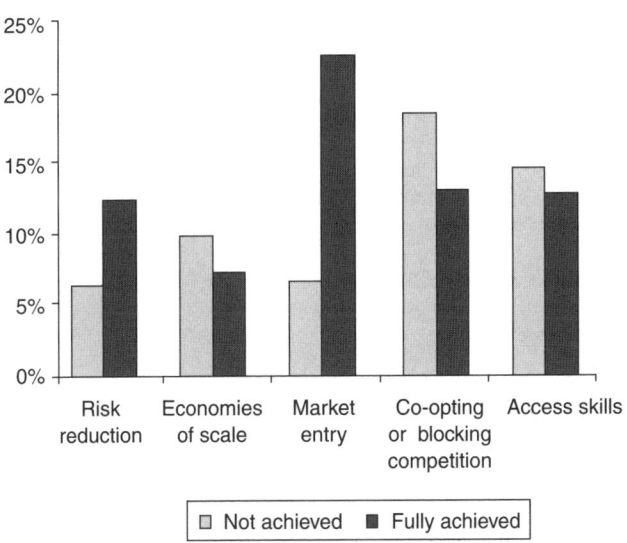

Appendix 2 Overview of experts interviewed (in alphabetic order)

John Bell
Director of Alliances
Royal Philips Corporation
Amsterdam, the Netherlands

Charles Billar
Alliance Manager
Oracle Corporation
De Meern, the Netherlands

Snehal Desai
Global Director of E-Business
The Dow Chemical Company
Midland, United States

Henk de Graauw
Director of Alliances
KLM-Air France
Amsterdam, the Netherlands

Aimé Heene
Associate Professor
Ghent University, De Vlerick School of Management
Ghent, Belgium

Ha Hoang
Associate Professor
INSEAD
Fontainebleau, France

Jan Jurriëns
Partner
Twynstra Gudde Management Consultants
Amersfoort, the Netherlands

Ard-Pieter de Man
Professor of Organization Science
CEO Centre for Global Corporate Positioning
Amsterdam, the Netherlands

Ron Sanchez
Professor of Strategy and Technology Management
IMD
Lausanne, Switzerland

Larraine Segil
CEO and alliance specialist
The Lared Group
Los Angeles, United States

Peter Thurlby
Director Alliance Management
GlaxoSmithKline
United Kingdom

Appendices 127

Wim Vanhaverbeke
Assistant Professor
Eindhoven University of Technology
Eindhoven, the Netherlands

Appendix 3 Top five reasons for strategic alliance failure

As mentioned, over recent years extensive scholarly attention has been paid to the impact of inter-firm factors on alliance performance (e.g. Geringer, 1991; Medcof, 1997; Cullen et al., 2000; Koza and Lewin, 2000). In our survey among 192 firms (see Appendix 4), we also asked respondents to what extent they considered different dyadic issues to be of critical importance to alliance success. As can be seen in the above figure, many respondents considered issues such as operational hurdles or a mismatch with a partner's culture and strategy of importance to make their strategic alliance succeed. For a more detailed review, we refer to Duysters and Heimeriks (2005).

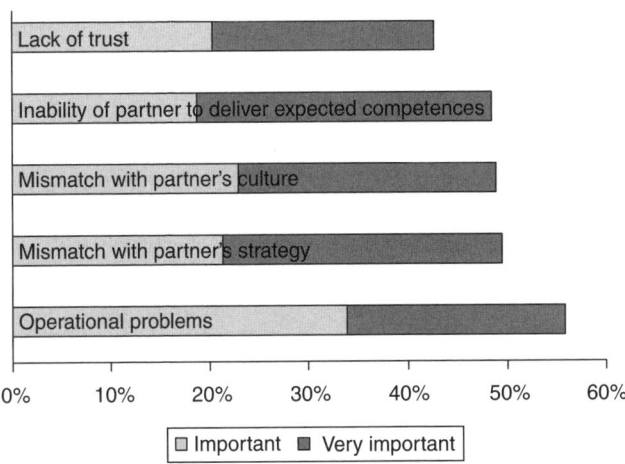

Appendix 4 Methodology

Survey

In line with numerous other studies in the area of alliance research, this study's quantitative analysis is mainly based on a survey technique to gather data on the organization of firms' alliance management processes (Anand and Khanna, 2000: 314). To this end, a survey questionnaire was developed in cooperation with a number of specialists. The survey was sent to 650 vice-presidents and alliance managers worldwide, who were responsible for managing the firm's alliance portfolio. The membership databases of the Internet Society (ISOC) and the Association of Strategic Alliance Professionals (ASAP) were used to direct our survey questionnaires to the right person. ISOC is an internationally organized association that addresses important issues to maintain the viability of the Internet in the future (see www.isoc.nl for more information). Based in North America and Europe ASAP aims to share knowledge in the area of alliances in order to help firms cope with recurring problems (see www.strategic-alliances.org for more information). The membership databases of these associations have a number of characteristics that support the objective of this study. First, ISOC and ASAP are associations that have attracted a large variety of firms worldwide from a wide range of industries. As a consequence of the above-average use of alliances in technology-intensive industries (see e.g. Hagedoorn, 2001), the majority of our respondents were active in ICT and service-related sectors. Second, the databases enabled us to address the mailing to VP's of alliances or – in the absence of this particular function – to top managers in charge of corporate alliance management. These persons were used as key informants on their firm's alliance activities and related management practices. As Tippins and Sohi (2003: 757) note, the use of key informants is currently the standard methodology in strategy research when it comes to information on corporate level issues (Philips, 1981; see e.g. Simonin, 1997; Kale et al., 2002).[1] In this study, they are assumed to be able to appropriately judge the performance of the alliance portfolio they manage as well as have a sufficient degree of awareness of the intra-firm mechanisms their firm uses. In this way, we reckon that the people addressed are considered to be sufficiently knowledgeable about the organization's alliance matters.

In line with earlier studies, this survey was used to collect data on managerial assessments of a firm's alliance portfolio performance (Tuchi, 1996; Kale et al., 2002). It was set up so as to optimize the response rate (Kanuk and Berenson, 1975; Pressley, 1980; Erdogan and Baker, 2002; Rea and Parker, 2002). Although in the absence of other factors, there is no relationship between response rate and non-response bias, non-response bias is an important barrier in business research (Hunt, 1990; Tanner, 1999). In order to optimize the study's response rate and to not unnecessarily impose restrictions on the generalizability of the results, the two most effective techniques for increasing response rates were taken into account: follow-up and the use of incentives (for an overview see Jobber and O'Reilly, 1998). So, despite the lack of maturity of literature on large-scale international mail surveys in comparison to domestic settings (Jobber and Saunders, 1988; Angur and Nataraajan, 1995; Harzing, 2000) and the ongoing debate about the required response rate in business research, various aspects were paid attention to so as to ensure we gathered sound data. These aspects relate to questionnaire design, reminder messages and incentives. First, with respect to questionnaire design, the questionnaire was developed along the steps proposed by Nunally and Bernstein (1994) and Churchill and Iacobucci (2001). This ensured that aspects such as questionnaire length, style of question and scoring were taken into account (see Special Issue of *Journal of Consumer Psychology*, 2001, 10(1, 2), pp. 55–69 and pp. 37–53, for an overview of critical issues in measurement and continuous and discrete variables repectively). In addition, fixed alternative responses or comparative scales were used to ask for facts (Greer et al., 2000). Moreover, the questionnaire was extensively pre-tested with various experts so as to finalize it and erase any inconsequent aspects or aspects that could potentially be wrongly interpreted. Two panels reviewed the measures used in the questionnaire. The first panel consisted of academic researchers, who verified for the consistency and construct operationalizations. The second panel contained professionals from a manufacturing firm and a high-tech firm, who mainly addressed issues in relation to clarity and relevance of the questions and the terminology used. Furthermore, respondents were assured that responses would be treated confidentially and that results would be presented in an aggregated format. Last, the questionnaire was put online (at www.alliancecapability.com) so as to ease the filling out of the questionnaire and decrease the effort to reply. The e-mails that were used as cover letters of the questionnaire were personalized (Larson and Chow, 2003). Following these steps, our efforts were pinpointed towards optimizing the technical format of the questionnaire and ensuring a minimum amount of effort on the side of our respondents.

Second, after the survey was sent out to the respondents, a reminder message was used in order to maximize the response rate (Dillman, 1978; Paxson, 1992). Various follow-up techniques can be used for follow-up or reminder messages (for an overview see Erdogan and Baker, 2002). Of these various techniques, we used the original replacement follow-up (ORF) technique, which includes the same e-mail message as the original message, since this is likely to encourage a high response rate. There are a number of reasons for this. First, the initial or original message may be simply discarded by the recipient. In this case, it will allow to function as a simple reminder, as it will confront the potential respondent with the same graphic imaging and lay-out, which is most likely to appear familiar. Second, since questionnaire fatigue is considered as one the prime aspects negatively influencing response rates (Bickart and Schmittlein, 1999; Harzing, 2000), resending the original message may also be interpreted by the recipient as a sign of commitment to the research on the side of the researcher.

Third, a relevant book on the topic as well as a copy of the study results was sent to those who cooperated in filling out the survey questionnaire, which served as an incentive. This was done to increase the perceived benefit of participating in the survey. Using these kinds of incentives has proved to contribute to the response rate (see e.g. Angur and Nataraajan, 1995; Cycyota and Harrison, 2002; Larson and Chow, 2003).

As mentioned earlier, the survey was conducted among 650 alliance managers and VPs, who together make up the total population of this study. After sending out the survey in two batches and a reminder message to all the potential respondents, I received 192 responses. This resulted in a response rate of 29.5 per cent. This response rate can be considered to be high in comparison to most international mail surveys, which obtain a rate between 6 per cent and 16 per cent (Harzing, 2000) and good in comparison to most research in strategic management (Snow and Thomas, 1994). However, it is equal to response rates obtained in various earlier alliance studies (see e.g. Kale et al., 2002; Reuer et al., 2002a; Zollo et al., 2002) and is very reasonable given the seniority of our respondents and the amount of surveys conducted in the area of alliances (Zollo et al., 2002). After data screening and removing outliers, the sample consisted of 192 firms from a variety of industries: chemicals (3%), ICT (17%), ICT services (26%), financial services (5%), other services (e.g. consultancies; 30%), pharmaceuticals and

Table App. 4.1 Distribution of firm size

	N	%
(1) Number of employees[a]		
1–500	81	42.2
500–1000	8	4.2
> 1000	101	52.6
Total	190	100
(2) Sales revenues (in US$)[b]		
Less than 1 million	46	24.0
1–100 million	44	22.9
100 million–1 billion	24	12.5
1–50 billion	68	35.4
> 50 billion	9	4.7
Total	191	100

[a] Two cases 'don't know'
[b] One case 'don't know'

biotechnology (3%), other manufacturing (10%) and public sector (e.g. education and non-profit organizations; 4%), the rest (2%) is missing data. In total, 82 per cent of the respondents are active in ICT and service-related sectors. In total, the 192 firms in our dataset report on approximately 2973 alliances.[2]

The next table shows the distribution of the variable 'firm size' of firms in our dataset, which was measured on the basis of two variables: number of employees and sales revenues.

Firm size was measured in both the number of employees and the firm's sales revenues. With respect to the number of employees, the dataset proved to consist of two relatively balanced sets of firms: 42.2 per cent of the respondents works for a parent firm having between 1 and 500 employees and 52.6 per cent has over 1000 employees. With respect to sales revenues, the largest amount of respondents, namely 35.4 per cent, is found in the category of US$ 1–50 billion worldwide sales per year. The rest is found in: 24.0 per cent below $1m, 22.9 per cent between $1–100m, 12.5 per cent between $100m–$1b, 4.7 per cent larger than $50b, and the rest is missing data.

To ensure that our data was not biased as a result of non-response, the data was screened to compare a number of respondent characteristics. These characteristics were investigated to understand if our sample was a good representation of the population. First of all, an analysis was performed to verify if any non-response bias was apparent using three variables to compare early versus late respondents. The three variables were: firm size measured as the number of employees of the parent company, firm size as measured by total worldwide sales revenues and alliance performance. Chi-square tests for each of these measures show that there is no difference between the different categories.[3] This demonstrates that there is a relatively equal division between small to medium-sized and large firms in terms of both number of employees and sales as well as alliance performance level when comparing early and late respondents. As late respondents can be assumed to be comparable to non-respondents (Kanuk and Berenson, 1975; Armstrong and Overton, 1977), this indicates that there was no significant non-response bias in our dataset. Second, the average alliance performance of our sample was 52 per cent, which is comparable to other studies on alliance performance (Park and Ungson, 2001). These results suggest that our sample is not skewed in terms of firm size or in terms of alliance performance, which implies that the validity of our dataset was not influenced as a consequence of non-response bias.

Expert interviews

In addition to the survey, in-depth expert interviews were conducted. For these interviews, twelve experts in the field of alliances and capability development were selected worldwide (see Appendix 2 for an overview of the experts interviewed). Within the group of experts, there was a sound division between practitioners (seven in number) and academics (five in number). However, some of the experts are active in academia and business. The experts interviewed were selected on the basis of their established reputation in the field and ability to sufficiently contribute to the goal of these interviews on the basis of their prior experience and related knowledge.

The interviews served two purposes. On the one hand, they allowed for a verification of the empirical findings. On the other hand, the interviews were aimed at validating and extending the argumentations for expected and unexpected results and the reasons why the study's findings were appropriate. Mirroring our findings against the opinion and insights of practitioners and academics should nurture stronger and more reliable results. The interviews consisted of two sections (part A and part B), were semi-structured and lasted between forty and sixty minutes. The interview questions were partly exploratory and mostly open-ended (Greer et al., 2000; see Appendix 5). Before interviewing the envisioned experts, a panel of interviewees allowed for informal pre-testing of the questionnaire (Churchill and Iacobucci, 2001). After the pre-tests, the interviews were recorded with the consent of the interviewees and thereafter transcribed to allow for comparison of the different interviews. Moreover, the results were summarized during the interview in order to ensure an adequate representation of the expert's answers. The results of these interviews were used to verify our findings. Analyses of the results were done by comparing individual arguments and comments of the interviewees to our findings and categorize any arguments given to provide additional support for our findings.

Explanatory variables

Given the infancy of the field of research, measurement of intra-firm mechanisms lying at the very roots of alliance capabilities is a challenging area. As mentioned, proxying alliance capabilities by the firm's number of prior alliances is a popular approach (Hoang et al., 2002; Kale et al., 2002; Zollo et al., 2002). However, in order to more meticulously examine the development of alliance capabilities at the micro-level, a more comprehensive measure for alliance capabilities is needed. Relying on expert input and in line with Draulans et al. (2003), this study has defined thirty intra-firm mechanisms that underlie the development of alliances capabilities. Figure 4.1 lists these mechanisms, which make up the explanatory or independent variables of this study. In line with the logic followed by Gittell (2002) and Miller (2003), these mechanisms reflect the way in which firms develop alliance capabilities. They essentially function as intra-firm stimuli aimed at enhancing alliance performance. Following Afuah (2000) and Kale et al. (2002), the investigation of these thirty key variables of alliance capability are represented by thirty single-item dummy variables. Consequently, the existence of a certain mechanism is measured by a categorical variable. For each mechanism we defined, we created a dummy variable to analyse its relation to different performance levels. This is called a binominal semantic differential scale (Bagozzi and Phillips, 1982; Jobson, 1992; Nunally and Bernstein, 1994). The semantic differential scale is a scale where the endpoints consist of two bipolar activities (i.e. 'good' versus 'bad' or 'yes' versus 'no'). In this study, we used a binominal scale to understand if firms have or do not have a certain mechanism in place. This type of scale is nominal and results in binary independent variables. This implies that either a firm has a certain mechanism ($X_c = 1$) or it does not have it ($X_c = 0$). In this way, the total set of mechanisms a firm has in place can be seen as a representation of its capability (Gittell, 2002) on basis of which differences between firms can be easily disseminated.

The underlying logic has been advanced in the early 1960s by Rotter (1966), who in a psychological study on the perception of causes of events made use of

Table App. 4.2 Intra-firm mechanisms

	Intra-firm mechanisms[a]
Functions	(1) Vice-President of alliances, (2) alliance department, (3) alliance specialist, (4) alliance manager, (5) gatekeeper, (6) local alliance manager
Tools	(7) internal alliance training, (8) external alliance training, (9) international alliance training (11) joint business planning, (12) alliance database, (13) use of intranet to disperse knowledge, (14) best practices, (15) culture programme, (16) partner programme, (17) individual alliance evaluation, (18) comparison of evaluations, (19) joint evaluations
Control and management processes	(20) responsibility level for alliances (a. top management, b. business development, c. marketing, d. M&A department, e. R&D, f. strategy), (21) rewards and bonuses for alliance managers, (22) rewards and bonuses for business managers, (23) formally structured knowledge exchange between alliance managers, (24) use of own knowledge (25) alliance metrics, (26) country-specific alliance policies
External parties	(27) consultant, (28) lawyer, (29) mediator, (30) financial expert

[a] See Appendix 5 for definitions of different mechanisms

a technique to define his construct. Rotter defined a 29-item instrument consisting of binary variables, which when one adds up the items generates a total score ranging from 0 to 29. The total score represents to what extent someone has a preference or interest (see also Lambin, 1993, the importance–performance matrix). For this study's purposes, despite the fact that it suffers from limitations such as the assumption that all mechanisms are equally important, we use the same logic to define a construct for measuring a firm's alliance capability for a number of reasons (see also Hopkins, 2004). First of all, using binary variables to measure whether a firm deploys a certain intra-firm mechanism provides an objective way to measure the issue under investigation. For instance, asking a respondent whether his firm has an alliance department can be answered straightforwardly by responding 'yes' or 'no'. In doing so, we follow a recent study by Knott (2003), who investigates the effect of franchise routines on franchise performance. Second, using alternative scales such as a Likert scale would seriously complicate the comparison and summing up of the individual mechanisms. Given the different nature of the mechanisms, it would have been practically impossible to use one definition of a Likert scale for all mechanisms (e.g. the use of intranet could be quantified by for instance daily or weekly use, the contribution of a vice-president would have to be measured differently). Therefore, in case we would have used different scales for the mechanisms, this would have resulted in difficulty to interpret results and substantial loss of information. Third, as this study seeks to examine the use of mechanisms by management aimed at alliance capability development and intends to gather data using a large-scale survey, it is also important to take into account the unruly nature of practice. Adding a third option to the 0–1 scale, for instance the option 'don't know' or 'no opinion', is not likely to improve the quality of our study results as there is little ambivalence in having or not having a mechanism in place. Moreover, adding such a category makes people more prone to opt for the alternative 'no opinion' (DeVellis, 1991; Baarda and De Goede, 1995). The option of ascribing different weights to different mechanisms was not considered appropriate, because of the different nature of the mechanisms and a lack of insight into the specific (quantitative) contribution each mechanism makes. Hence, given these arguments, we reckon that the use of a binominal semantic differential scale suits the purposes of this study, as it allows us to examine the extent to which firms make use of internal mechanisms to develop alliance capabilities.

Dependent variable

Triggered by the dissatisfaction with performance of many alliances (Khanna et al., 1998), the topic of alliance performance and its measurement has been dealt with extensively over the last years. Although this area has been baptized as being 'challenging' due to measurement problems and data access (Anderson, 1990; Gulati, 1998), various studies have used different measures and levels of analysis (for a critical review see Gulati, 1998; for an overview see Park and Ungson, 2001). With respect to measurement, Venkatraman and Ramanujam (1986) propose three groups of measures: financial, operational and organizational effectiveness performance. The first group includes measures such as profitability and growth (e.g. Parkhe, 1993; Hagedoorn and Schakenraad, 1994;

Aulakh et al., 1996; Combs and Ketchen, 1999; Sarkar et al., 2001). Longevity, survival and duration are part of the second group and are therefore examples of operational performance measures (e.g. Killing, 1983; Harrigan, 1988a; Kogut, 1988). The third and most common way to measure alliance performance is to use organizational effectiveness measures. These measures determine the overall satisfaction with the alliance or the extent to which objectives have been met (e.g. Geringer and Hebert, 1991; Mohr and Spekman, 1994). Whereas the former two groups of measures are objective, the third group is more subjective.

Various studies have investigated the need to use objective, subjective or a composite index to measure alliance performance (e.g. Arino, 2003). Geringer and Hebert (1991) have shown that objective and subjective measures tend to be highly correlated. In spite of early criticism on the use of managerial assessments as a measure for alliance performance, there is an emerging consensus that managerial assessments of performance provide a sound reflection of alliance performance (Kale et al., 2002). Given the fact that companies form alliances for specific reasons, asking alliance managers to what extent the stated alliance objectives were achieved, is an effective and scientifically established manner to assess the success of an alliance (Geringer and Herbert, 1991; Tuchi, 1996; Kale and Singh, 1999).

With respect to the level of analysis used, earlier studies relied primarily on measuring the performance of the individual alliance or on measuring the partner benefits from the alliance (Olk, 2002). Using the individual alliance as the unit of analysis provides an indication of how the entity performs, whereas the partner perspective allows researchers to differentiate between the assessments of different partners. Especially the latter type level of analysis has been used in studies focusing on knowledge transfer *between* firms (e.g. Jap, 2001). An obvious detriment to using this level of analysis is that each alliance is treated as a single and independent transaction (Doz and Prahalad, 1991).

However, as researches have recently started to analyse knowledge transfer *within* firms, doubts arise whether an alliance or partner level of analysis is the appropriate level to measure alliance performance (Levinthal, 2000; Duysters et al., 2002b; Sarkar et al., 2004). Using the performance of a firm's alliance portfolio as a level of analysis is preferred for a number of reasons. First, it allows us to analyse the *average* impact of a firm's alliance capability on its alliance performance. This is in line with Ray et al. (2004), who suggest that performance is only a viable dependent when it represents the specific business processes the study seeks to investigate. We follow their argumentation, as this study measures whether alliance capabilities explain persistent heterogeneity in firm alliance performance. Second, using the firm's alliance portfolio as dependent variable is more likely to average out biases than when a firm's alliance capability is linked to its performance in one alliance. The impact of a firm's alliance capability is by nature not restricted to one alliance but is centred on the creation of a firm-wide ability to deal with its entire alliance portfolio. Third, the performance of a firm's alliance is not an isolated issue, but should be seen in the context of a firm's alliance experience (Gulati, 1998). When it comes to developing alliance capabilities, it is important to leverage knowledge across a firm's alliances by considering alliances as a portfolio rather than a separate activity (Lorenzoni and Baden Fuller, 1995). Isolation of an alliance by viewing it as a stand-alone activity would unnecessarily limit the firm's learning abilities

(Khanna et al., 1998). Last, it is worth mentioning that, for this study's purposes, it would be illogical to include additional performance items (such as learning or relationship quality) given the fact that we investigate the performance of a firm's alliance portfolio. These items in general relate to performance in individual alliances and can be considered less useful when analysing a firm's alliance portfolio. For all of these reasons, we follow Anand and Vassalo (2002) and use the performance of the entire alliance portfolio rather than the performance of an individual alliance, as we argue it allows for a better understanding of the role alliance capabilities play.

In this study, alliance performance is defined as the percentage of alliances where the firm's initial goals were realized, which is in line with earlier studies (Hamel et al., 1989; Hamel, 1991; Zollo et al., 2002). It is measured as a composite of a firm's alliance portfolio performance over the period 1997 to 2001 and therefore reflects the percentage of a firm's alliances in its alliance portfolio that was considered successful over this period. Following Geringer (1988) and Parkhe (1993), a 5-point interval scale with integers ranging from 1 to 5 (1 = 0%–20%, 2 = 21%–40%, ..., 5 = 81%–100%) was used to measure alliance performance (see DeVellis, 1991 and Special Issue of *Journal of Consumer Psychology*, 2001, **10**(1, 2), pp. 55–69, for an overview of critical issues in measurement). We also added a category 'don't know' as an option. This scale allows respondents to rate the degree to which alliances in the firm's alliance portfolio reach their initial objectives and can be seen as an indicator of overall performance satisfaction (Arino, 2003).

Appendix 5 Summary of survey items

Please indicate which of the following mechanisms exist in your company to support alliance management.

	In place
1. Vice-President of alliances	☐
2. Alliance department	☐
3. Alliance specialist	
a. At top management level only	☐
b. At middle management level only	☐
c. At both levels	☐
4. Alliance manager	☐
5. Gatekeeper	☐
6. Formal alliance training	
a. Internal training	☐
b. External training	☐
7. Standard partner selection approach	
8. Joint business planning	☐
9. Metrics	☐
10. Alliance database	
a. Accessible for top management only	☐
b. Accessible to all involved	☐
11. Alliance best practices	☐
12. Culture programme	☐
13. Partner programme	
a. Yes, and allows partner to access information via the internet	☐
b. Yes, but it does not allow partner to access information via the internet	☐
14. Evaluation techniques	
a. Each alliance is evaluated individually	☐
b. Compary alliances are compared	☐
15. Joint evaluation with partners	☐
16. The marjority of alliances are formed via:	
a. A formal, 'top-down' process	☐
b. An informal, 'bottom-up' process	☐

17. The main responsibility for alliances lies with:

    a. Top management ☐

    b. Business development ☐

    c. Marketing ☐

    d. Mergers and acquisition department ☐

    e. Researc and development ☐

    f. Strategy ☐

    g. Other (specify)

18. Rewards and bonuses for alliance managers are tied to alliance success ☐
19. Rewards and bonuses for business managers are tied to alliance success ☐
20. Alliance managers from different units/divisions formally exchange their experiences ☐
21. Use of own (international) alliance knowledge ☐
22. International alliance management training for alliance managers ☐
23. Country-specific alliance policies ☐
24. Local alliance managers ☐
25. Consultants ☐
26. Legal experts ☐
27. Mediators ☐
28. Financial experts ☐
29. Other external sources (specify)

Appendix 6 Test of equality of group means

	Wilks' lambda	F-value	Sig.
VP of alliances (1)	0.930	10.285	.002**
Alliance department (2)	0.975	3.476	.034*
Alliance specialist (3)	0.989	1.488	.225
Alliance manager (4)	0.948	7.578	.007**
Gatekeeper (5)	0.992	1.146	.286
Local alliance managers (6)	0.977	3.224	.075+
Internal alliance training (7)	0.993	0.986	.327
External alliance training (8)	0.975	3.448	.065+
International alliance training (9)	0.989	1.504	.222
Partner selection programme (10)	0.951	7.099	.009**
Joint business planning (11)	0.999	0.080	.778
Alliance database (12)	0.897	15.758	.000***
Use of intranet to disperse alliance knowledge (13)	0.935	9.514	.002**
Alliance best practices (14)	0.975	3.538	.062+
Culture programme (15)	1.000	0.003	.956
Partner programme (16)	0.994	0.882	.366
Individual alliance evaluation (17)	0.960	5.777	.018*
Comparison of alliance evaluations (18)	0.998	0.303	.583
Joint alliance evaluation (19)	0.959	5.825	.017*
Rewards for alliance managers tied to alliance performance (21)	0.982	2.535	.114
Rewards for business managers tied to alliance performance (22)	0.983	2.414	.123
Formally structured knowledge exchange between alliance managers (23)	0.957	6.102	.015*
Use of own (international) alliance knowledge (24)	0.948	7.578	.007**
Alliance metrics (25)	0.963	5.196	.024*
Country-specific alliance policies (26)	0.999	0.157	.693
Consultants (27)	0.986	1.992	.160
Legal experts (28)	0.999	0.177	.675
Mediators (29)	0.973	3.796	.053+
Financial experts (30)	0.991	1.247	.266

*** $p < .001$; ** $p < .01$; * $p < .05$; + $p < .10$

Appendix 7 Pearson correlation matrix

	1	2	3	4	5	6	7
1. SUCADJ	1						
2. VP	.219**	1					
3. DEP	.101	.59**	1				
4. SPEC	−.111	−.49**	−.43**	1			
5. MANAGER	.112	.444**	.594**	−.318**	1		
6. GATEKP	.074	.131	.221**	−.199**	.29**	1	
7. LOCALMAN	.072	.332**	.488**	−.213**	.459**	.249**	1
8. INTTRAIN	.028	.249**	.359**	−.248**	.331**	.159*	.422**
9. EXTTRAIN	.139	.133	.094	−.057	.147*	.065	.153*
10. INTCULTR	.149*	.146*	.155*	−.132	.15*	.116	.107
11. PARTSEL	.166*	.428**	.413**	−.293**	.362**	.190**	.264**
12. JPB	−.010	.200**	.334**	−.169*	.251**	.099	.295**
13. DATABS	−.238**	−.442**	−.553**	.372	−.515**	−.202**	−.385**
14. INTRANT	.164*	.275**	.388**	−.32**	.365**	.179*	.289**
15. BESTPRAC	.171*	.169*	.194**	−.152*	.241**	.197**	.255**
16. CULTPROG	.038	.023	−.059	.000	.059	.116	.141
17. PPG	−.009	−.193**	−.296**	.178*	−.201**	−.209**	−.153*
18. EVALIND	.161*	.251**	.31**	−.234**	.346**	.118	.199**
19. EVALCOMP	.014	.25**	.394**	−.255**	.327**	.165*	.261**
20. JOINTEV	.136	.149*	.167*	−.117	.235**	.141	.250**
21. REWALLM	.098	.431**	.519**	−.363**	.458**	.079	.475**
22. REWBUSM	.141	.174*	.15*	−.096	.131	.070	.142*
23. FORMEXCH	.117	.251**	.395**	−.257**	.395**	.254**	.485**
24. KNOWUSE	.196**	.215**	.122	−.288**	.171*	−.024	.297**
25. METRICS	.140	.276**	.336**	−.231**	.362**	.277**	.322**
26. CNTRYPOL	.035	.2**	.292**	−.182*	.296**	.118	.325**
27. CONSULT	.105	.000	−.063	.040	−.002	−.028	−.113
28. LEGALEXP	−.026	−.099	−.096	.126	−.141	−.023	−.107
29. MEDIATE	.211**	−.044	−.155*	.094	−.043	.037	−.078
30. FINANCE	.085	−.024	−.106	.119	−.115	.075	.018

Continued

Appendix 7 Continued

	8	9	10	11	12	13	14
1. SUCADJ							
2. VP							
3. DEP							
4. SPEC							
5. MANAGER							
6. GATEKP							
7. LOCALMAN							
8. INTTRAIN	1						
9. EXTTRAIN	.088	1					
10. INTCULTR	.181**	.189*	1				
11. PARTSEL	.278**	.148*	.101	1			
12. JPB	.190**	.142*	.061	.344**	1		
13. DATABS	−.471**	−.112	−.179*	−.472**	−.185*	1	
14. INTRANT	.326**	.134	.026	.333**	.26**	−.372**	1
15. BESTPRAC	.463**	.354**	.206**	.329**	.238**	−.267**	.317**
16. CULTPROG	.147*	.030	.288**	.071	.152*	.074	−.004
17. PPG	−.194**	.024	−.028	−.336**	−.263**	.259**	−.197**
18. EVALIND	.166*	.108	.038	.279**	.218**	−.282**	.269**
19. EVALCOMP	.382*	.147*	.146*	.294**	.248**	−.366**	.242**
20. JOINTEV	.286**	.105	.063	.241**	.327**	−.173*	.276**
21. REWALLM	.34*	.013	.143*	.264**	.281**	−.47**	.252**
22. REWBUSM	.053	−.064	−.054	.117	.028	−.073	.051
23. FORMEXCH	.291**	.261**	.127	.257**	.225**	−.362**	.263**
24. KNOWUSE	.191**	.107	.169*	.242**	.209**	−.281*	.178*
25. METRICS	.406**	.326**	.217*	.388**	.285**	−.349**	.234**
26. CNTRYPOL	.223**	.05	.099	.240**	.268**	.317**	.189**
27. CONSULT	.091	.094	.124	.023	−.086	−.054	−.094
28. LEGALEXP	−.025	−.123	−.090	−.009	−.032	.095	−.105
29. MEDIATE	−.075	.251**	.272**	−.086	−.074	.012	−.076
30. FINANCE	.052	−.131	.071	.018	−.077	.100	−.129

15	16	17	18	19	20	21	22	23
1								
.238**	1							
−.093	0.17	1						
.199*	.166*	−.125	1					
.282**	.038	−.305**	.015	1				
.229**	.248**	−.140	.192**	.237**	1			
.146*	.016	−.221**	.131	.359**	.186*	1		
.126	.027	−.076	.158*	.055	.127	.184*	1	
.306**	.094	−.173*	.264**	.274**	.175*	.4**	.121	1
.227*	.047	−.156*	.1	.147*	.131	.205**	.019	.276**
.448**	.186**	−.171*	.258**	.337**	.274**	.229**	.014	.311**
.158*	.099	−.254**	.109	.188**	.188**	.259**	.076	.280**
.023	.062	.052	.139	−.024	.082	.023	.077	−.003
−.125	.098	−.016	−.048	−.019	.070	−.103	−.005	−.065
.190**	.056	.086	−.042	−.062	−.040	−.066	−.099	.01
−.085	.167*	.048	.047	−.05	.035	−.016	.123	−.007

Continued

Appendix 7 Continued

	24	25	26	27	28	29	30
1. SUCADJ							
2. VP							
3. DEP							
4. SPEC							
5. MANAGER							
6. GATEKP							
7. LOCALMAN							
8. INTTRAIN							
9. EXTTRAIN							
10. INTCULTR							
11. PARTSEL							
12. JPB							
13. DATABS							
14. INTRANT							
15. BESTPRAC							
16. CULTPROG							
17. PPG							
18. EVALIND							
19. EVALCOMP							
20. JOINTEV							
21. REWALLM							
22. REWBUSM							
23. FORMEXCH							
24. KNOWUSE	1						
25. METRICS	.152*	1					
26. CNTRYPOL	.268**	.237**	1				
27. CONSULT	.076	.060	−.043	1			
28. LEGALEXP	−.064	−.104	−.063	.063	1		
29. MEDIATE	.034	.110	−.067	.027	−.021	1	
30. FINANCE	−.047	−.032	−.066	.135	.415**	−.055	1

** $p < .01$; * $p < .05$

Appendix 8 Variance matrix of mechanisms

	DUMSUC01 = 0 (N = 52)			DUMSUC01 = 1 (N = 87)		
	Mean	Std. dev.	SE	Mean	Std. dev.	SE
VP***	.2692	.44789	.06211	.5402	.50127	.05374
DEP**	.3654	.48624	.06743	.5517	.50020	.05363
SPEC	.7115	.45747	.06344	.6092	.49076	.05261
MANAGER***	.3846	.49125	.06812	.6207	.48803	.05232
GATEKP	.1346	.34464	.04779	.2069	.40743	.04368
LOCALMAN*	.1731	.38200	.05297	.3103	.46532	.04989
INTTRAIN	.2115	.41238	.05719	.2874	.45515	.04880
EXTTRAIN*	.2692	.44789	.06211	.4253	.49725	.05331
INTCULTR	.1154	.32260	.04474	.1954	.39881	.04276
PARTSEL***	.4038	.49545	.06871	.6322	.48501	.05200
JPB	.4808	.50450	.06996	.5057	.50287	.05391
DATABS***	.8269	.38200	.05297	.5057	.50287	.05391
INTRANT***	.3269	.47367	.06569	.5862	.49537	.05311
BESTPRAC*	.2885	.45747	.06344	.4483	.50020	.05363
CULTPROG	.1346	.34464	.04779	.1379	.34683	.03718
PPG	.9231	.26907	.03731	.8736	.33427	.03584
EVALIND**	.5000	.50488	.07001	.7011	.46041	.04936
EVALCOMP	.2115	.41238	.05719	.2529	.43718	.04687
JOINTEV**	.2885	.45747	.06344	.4943	.50287	.05391
REWALLM	.2692	.44789	.06211	.4023	.49320	.05288
REWBUSM	.0962	.29768	.04128	.0962	.29768	.04128
FORMEXCH**	.1923	.39796	.05519	.3908	.49076	.05261
KNOWUSE***	.3846	.49125	.06812	.6207	.48803	.05232
METRICS**	.2885	.45747	.06344	.4828	.50260	.05388
CNTRYPOL	.1923	.39796	.05519	.2644	.44355	.04755
CONSULT	.3269	.47367	.06569	.4483	.50020	.05363
LEGALEXP	.4038	.49545	.06871	.3678	.48501	.05200
MEDIATE*	.0000	.0000	.000	.0690	.25486	.02732
FINANCE	.3077	.46604	.06463	.4023	.49320	.05288

*** $p < .01$; ** $p < .05$; * $p < .1$

Appendix 9 Classification matrix (predicted group membership)

		DUMSUC01	0	1	Total
0 = 0%–40%	Count	0	27	21	48
		1	16	53	69
		ungrouped cases	19	25	49
1=61%–100%	%	0	56.3	43.8	100
		1	23.2	76.8	100
		ungrouped cases	40.8	59.2	100

A total of 68.4 per cent of the original grouped cases is correctly classified.

Appendix 10 Robustness checks for discriminant analysis

Table App. 10.1 Box's M test of equality of covariance matrices Log determinants

0 = 0%–40%; 1 = 61%–100%	Rank	Log determinant
0	6	–1.997
1	6	–1.258
Pooled within groups	6	–1.338

Test results

Box's M		25.480
F	Approx.	1.142
	df1	21
	df2	37568.139
	Sig.	.294

The Box's M test verifies whether the variance-covariance matrices are homogeneous (see e.g. Knudsen and Madsen, 2002; Von Taysen, 2003).[4] The results indicate a Box's M value of 25.480 and a *p*-value of .294, although this value lies above the critical value of .05, which provides strong evidence that the matrices do not differ among the two performance groups (Hair et al., 1998). Moreover, as sample sizes of the two groups are reasonably comparable while having reasonable homogeneity of variance given the two-tailed tests, the robustness of the results does not seem to be negatively influenced.

Table App. 10.2 Hit ratio
See Appendix 9: 68.4 per cent of the original grouped cases is correctly classified.

Table App. 10.3 Variance matrix of mechanisms (for DUMSUC01 = 0 and DUMSUC01 = 1)
See Appendix 8.

Table App. 10.4 Pearson correlation matrix
See Appendix 7: nine predictors are significantly related to the dependent variable at the 5 per cent level.

Appendix 11 Mean differences by experience level

	Mean(sd)					
	Low experience group(N = 88)	Moderate experience group (N = 47)	High experience group(N = 31)	F-test[a]	Eta sq[b]	F-test[c]
Control						
Firm size				6.937***	.078	
ICT industry				.929	.011	
Service industry				1.683	.020	
Factor 1[d]	.205	.381	.597			
Organization level Learning mechanisms	2.05(2.21)	3.81(2.79)	5.97(2.23)	32.388***	.284	4.369**
Factor 2[e]	.220	.298	.348			
Group level learning mechanisms	1.10(1.31)	1.19(1.32)	1.74(1.39)	3.120*	.037	3.878**
Interaction effect						
Factor 1*factor 2	3.70(6.93)	7.17(9.75)	11.456(10.15)	10.31***	.111	1.791
Performance						
Alliance performance	2.78	3.67	3.37	7.713***		

*** $p < .001$; ** $p < .01$; * $p < .05$

Continued

Appendix 11 Continued

[a] T-test for mean difference
[b] Eta is a measure of association and reflects the proportion of variance in the dependent variable (alliance experience) that is explained by differences among groups. It is the ratio of the between-groups sum of squares and the total sum of squares.
[c] One-way ANOVA on alliance performance
[d] The number of mechanisms included in this factor is 10, therefore the average of this factor is divided by ten to obtain a comparable figure with group-level learning mechanisms.
[e] The number of mechanisms included in this factor is 5, therefore the average of this factor is divided by five to obtain a comparable figure with organization-level learning mechanisms.

Notes

1 Introduction

1. This study finds that alliance success also depends on the goal of the alliance (see Appendix 1).

2 A Literature Review of Alliance Research

1. Although it is a related topic, we leave the field of study which is dedicated to analysing alliance networks undiscussed. This field of study also has paid attention to alliance portfolios (see e.g. Gomes-Casseres, 1996; Lemmens, 2003; Beerkens, 2004; De Man, 2004).
2. Our study confirms that dyadic factors are important antecedents of alliance performance (see Appendix 3). Moreover, we acknowledge that some dyadic factors may be positively influenced by intra-firm mechanisms (for a more elaborate overview see also Heimeriks and Schreiner (2002b).
3. For a comparison of principles underlying transaction cost theory, RBV and social exchange theory, we refer to Das and Teng (2002a: 455).
4. As it is not the intention of this study to provide a complete overview or discussion of developments in strategic management, we refer to Conner (1991) and Sanchez and Heene (1997) for a more complete overview of developments in streams of research in the field of strategic management.
5. Nelson and Winter (1982: 10) underscore the need for a dynamic or evolutionary element in organization theory when suggesting that pure economic reasoning has become an orthodoxy as 'much of contemporary economic theory appears faintly anachronistic...It is as if economics has never really transcended the experiences of its childhood.'
6. As it is not our intention to provide an extensive overview of the vast amounts of literature on RBV and DCV, we wish to refer to other texts for more elaborate reviews (Peteraf, 1993; Teece et al., 1997; Dosi et al., 2000a; Fujimoto, 2000).
7. Although extensively investigated in the context of the DCV, other theories such as the RBV and OL theory have also used this concept to explain a firm's rent-generation capacity.
8. For a more extended overview of specific contributions of the CBV, we refer to Prahalad and Hamel (1990), Hamel and Heene (1994) and De Leo (1994).
9. As a firm's ability to share knowledge is limited and influenced by all kinds of limitations and factors, such as organizational forgetting (Martin de Holan and Philips, 2003), tacitness (Tsoukas, 2003), stickiness (Szulanski, 1996) and the link between individual and organizational learning (Lorino, 2001), knowledge sharing should certainly not be seen as a goal in itself (Grant, 1996b).
10. Organizational learning theory has also paid significant attention to learning barriers such as turnover, organizational forgetting, memory, fragmented

learning, competence traps, communication, tacitness and superstitious learning (see e.g. Stata, 1989; Senge, 1990b; Levinthal and March, 1993; Argyris, 1994).
11. For a complete overview of theories and paradigms related to the field of strategy research, we refer to Lewin and Volberda (1999).

3 Describing the Phenomenon: Alliance Capabilities

1. For more elaborate reviews, see Sanchez et al. (1996b), Dosi et al. (2000a) and Sanchez (2001c).
2. For an extensive discussion on characteristics, typologies and definitions of 'knowledge', we refer to Polanyi (1962), Winter (1987), Nonaka (1994) and Spender (1996).
3. In OL theory, this is also referred to as the exploitation–exploration dilemma (March, 1991).

4 Towards a Micro-level Understanding of Alliance Capabilities

1. For a critical overview of the use of discriminant analysis, we refer to Crask and Perreault (1977) and Huberty (1984).
2. Please note that this analysis includes 139 of the 192 cases since the average performance group (41%–60%) was left out of the analysis and the variables related to the responsibility levels were left out due to measurement constraints.
3. The canonical correlation coefficient is related to the eigenvalue and can be calculated using the following formula:

$$r_i = \sqrt{\frac{\lambda_i}{1+\lambda_i}}$$

where i denotes the discriminant function and λ_i the eigenvalue (Klecka, 1980).
4. The standardized coefficients reflect the relative importance of a variable. It can be computed as follows:

$$c_i = u_i \sqrt{\frac{w_{ii}}{n-g}}$$

where u_i is the unstandardized coefficient, w_{ii} is the sum of squares for variable i, n is the total number of cases and g is the number of groups. The obvious disadvantage is that the standardized coefficients are affected by relationships with other variables.
5. For a more elaborate discussion on critical issues in exploratory factor analysis with dichotomous items, we refer to Bernstein et al. (1988), Nunally and Bernstein (1994) and McLeod et al. (2001).
6. For dichotomous items, this is also referred to as the KR20 formula (Kuder and Richardson, 1937; Moll, 1995; Yaffee, 1998).

7. In this context, it seems relevant to mention that the predictors in this study all refer to the internal process of alliance capability development. Inherently, this excludes all external factors influencing a firm's performance, including for instance the alliance capabilities of the partner, competitive pressures and technological challenges. We are therefore less likely to find very high correlations, as this study focuses on internal organization drivers of alliance performance.
8. An additional analysis was performed to verify if – as suggested in Section 4.4 – firms use different mechanisms at different experience levels. The results are shown in Appendix 11 and confirm that firms at different experience levels use different combinations of group-level and organization-level learning mechanisms. These findings are in line with results of earlier studies (e.g. Harbison and Pekar, 1998b; Draulans et al., 2003).
9. The 4I framework is summarized by Mintzberg et al. (1998) (in Vera and Crossan, 2004: 225): '*Intuiting* is a subconscious process that occurs at the level of the individual. It is the start of learning and must happen in a single mind. *Interpreting* then picks up on the conscious elements of this individual learning and shares it at the group level. *Integrating* follows to change collective understanding at the group level and bridges to the level of the whole organization. Finally, *institutionalizing* incorporates that learning across the organization by imbedding it in its systems, structures, routines and practices' (1998: 212).

5 An Analysis of the Alliance Capability Development Process

1. This chapter is partly based on 'Alliance capability as mediator between experience and alliance performance: an empirical investigation into the alliance capability development process' by Heimeriks and Duysters (2007). Part of this chapter is reprinted with permission of the *Journal of Management Studies*. Copyright 2007 Blackwell Publishing.
2. For a comparison of these theories, we refer to Teece et al. (1994) and Sanchez (2001a).
3. For an extensive overview of the concept 'routines', we refer to Nelson and Winter (1982), Prahalad and Hamel (1990), Cohen et al. (1996) and Coriat (2000).
4. This was also confirmed during the expert interviews, in which we verified for face validity with respect to the operationalization of alliance capability used in this study. Please refer to Appendix 4 for a more elaborate discussion on construct validity.
5. A number of additional analyses were performed to verify for any biases in the methodology used. This means the hypotheses were also tested using binary logistic regression; the results were comparable.
6. We prefer the likelihood ratio test to alternative tests such as the Wald test as various studies express doubts with respect to the latter test (see e.g. Hauck and Donner, 1977; Menard, 1995).
7. This procedure tests the following formulas: $Y_{success}$ = fn (experience), $Y_{mechanisms}$ = fn (experience) and $Y_{success}$ = fn (experience, mechanisms).
8. In order to ensure sound results, additional logistic regression analyses were performed using another independent variable for mechanisms, which

consisted of only the significant mechanisms as was concluded from Chapter 5. So, this independent variable was defined as a composite variable consisting of eleven instead of fifteen intra-firm mechanisms. As expected, the results showed comparable significance levels for all independent variables.

9. We also tested whether alliance capability has a moderating effect on experience using the procedure suggested by Sharma et al. (1981); these results also suggested to reject hypothesis 3B.
10. Simonin (1997) also finds that collaborative know-how mediates between alliance experience and performance and concludes that experience must be internalized to engender future collaborative benefits. However, he falls short of identifying and measuring the intra-firm mechanisms that help internalize this know-how.

6 Conclusions, Implications, Limitations and Future Research

1. For an overview and comparison of definitions of strategic alliances, we refer to Douma (1997).

Appendices

1. Although we carefully selected the key informants involved, there are a number of limitations to the use of key informants. For instance, making use of key informants implies that one asks for perceptions thereby potentially creating bias in the data gathered. We refer to Philips (1981), John and Reve (1982) and Frechtling (2002) for a critical overview of pros and cons of using key informants. Overall, different scholars define different opinions about the utility of the key informant approach. However, despite these varying opinions on its influence on the validity and reliability of the data gathered, using key informants to gather subjective information on organizational issues has become an accepted practice in management research and consensus seems to have been established with respect to the fact that subjective information correlates highly with objective information (Geringer and Hebert, 1991; Kale et al., 2002; Tippins and Sohi, 2003). Although we tried to carefully select our respondents, the drawbacks of using a single-respondent survey should be not negated and therefore poses a limitation to this study.
2. The variable measuring the number of alliances consists of five categories (see Appendix 4). For the last category (> 40 alliances), the average was set at 50 alliances. Hence, the total number of alliances is an estimate of 2973 alliances.
3. None of the three variables was significant at the 5 per cent level. The chi-square statistic shows a χ^2-value of 2.386 (p-value is 0.122) for number of employees, a χ^2-value of 1.947 (p-value is 0.163) for sales revenues and a χ^2-value of 3.133 (p-value is 0.077) for alliance performance. Therefore, no significant correlations were found between item scores and survey response time.
4. Multicollinearity is not an issue here, as SPSS protects against this by means of tolerance (Tabachnick and Fidell, 2001).

References

Abramson, NR. and Ai, JX. 1999. Canadian companies doing business in China: key success factors. *Management International Review* **39**: 7–35.

Accenture, The Conference Board. 2001. *The CEO Challenge: Top marketplace and management issues 2001*. www.accenture.com/xdoc/en/ideas/RR-_1286_ACC_ES.pdf. Accessed 18 December 2001.

Accenture Consulting. 2002. Grasping the Capability. The Point **2**(1): 1–10. http://www.partneringintelligence.com/resources/ThePointGrasping the Capability.pdf. Accessed 27 April 2002.

Afuah, A. 2000. How much do your co-opetitors' capabilities matter in the face of technological change?. *Strategic Management Journal* **21**(3): 387–404.

Agresti, A. 1990. *Categorical Data Analysis*. John Wiley: New York.

Aiken, LS. and West, SG. 1991. *Multiple Regression: Testing and Interpreting Interactions*. Sage: Newbury Park, CA.

Aldrich, HE. 1999. *Organizations Evolving*. Sage Publications: London.

Alliance Analyst. 1994. *Two Grandmasters at the Extremes*. November 1994. NewCap Communications: Philadelphia, PA.

Alliance Analyst. 1996a. *Managing Alliances – Skills for the Modern Era*. March 1996. NewCap Communications: Philadelphia, PA.

Alliance Analyst. 1996b. *Outsider in the Middle*. July 1996. NewCap Communications: Philadelphia, PA.

Alliance Analyst. 1999a. *Welshing the Knowledge Rabbit*. May 1999. NewCap Communications: Philadelphia, PA.

Alliance Analyst. 1999b. *A Structure for Collaboration*. December 1999. NewCap Communications: Philadelphia, PA.

Almeida, P., Song, J. and Grant, RM. 2002. Are firms superior to alliances and markets? An empirical test of cross-border knowledge building. *Organization Science* **13**(2): 147–161.

Alza Corporation. 2004. http://www.alza.com/alza/media, http://www.alza.com/pdf/vol_2_4.pdf. Accessed 2 April 2004.

Amburgey, TL. and Miner, AS. 1992. Strategic momentum: the effects of repetitive, positional, and contextual momentum on merger activity. *Strategic Management Journal* **13**: 335–348.

Amburgey, TL., Kelly, D. and Barnett, WP. 1993. Resetting the clock: the dynamics of organizational change and failure. *Administrative Science Quarterly* **38**(1): 51–73.

Amit, R. and Schoemaker, PJH. 1993. Strategic assets and organizational rent. *Strategic Management Journal* **14**(1): 33–46.

Anand, BN. and Khanna, T. 2000. Do firms learn to create value? The case of alliances. *Strategic Management Journal* **21**(3): 295–315.

Anand, J. and Vassolo, RS. 2002. An examination of dynamic capabilities: is evolutionary theory under-determined? Paper presented at SMS Conference, Paris.

Anderson, E. 1990. Two firms, one frontier: on assessing joint venture performance. *Sloan Management Review* **31**(2): 19–30.

Anderson, JE., Hakansson, H. and Johanson, J. 1994. Dyadic business relationships within a business network context. *Journal of Marketing* **58**(4): 1–15.

Angur, MG. and Nataraajan, R. 1995. Do source of mailing and monetary incentives matter in international industrial mail surveys? *Industrial Marketing Management* **24**: 351–357.

Appleyard, MM. 2002. Cooperative knowledge creation: the case of buyer-supplier co-development in the semiconductor industry. In *Cooperative Strategies and Alliances*. Contractor, FJ. and Lorange, P. (eds). Elsevier Science: Oxford: 381–418.

Appleyard, MM., Hatch, NW. and Mowery, DC. 2000. Managing the development and transfer of process technologies in the semiconductor manufacturing industry. In *The Nature and Dynamics of Organizational Capabilities*. Dosi, G., Nelson, RR. and Winter, SG. (eds). Oxford University Press: New York: 183–207.

Argote, L. 1999. *Organizational Learning: Creating, Retaining, and Transferring Knowledge*. Kluwer Academic: Boston, MA.

Argote, L. and Darr, E. 2000. Repositories of knowledge in franchise organizations: individual, structural, and technological. In *The Nature and Dynamics of Organizational Capabilities*. Dosi, G., Nelson, RR. and Winter, SG. (eds). Oxford University Press: Oxford, New York: 51–68.

Argote, L. and Epple, D. 1990. Learning curves in manufacturing. *Science* **247**: 920–924.

Argote, L. and Ingram, P. 2000. Knowledge transfer: a basis for competitive advantage in firms. *Organizational Behavior and Human Decision Processes* **82**: 150–169.

Argyris, C. 1977. Double loop learning in organizations. *Harvard Business Review* **15**(5): 115–125.

Argyris, C. 1994. Good communication that blocks learning. In *Harvard Business Review on Organization Learning*. Harvard Business School Press: Boston, MA: 87–109.

Arino, A. 2003. Measures of collaborative venture performance: an analysis of construct validity. *Journal of International Business Studies* **34**(1): 66–79.

Arino, A., Abramov, M., Skorobogatykh, I., Rykounina, I. and Vilà, J. 1997. Partner selection and trust building in West European–Russian joint ventures, a Western perspective. *International Studies of Management & Organizations* **27**(1): 19–37.

Arino, A., De la Torre, J. and Ring, PS. 2001. Relational quality: managing trust in corporate alliances. *California Management Review* **44**(1): 109–131.

Armstrong, JS. and Overton, TS. 1977. Estimating nonresponse bias in mail surveys. *Journal of Marketing Research* **14**: 396–402.

Arrow, KH. 1962. The economic implications of learning by doing. *Review of Economic Studies* **29**: 166–170.

Arthur D. Little. 2001. *Partnering – Challenges for the Old and New Economy*. Facts, assessments, recommendations based on a global Arthur D. Little survey.

Asher, HB. 1976. *Causal Modeling*. Sage: Beverly Hills, CA.

Aulakh, P., Kotabe, M. and Sahay, A. 1996. Trust and performance in cross-border marketing partnerships: a behavioral approach. *Journal of International Business Studies*, Special Issue **27**(5): 1005–1033.

Baarda, DB, Goede, de MPM. 1995. *Basisboek Methoden en Technieken*. Stenfert Kroese: Houten.
Bagozzi, RP. 1981. Attitudes, intentions, and behavior: a test of some key hypotheses. *Journal of Personality and Social Psychology* **41**: 607–627.
Bagozzi, RP. and Phillips, LW. 1982. Representing and testing organizational theories: a holistic construal. *Administrative Science Quarterly* **27**(3): 459–489.
Bakker, HJC. and Helmink, JWA. 2000. *Successfully Integrating Two Businesses*. Gower Publishing Ltd: Brookfield.
Bamford, JD. and Ernst, D. 2002. Managing an alliance portfolio. *The McKinsey Quarterly* **3**: 29–39.
Bamford, JD. and Ernst, D. 2003. Growth of alliance capabilities. In *Mastering Alliance Strategy: A Comprehensive Guide to Design, Management, and Organization*. Bamford, JD., Gomes-Casseres, B. and Robinson, MS. (eds). Jossey-Bass: San Francisco, CA: 321–333.
Bamford, JD., Gomes-Casseres, B. and Robinson, MS. 2003. *Mastering Alliance Strategy: A Comprehensive Guide to Design, Management, and Organization*. Jossey-Bass: San Francisco, CA.
Barnett, WP. and Burgelman, RA. 1996. Evolutionary perspectives on strategy. *Strategic Management Journal*, Special Issue **17**: 5–19.
Barney, JB. 1986. Strategic factor markets: expectations, luck, and business strategy. *Management Science* **32**(10): 1231–1241.
Barney, JB. 1991. Firm resources and sustained competitive advantage. *Journal of Management* **17**: 99–120.
Barney, JB. 2002. *Gaining and Sustaining Competitive Advantage*, 2nd edn. New Jersey: Prentice Hall.
Barney, JB. and Ouchi, W. (eds). 1986. *Organizational Economics: Toward a New Paradigm for Studying and Understanding Organizations*. Jossey-Bass: San Francisco, CA.
Barney, JB., Wright, M. and Ketchen, DJ. jr. 2001. The resource-based view of the firm: ten years after 1991. *Journal of Management*, Special Issue **27**(6): 625–641.
Baron, RM. and Kenny, DA. 1986. The moderator-mediator variable distinction in social psychological research: conceptual, strategic, and statistical considerations. *Journal of Personality and Social Psychology* **51**: 1173–1182.
Barringer, B. and Harrison, J. 2000. Walking the tightrope: creating value through interorganizational relationships. *Journal of Management* **26**(3): 367–404.
Bartholomew, DJ. 1987. *Latent Variable Models and Factor Analysis*. Oxford University Press: New York.
Beerkens, B. 2004. External acquisition of technology. Exploration and exploitation in international innovation networks. PhD thesis. Eindhoven Centre for Innovation Studies (ECIS). Eindhoven University Press, the Netherlands.
Bekkers, R., Duysters, G. and Verspagen, B. 2002. Intellectual property rights, strategic technology agreements and market structure: the case of GSM. *Research Policy* **31**: 1141–1161.
Bereiter, C. and Scardamalia, M. 1993. *Surpassing Ourselves: An Inquiry into the Nature and Implications of Expertise*. Open Court: Chicago, IL.
Bernstein, IH., Garbin, C. and Teng, G. 1988. *Applied Multivariate Analysis*. Springer-Verlag: New York.

Bernstein, IH. and Teng, G. 1989. Factoring items and factoring scales are different: spurious evidence for multidimensionality due to item categorization. *Psychological Bulletin* **105**: 467–477.

Beugelsdijk, S., Noorderhaven, NG. and Koen, CI. 2002. Organization culture and relationship skills. *Organization Studies* **27**(6): 833–854.

Bierly, P. and Chakrabarti, A. 1996. Generic knowledge strategies in the U.S. pharmaceutical industry. *Strategic Management Journal* **17**(S2): 123–135.

Bickart, B. and Schmittlein, D. 1999. The distribution of survey contact and participation in the United States: constructing a survey-based estimate. *Journal of Marketing Research* **36**(2): 286–294.

Bleeke, J. and Ernst, D. 1991. The way to win in cross-border alliances. *Harvard Business Review* **69**(6): 127–135.

Bleeke, J. and Ernst, D. 1993. *Collaborating to Compete*. John Wiley and Sons: New York.

Bleeke, J. and Ernst, D. 1995. Is your strategic alliance really a sale? *Harvard Business Review* **73**(1): 97–105.

Boddy, D., MacBeth, D. and Wagner, B. 2001. Implementing cooperative strategy. A model from the private sector. In *Cooperative Strategy, Economic, Business, and Organizational Issues*. Faulkner, D. and De Rond, M. (eds). Oxford University Press: New York, 193–211.

Boersma, MF. 1999. Developing trust in international joint ventures. PhD dissertation. Research Institute Systems: Groningen.

Bogaert, I., Martens, R. and Van Cauwenbergh, A. 1994. Strategy as a situational puzzle: the fit of components. In *Competence-Based Competition*. Hamel, G. and Heene, A. (eds). John Wiley & Sons: Chichester: 57–74.

Bohn, RE. 1994. Measuring and managing technological knowledge. *Sloan Management Review* **32**: 61–73.

Bollen, KA. 1989. *Structural Equations with Latent Variables*. John Wiley: New York.

Boisot, MH. 1995. Is your firm a creative destroyer? Competitive learning and knowledge flows in the technological strategies of firms. *Research Policy* **24**: 489–506.

Boone, PF. 1997. Managing intracorporate knowledge sharing. PhD dissertation. Erasmus Universiteit Rotterdam: Eburon.

Borker, M., De Man, A-P. and Weeda, P. 2004. Embedding alliance competence: alliance offices. In *Fostering Execution*. Van der Zee, H. and Strikwerda, H. (eds). Nolan Norton Annual, De Meern, Nolan Norton & Co, 84–92.

Brown, JS. and Duguid, P. 1991. Organizational learning and communities of practice: toward a unified view of working, learning, and innovation. *Organization Science* **2**(1): 40–57.

Brown, JS. and Duguid, P. 2001. Creativity versus structure: a useful tension. *MIT Sloan Management Review* **42**: 93–94.

Bruderer, E. and Singh, JV. 1996. Organizational evolution, learning, and selection: a genetic-algorithm-based model. *Academy of Management Journal* **39**(5): 1322–1349.

Büchel, B. and Killing, P. 2002. Interfirm cooperation throughout the joint venture life cycle: impact on joint venture performance. In *Cooperative Strategies and Alliances*. Contractor, FJ. and Lorange, P. (eds). Elsevier Science: Oxford: 751–772.

Callahan, J. and MacKenzie, S. 1999. Metrics for strategic alliance control. *R&D Management* **9**(4): 365–378.
Campbell, D. 1969. Variation and selective retention in socio-cultural evolution. *General Systems* **16**: 69–85.
Carlile, PR., Rebentisch, ES. 2003. Into the black box: the knowledge transformation cycle. *Management Science* **49**(9): 1180–1195.
Carroll, JS., Rudolph, JW. and Hatakenaka, S. 2003. Learning from organizational experience. In *Handbook of Organizational Learning and Knowledge Management*. Easterby-Smith, M. and Lyles, MA. (eds). Blackwell: Oxford: 575–600.
Caves, RE. 1980. Industrial organization, corporate strategy and structure. *Journal of Economic Literature* **58**: 64–92.
Chan, S., Kesinger, J., Keown, A. and Martin, J. 1997. Do strategic alliances create value? *Journal of Financial Economics* **46**: 199–221.
Chandler, AD. jr., Hagström, P. and Solvell O. (eds). 1999. *The Dynamic Firm: The Role of Technology, Strategy, Organization, and Regions*. Oxford University Press: New York.
Chiesa, V. and Manzini, R. 1997. Competence levels within firms: a static and dynamic analysis. In *Competence-Based Strategic Management*, Heene, A. and Sanchez, R. (eds). John Wiley & Sons: Chichester: 195–214.
Churchill, GA. 1979. A paradigm for developing better measures of marketing constructs. *Journal of Marketing Research* **16**(2): 64–73.
Churchill, GA. and Iacobucci, D. 2001. *Marketing Research: Methodological Foundations*, 8th edn. South-Western College Publishing: Mason, OH.
Clark, K. and Fujimoto, T. 1991. *Product Development Performance: Strategy, Organization and Management in the World Auto Industries*. Harvard Business School Press: Cambridge, MA.
Clegg, G. 1999. Alliances alive, but not necessarily well. *Australian Financial Review* October 1999.
Coase, RE. 1937. The nature of the firm. *Economica* **4**: 386–405.
Cohen, M. and Bacdayan, P. 1994. Organizational routines are stored as procedural memory: evidence from a laboratory study. *Organization Science* **5**: 554–568.
Cohen, MD., Burkhart, R., Dosi, G., Egidi, M., Marengo, L., Warglien, M., Winter, S. and Coriat, S. 1996. Routines and other recurring action patterns of organizations: contemporary research issues. *Industrial and Corporate Change* **5**: 653–698.
Cohen, WM. and Levinthal, DA. 1989. Innovation and learning: the two faces of R&D. *The Economic Journal* **99**: 569–596.
Cohen, WM. and Levinthal, DA. 1990. Absorptive capacity: a new perspective on learning and innovation. *Administrative Science Quarterly* **35**: 128–152.
Collis, DJ. 1991. A resource-based analysis of global competition: the case of the bearings industry. *Strategic Management Journal* **12**(6): 49–68.
Collis, DJ. 1994. Research note: how valuable are organizational capabilities? *Strategic Management Journal*, Winter Special Issue **15**: 143–152.
Combs, JG. and Ketchen, DJ. jr. 1999. Explaining inter-firm cooperation and performance: toward a reconciliation of predictions from the resource-based view and organizational economics. *Strategic Management Journal* **20**: 867–888.

Comrey, AL. and Lee, HB. 1992. *A First Course in Factor Analysis*, 2nd edn. Lawrence Erlbaum Associates Publishers: Hillsdale, NJ.

Conlon, DE. and Sullivan, DP. 1999. Examining the actions of organizations in conflict: evidence from the Delaware court of chancery. *Academy of Management Journal* 42(3): 319–329.

Conner, KR. 1991. A historical comparison of resource-based theory and five schools of thought within industrial organization economics: do we have a new theory of the firm? *Journal of Management* 17(1): 121–154.

Conner, KR. and Prahalad, C. 1996. A resource-based theory of the firm: knowledge versus opportunism. *Organization Science* 7: 477–501.

Contractor, FJ. and Lorange, P. 1998. Competition versus cooperation: a benefit/cost framework for choosing between fully owned investments and cooperative relationships. *Management International Review*, Special Issue 28: 5–18.

Contractor, FJ. and Lorange, P. (eds). 1988. *Cooperative Strategies in International Business*. Lexington: Lexington Books.

Contractor, FJ. and Lorange, P. (eds). 2002. *Cooperative Strategies and Alliances*. Elsevier Science: Oxford.

Coriat, B. 2000. The 'abominable Ohno production system'. Competences, monitoring, and routines in Japanese production. In *The Nature and Dynamics of Organizational Capabilities*. Dosi, G., Nelson, RR. and Winter, SG. (eds). Oxford University Press: Oxford, New York: 213–243.

Coriat, B. and Dosi, G. 1999. Learning how to govern and learning how to solve problems: on the co-evolution of competences, conflicts and organizational routines. In *The Dynamic Firm: The Role of Technology, Strategy, Organization, and Regions*. Chandler, AD. jr., Hagström, P. and Solvell, O. (eds). Oxford University Press: New York: 103–133.

Corporate Strategy Board. 2000. *Institutionalizing Alliance Capabilities. A Platform for Repeatable Success*. http://www.partneringintelligence.com/resources/InstitutionalizingAllianceCapabilities.pdf. Accessed 15 July 2001.

Cote, J. 2001. Structural equations modeling. *Journal of Consumer Psychology* 10(1–2): 93–94.

Crask, M. and Perreault, W. 1977. Validation of discriminant analysis in marketing research. *Journal of Marketing Research* 14(2): 60–68.

Cronbach, LJ. and Meehl, PE. 1955. Construct validity in psychological test. *Psychological Bulletin* 52: 281–302.

Crossan, M., Lane, H. and White, R. 1999. An organizational learning framework: from intuition to institution. *Academy of Management Review* 24(3): 522–538.

Cullen, JB., Johnson, JL. and Sakano, T. 2000. Success through commitment and trust: the soft side of strategic alliance formation. *Journal of World Business* 35: 223–241.

Cycyota, CS. and Harrison, DA. 2002. Enhancing survey response rates at the executive level: are employee- or consumer-level techniques effective? *Journal of Management* 28(2): 151–176.

Cyert, RM. and March, JG. 1963. *A Behavioral Theory of the Firm*. Prentice-Hall: Englewood Cliffs, NJ.

Das, TK. and Teng, B-S. 2000a. A resource-based theory of strategic alliances. *Journal of Management* 26(1): 31–61.

Das, TK. and Teng, B-S. 2000b. Instabilities of strategic alliances: an internal tensions perspective. *Organization Science* **11**(1): 77–101.

Das, TK. and Teng, B-S. 2002a. A social exchange theory of strategic alliances. In *Cooperative Strategies and Alliances*. Contractor, FJ. and Lorange, P. (eds). Elsevier Science: Oxford: 439–460.

Das, TK. and Teng, B-S. 2002b. The dynamics of alliance conditions in the alliance development process. *Journal of Management Studies* **39**(5): 725–746.

David, RJ. and Han, S-K. 2004. A systematic assessment of the empirical support for transaction cost economics. *Strategic Management Journal* **25**(1): 39–58.

Davies, H. and Walters, P. 2004. Emergent patterns of strategy, environment and performance in a transition economy. *Strategic Management Journal* **25**(4): 347–364.

DeCoster, J. 2003. Overview of factor analysis. White paper. Free University, Amsterdam.

Deeds, DL. and Hill, CWL. 1996. Strategic alliances and the rate of new product development: an empirical study of entrepreneurial biotechnology firms. *Journal of Business Venturing* **11**: 41–55.

De Leo, F. 1994. Understanding the roots of your competitive advantage. From product/market competition to competition as a multiple-layer game. In *Competence-Based Competition*. Hamel, G. and Heene, A. (eds). John Wiley & Sons: Chichester: 35–55.

De Man, A-P. 2001. The future of alliance capability: towards a basic necessity for firm survival? White paper CGCP. http://www.cgcp.nl/papers/futurecapability.pdf. Accessed 9 November 2001.

De Man, A-P. 2004. A movable feast? Competition in the network economy. Inaugural lecture 28 May 2004. Department of Technology Management, Eindhoven University of Technology.

De Man, A-P., Duysters, GM. and Vasudevan, A (eds). 2001. *The Allianced Enterprise, Global strategies for corporate collaboration*. Imperial College Press: London.

Demetz, H. 1991. The theory of the firm revisited. In *The Nature of the Firm*. Williamson, OE., Winter, SG. and Coase, RH. (eds). Oxford University Press: New York.

Dent, SM. 1999. *Partnering Intelligence, Creating Value for Your Business by Building Strong Alliances*. Davies Black Publishing: Palo Alto.

DeVellis, R. 1991. *Scale Development: Theory and Applications*. Sage: Newbury Park, CA.

De Wit, B. and Meyer, R. 1994. *Strategy: Process, Content, Context*. West Publishing: New York.

Dickson, PR. 1996. The static and dynamic mechanisms of competition: a comment on Hunt and Morgan's comparative advantage theory. *Journal of Marketing* **60**(4): 102–106.

Dierickx, I. and Cool, K. 1989. Asset stock accumulation and sustainability of competitive advantage. *Management Science* **35**(12): 1504–1511.

Dillman, DA. 1978. *Mail and Telephone Surveys: The Total Design Method*. John Wiley: New York.

Dosi, G., Nelson, RR. and Winter, SG. (eds). 2000a. *The Nature and Dynamics of Organizational Capabilities*. Oxford University Press: New York.

Dosi, G., Nelson, RR. and Winter, SG. 2000b. Introduction: the nature and dynamics of organizational capabilities. In *The Nature and Dynamics of Organizational Capabilities*. Dosi, G., Nelson, RR. and Winter, SG. (eds). Oxford University Press: New York: 1–22.

Douma, MU. 1997. Strategic alliances, fit or failure. PhD dissertation. Drukkerij Elinkwijk: Utrecht.

Doz, YL. 1996. The evolution of cooperation in strategic alliances: initial conditions or learning processes? *Strategic Management Journal*, Special Issue 17(3): 55–83.

Doz, YL. and Hamel, G. 1998. *Alliance Advantage, The Art of Creating Value through Partnering*. Harvard Business School Press: Boston, MA.

Doz, YL. and Prahalad, CK. 1991. Managing DMNCs: a search for a new paradigm. *Strategic Management Journal* 12: 145–164.

Draulans, J., De Man, A-P. and Volberda, HW. 1999. Alliantievaardigheid: een bron van concurrentievoordeel. *Holland/Belgium Management Review* 63(1): 52–59.

Draulans, J., De Man, A-P. and Volberda, HW. 2003. Building alliance capability: management techniques for superior alliance performance. *Long Range Planning* 36(2): 151–166.

Dussauge, P. and Garrette, B. 1995. Determinants of success in international strategic alliances: evidence from the global aerospace. *Journal of International Business Studies* 6(3): 505–530.

Dussauge, P., Garrette, B. and Mitchell, W. 2002. The market share impact of inter-partner learning in alliances: evidence from the global auto industry. In *Cooperative Strategies and Alliances*. Contractor, FJ. and Lorange, P. (eds). Elsevier Science: Oxford: 707–728.

Dutton, JM. and Thomas, A. 1984. Treating progress functions as a managerial opportunity. *Academy of Management Review* 9: 235–247.

Duysters, G. 2001. *Partner or Perish, Surviving the Network Economy*. Inaugural lecture 22 June. Eindhoven University of Technology.

Duysters, G. and Hagedoorn, J. 2000. A note on organizational modes of strategic technology partnering. *Journal of Scientific & Industrial Research* 58: 640–649.

Duysters, GM. and Hagedoorn, J. 2001. Do company strategies and structures converge in global markets? Evidence from the computer industry. *Journal of International Business Studies* 32(2): 247–256.

Duysters, GM. and Heimeriks, KH. 2002a. The influence of alliance capabilities on alliance performance: an empirical investigation. Paper presented at SMS Conference, Rotterdam.

Duysters, GM. and Heimeriks, KH. 2002b. New frontiers in alliance research. Proposal for Organization Science Winter Conference 2003, Steamboat, CO.

Duysters, GM. and Heimeriks, KH. 2005. Developing alliance capabilities in a new era. In *Advances in Applied Business Strategy, Vol. 8, Competence Perspectives on Managing Interfirm Interactions*. Sanchez, R. and Heene, A. (eds). Elsevier: Oxford: 151–167.

Duysters, GM., Kok, G. and Vaandrager, M. 1999a. Crafting strategic technology partnerships. *R&D Management* 29: 343–351.

Duysters, GM., De Man, A-P. and Wildeman, L. 1999b. A network approach to alliance management. *European Management Journal* 17(2): 182–187.

Dyer, JH. 2000. *Collaborative Advantage, Winning through Extended Enterprise Supplier Networks.* Oxford University Press: New York.

Dyer, JH. and Chu, W. 2000. The determinants of trust in supplier-automaker relationships in the U.S., Japan, and Korea. *Journal of International Business Studies* 31(2): 259–285.

Dyer, JH., Kale, P. and Singh, H. 2001. How to make strategic alliances work. Developing a dedicated alliance function is key to building the expertise needed for competitive advantage. *Sloan Management Review* 42(4): 37–43.

Dyer, JH. and Nobeoka, K. 2000. Creating and managing a high-performance knowledge-sharing network: the Toyota case. *Strategic Management Journal* 21(3): 345–367.

Dyer, JH. and Singh, H. 1998. The relational view: cooperative strategy and sources of inter-organizational competitive advantage. *Academy of Management Review* 23(4): 660–679.

Eisenhardt, KM. and Martin, JA. 2000. Dynamic capabilities: what are they?. *Strategic Management Journal*, Special Issue 21(10–11): 1105–1121.

Eisenhardt, KM. and Schoonhoven, CB. 1996. Resource-based view of strategic alliance formation: strategic and social effects of entrepreneurial firms. *Organization Science* 7: 136–150.

Erdogan, BZ. and Baker, MJ. 2002. Increasing mail survey response rates from an industrial population. A cost-effectiveness analysis of four follow-up techniques. *Industrial Marketing Management* 31: 65–73.

Financial Times. 2000. Mastering management. Strategy must lie at the heart of alliances. 16 October 2000. By B. Gomes-Casseres. Accessed 9 March 2004.

Financial Times. 2004a. Experience is 'key to putting theory into practice'. 1 June 2004.

Financial Times. 2004b. Tantalised by the promise of wisdom. 26 August 2004.

Financial Times. 2004c. Drucker managed to do it first. 16 November 2004.

Fiol, CM. and Lyles, MA. 1985. Organizational learning. *Academy of Management Review* 10(4): 803–813.

Flaherty, MT. 2000. Limited inquiry and intelligent adaptation in semiconductor manufacturing. In *The Nature and Dynamics of Organizational Capabilities.* Dosi, G., Nelson, RR. and Winter, SG. (eds). Oxford University Press: New York: 99–123.

Florida, R. and Kenney, M. 2000. Transfer and replication of organizational capabilities: Japanese transplant organizations in the United States. In *The Nature and Dynamics of Organizational Capabilities.* Dosi, G., Nelson, RR. and Winter, SG. (eds). Oxford University Press: New York: 281–307.

Forbes Magazine. 2001. The Forbes Magnetic 40. 21 May 2001.

Foss, NJ. (ed). 1997a. *Resources, Firms and Strategies, A Reader in the Resource-Based Perspective.* Oxford University Press: Oxford.

Foss, NJ. 1997b. Resources and strategy: a brief overview of themes and contributions. In *Resources, Firms and Strategies, A Reader in the Resource-Based Perspective.* Foss, NJ. (ed.). Oxford University Press: Oxford: 3–18.

Foss, NJ. 2000. Equilibrium versus evolution in the resource-based perspective. In *Resources, Technology and Strategy.* Foss, NJ. and Robertson, PL. (eds). Routledge: London : 11–30.

Foss, NJ. and Robertson, PL. 2000. *Resources, Technology and Strategy.* Routledge: London.

Frechtling, J. 2002. *The 2002 User Friendly Handbook for Project Evaluation.* National Science Foundation. Directorate for Education and Human Resources. http://www.nsf.gov/pubs/2002/nsf02057/nsf02057_1.pdf. Accessed 28 June 2003.

Freidheim, C. 1998. *The Trillion-Dollar Enterprise. How the Alliance Revolution will Transform Global Business.* Perseus Books: Cambridge, MA.

Fujimoto, T. 1999. Reinterpreting the resource-capability view of the firm: a case of the development-production systems of the Japanese automakers. In *The Dynamic Firm: The Role of Technology, Strategy, Organization, and Regions.* Chandler, AD. jr. Hagström, P. and Solvell, O. (eds). Oxford University Press: New York: 15–44.

Fujimoto, T. 2000. Evolution of manufacturing systems and ex post dynamic capabilities: a case of Toyota's assembly operations. In *The Nature and Dynamics of Organizational Capabilities.* Dosi, G., Nelson, RR. and Winter, SG. (eds). Oxford University Press: Oxford, New York: 244–280.

Galbraith, J. 1973. *Designing Complex Organizations.* Addison-Wesley: Reading, MA.

Garcia-Pont, C. and Nohria, N. 2002. Local versus global mimetism: the dynamics of alliance formation in the automobile industry. *Strategic Management Journal* 23(4): 307–321.

Garson, GD. 1999. http://www2.chass.ncsu.edu/garson/pa765/reliab.htm#intraclass. Accessed 10 July 2003.

Garvin, DA. 1987. Building a learning organization. In *Harvard Business Review on Knowledge Management.* Harvard Business Review Press (ed.) Harvard Business School Press: 47–80.

Gerbing, DW. and Anderson, JC. 1988. An updated paradigm for scale development incorporating unidimensionality and its assessment. *Journal of Marketing* 25: 186–192.

Geringer, M. 1988. *Joint Venture Partner Selection: Strategies for Developed Countries.* Quorum: Westport, CT.

Geringer, JM. 1991. Strategic determinants of partner selection criteria in international joint ventures. *Journal of International Business Studies* 22(1): 41–62.

Geringer, JM. and Hebert L. 1991. Measuring performance of international joint ventures. *Journal of International Business Studies* 22(2): 249–263.

Ghoshal, S. and Bartlett, CA. 1999. *The Individualized Corporation: A Fundamentally New Approach to Management.* HarperBusiness: New York.

Ghosn, C. 2002. Saving the business without losing the company. *Harvard Business Review* 80(1): 37–45.

Gittell, JH. 2002. Coordinating mechanisms in care provider groups: relational coordination as a mediator and input uncertainty as a moderator of performance effects. *Management Science* 48(11): 1408–1426.

Glazer, R. 1991. Marketing in an information-intensive environment: strategic implications of knowledge as an asset. *Journal of Marketing* 55: 1–19.

Gomes-Casseres, B. 1996. *The Alliance Revolution: The New Shape of Business Rivalry.* Harvard University Press: Cambridge, MA.

Gorsuch, RL. 1983. *Factor Analysis.* Lawrence Erlbaum Associates: Hillsdale, NJ.

Grant, RM. 1991. The resource based theory of competitive advantage: implications for strategy formulation. *California Management Review* 33(3): 114–135.

Grant, RM. 1995. A knowledge-based theory of inter-firm collaboration. Academy of Management, Best Paper Proceedings: 17–22.
Grant, RM. 1996a. Prospering in dynamically competitive environments: organizational capability as knowledge integration. *Organization Science* 7(4): 375–387.
Grant, RM. 1996b. Toward a knowledge-based theory of the firm. *Strategic Management Journal*, Special Issue 17: 109–122.
Grant, RM. 1998. *Contemporary Strategy Analysis: Concepts, Techniques, Applications*, 3rd edn. Basil Blackwell: Cambridge, MA.
Grant, RM. and Baden-Fuller, C. 2002. The knowledge-based view of strategic alliance formation: knowledge accessing *versus* organizational learning. In *Cooperative Strategies and Alliances*. Contractor, FJ. and Lorange, P. (eds). Elsevier Science: Oxford: 419–436.
Greer, TV., Chuchinprakarn, N. and Seshadri, S. 2000. Likelihood of participating in mail survey research. *Industrial Marketing Management* 29: 97–109.
Grindley, PC. and Teece, DJ. 1997. Managing intellectual capital: Licensing in semiconductors and electronics. *California Management Review* 39(2): 8–41.
Gueth, A. 2001. Entering into an alliance with big pharma. *Pharmaceutical Technology* October: 132–135.
Gulati, R. 1995. Social structure and alliance formation patterns: a longitudinal analysis. *Administrative Science Quarterly* 40(4): 619–652.
Gulati, R. 1998. Alliances and networks. *Strategic Management Journal* 19: 293–317.
Gulati, R. 1999. Network location and learning: the influence of network resources and firm capabilities on alliance formation. *Strategic Management Journal* 20(5): 397–420.
Hagedoorn, J. 2001. Inter-firm R&D partnerships – an overview of major trends and patterns since 1960. Paper presented at the ECIS Conference, Eindhoven, the Netherlands.
Hagedoorn, J. and Schakenraad, J. 1994. The effect of strategic technology alliances on company performance. *Strategic Management Journal* 15: 291–309.
Hagström, P. and Chandler, AD. jr. 1999. Perspectives on firm dynamics. In *The Dynamic Firm: The Role of Technology, Strategy, Organization, and Regions*. Chandler, AD. jr., Hagström, P. and Solvell, O. (eds). Oxford University Press: New York: 1–12
Hair, JF., Anderson, RE. and Tatham, RL. 1998. *Multivariate Data Analysis*. Macmillan: New York.
Hamel, G. 1991. Competition for competence and interpartner learning within international strategic alliances. *Strategic Management Journal* 12(Summer): 83–103.
Hamel, G. 1994. The concept of core competence. In *Competence-Based Competition*. Hamel, G. and Heene, A. (eds). John Wiley & Sons: Chichester: 11–33.
Hamel, G., Doz, Y. and Prahalad, C. 1989. Collaborate with your competitors and win. *Harvard Business Review* 67(1): 133–139.
Hamel, G. and Heene A. (eds). 1994. *Competence-Based Competition*. John Wiley & Sons: Chichester.
Hannan, M. and Freeman, J. 1984. Structural inertia and organizational change. *American Sociological Review* 49: 149–164.
Hansen, MT. 2002. Knowledge networks: explaining effective knowledge sharing in multiunit companies. *Organization Science* 13(3): 232–248.

Hansen, MT., Nohria, N. and Tierney, T. 1999. What's your strategy for managing knowledge? *Harvard Business Review* **77**(2): 106–116.

Harbison, JR. and Pekar, P. jr. 1998a. *Smart Alliances, A Practical Guide to Repeatable Success*. BoozAllen & Hamilton. Jossey-Bass Publishers: San Francisco.

Harbison, JR. and Pekar, P. jr. 1998b, *Institutionalizing Alliance Skills: Secrets of Repeatable Success*, 3rd in a Series of Viewpoints on Alliances. BoozAllen Hamilton: Los Angelos, CA.

Harbison, JR., Pekar, P. jr., Viscio, A. and Moloney, D. 2000. *The Allianced Enterprise: Breakout Strategy for the New Millennium*. BoozAllen & Hamilton: Los Angelos, CA.

Hargadon, A. and Sutton, R. 1997. Technology brokering and innovation in a product development firm. *Administrative Science Quarterly* **42**: 716–749.

Harrigan, KR. 1985. *Strategic Flexibility: A Management Guide for Changing Times*. Lexington Books: Lexington, MA.

Harrigan, KR. 1986. *Managing for Joint Venture Success*. Lexington Books: Lexington, MA.

Harrigan, KR. 1988a. Joint ventures and competitive strategy. *Strategic Management Journal* **9**: 141–158.

Harrigan, KR. 1988b. Strategic alliances and partner asymmetries. *Management International Review*, Special Issue **28**: 53–72.

Harrison, JS., Hitt, MA., Hoskisson, RE. and Ireland, RD. 2002. Resource complementarity in business combinations: extending the logic to organizational alliances. *Journal of Management*, Special Issue **7**(6): 679–690.

Harvard Business Review Press (ed.). 1987. *Harvard Business Review on Knowledge Management*. Harvard Business School Press.

Harvard Business Review Press (ed.). 2002. *Harvard Business Review on Strategic Alliances*. Harvard Business School Press.

Harzing, A-W. 2000. Cross-national industrial mail surveys. Why do response rates differ between countries? *Industrial Marketing Management* **29**: 243–254.

Hauck, WW. and Donner, A. 1977. Wald's test as applied to hypotheses in logit analysis. *Journal of the American Statistical Association* **82**: 1110–1117.

Hayes, RH. and Clark, KB. 1986. Why some factories are more productive than others. *Harvard Business Review* **64**(5): 66–73.

Heath, T. 2001. Structural equations modeling. *Journal of Consumer Psychology* **10**(1–2): 94–97.

Hedlund, G. 1992. A model of knowledge management and the global N-form corporation. White paper. Stockholm School of Economics.

Heene, A. 1994. Preface. In *Competence-Based Competition*. Hamel, G. and Heene, A. (eds). Wiley: New York: 25–28.

Heene, A. and Sanchez, R. (eds). 1997. *Competence-Based Strategic Management*. John Wiley & Sons: Chichester.

Heimeriks, KH. and Duysters, GM. 2007. Alliance capability as mediator between experience and alliance performance: an empirical investigation into the alliance capability development process. *Journal of Management Studies* **44**(1): 25–49.

Heimeriks, KH. and Schreiner, M. 2002a. The influence of relational quality and alliance capacity on alliance performance: a conceptual framework. Paper presented at the SMS Conference, Paris.

Heimeriks, KH. and Schreiner, M. 2002b. Alliance capability, collaboration quality, and alliance performance: an integrated approach. White paper. Eindhoven University of Technology, University of St. Gallen.

Helfat, C. 1997. Know-how and asset complementarity and dynamic capability accumulation: the case of R&D. *Strategic Management Journal* **18**: 339–360.

Helfat, C. 2000. Guest editor's introduction to the special issue: the evolution of firm capabilities. *Strategic Management Journal*, Special Issue **21**: 955–959.

Helfat, C. 2003. *The SMS Blackwell Handbook of Organizational Capabilities*. Blackwell: Oxford.

Helfat, C. and Peteraf, MA. 2003. The dynamic resource-based view: capability lifecycles. *Strategic Management Journal* **24**(10): 997–1010.

Helleloid, D. and Simonin, B. 1994. Organizational learning and a firm's core competence. In *Competence-Based Competition*. Hamel, G. and Heene, A. (eds). John Wiley & Sons: Chichester.

Henderson, RM. 1995. The evolution of integrative capability: Innovation in cardiovascular drug discovery. *Industrial and Corporate Change* **3**: 607–630.

Henderson, R. and Clark, K. 1990. Architectural innovation: the reconfiguration of existing product technologies and the failure of established firms. *Administrative Science Quarterly* **35**: 9–30.

Henderson, R. and Cockburn, I. 1994. Measuring competence? Exploring firm effects in pharmaceutical research. *Strategic Management Journal*, Special issue **15**: 63–84.

Henderson, R. and Cockburn, I. 2000. Measuring competence? Exploring firm effects in drug discovery. In *The Nature and Dynamics of Organizational Capabilities*. Dosi, G., Nelson, RR. and Winter, SG. (eds). Oxford University Press: Oxford, New York: 155–182.

Hergert, M. and Morris, D. 1988. Trends in international collaborative agreements. In *Cooperative Strategies in International Business*. Contractor, F. and Lorange, P. (eds). Lexington Books: Lexington, MA: 99–109.

Hill, RC. and Hellriegel, D. 1994. Critical contingencies in joint venture management: some lessons for managers. *Organization Science* **5**: 594–607.

Hinkin, TR. 1995. A review of scale development practices in the study of organizations. *Journal of Management* **21**(5): 967–988.

Hirsch, WZ. 1952. Manufacturing progress functions. *Review of Economic and Statistics* **34**(2): 143–155.

Hirschmann, WB. 1964. Profit from the learning curve. *Harvard Business Review* **42**: 125–139.

Hitt, MA. and Ireland, RD. 1985. Corporate distinctive competence, strategy, industry and performance. *Strategic Management Journal* **6**(3): 273–293.

Hladik, K. 1985. *International Joint Ventures: An Economic Analysis of U.S. – Foreign Business Partnerships*. Lexington Books: Lexington, MA.

Hoang, HT. 2001. The impact of organizational and alliance-based complexity on the development of alliance capacity. White paper. INSEAD.

Hoang, HT., Rothaermel, FT. and Simac, S. 2002. Alliance experience and collaborative R&D performance in the pharmaceutical industry. Paper presented at the SMS Conference, Paris.

Holm, DB., Eriksson, K. and Johanson, J. 1999. Creating value through mutual commitment to business network relationships. *Strategic Management Journal* **20**: 467–486.

Hopkins, WG. 2004. A new view of statistics. www.sportsci.org/resource/stats/index.html.
Hosmer, DW. and Lemeshow, S. 2000. *Applied Logistic Regression*, 2nd edn. Wiley Interscience: New York.
Huber, GP. 1991. Organizational learning: the contributing process and the literatures. *Organization Science* 2: 88–115.
Huberman, BA. 1996. The dynamics of organizational leaning. Working paper. Xerox Palo Alto Research Center: Palo Alto, CA.
Huberty, CJ. 1984. Issues in the use and interpretation of discriminant analysis. *Psychological Bulletin* 95: 156–171.
Huberty, CJ. and Barton, RM. 1989. An introduction to discriminant analysis. *Measurement and Evaluation in Counseling and Development* 22: 158–168.
Hunt, S. 1990. Commentary on an empirical investigation of a general theory of marketing ethics. *Journal of the Academy of Marketing Science* 18: 173–177.
Hunt, SD. and Morgan, RM. 1996. The resource-advantage theory of competition: dynamics, path dependencies, and evolutionary dimensions. *Journal of Marketing* 60(4): 107–114.
Ingram, P. and Baum, JAC. 1997. Opportunity and constraint: organizations learning from the operating and competitive experience of industries. *Strategic Management Journal*, Special Issue 18: 75–98.
Inkpen, AC. 1996. Creating knowledge through collaboration. *California Management Review* 39(1): 123–140.
Inkpen, AC. 1998a. Knowledge management processes and international joint ventures. *Organization Science* 9(4): 454–468.
Inkpen, AC. 1998b. Learning and knowledge acquisition through international strategic alliances. *Academy of Management Executive* 12(4): 69–80.
Inkpen A. 1998c. Learning, knowledge acquisition, and strategic alliances. *European Management Journal* 16(2): 223–229.
Inkpen, AC. 2000. A note on the dynamics of learning alliances: competition, cooperation and relative scope. *Strategic Management Journal* 21: 775–779.
Inkpen, AC. 2002. Learning, knowledge management, and strategic alliances: so many studies, so many unanswered questions. In *Cooperative Strategies and Alliances*. Contractor, FJ. and Lorange, P. (eds). Elsevier Science: Oxford: 267–289.
Inkpen, AC, Beamish PW. 1997. Knowledge, bargaining power and international joint venture stability. *Academy of Management Review* 22: 177–202.
Inkpen, AC. and Crossan, MM. 1995. Believing is seeing: joint ventures and organizational learning. *Journal of Management Studies* 32: 595–618.
Inkpen, AC. and Dinur, A. 1998. Knowledge management processes and international joint ventures. *Organization Science* 9(4): 454–468.
Ireland, RD., Hitt, M. and Vaidyanath, D. 2002. Alliance management as a source of competitive advantage. *Journal of Management* 28(3): 413–446.
Irwin, JR. and McClelland, GH. 2001. Misleading heuristics and moderated multiple regression models. *Journal of Marketing Research* 38(1): 100–109.
Jacobides, MG. and Winter, SG. 2004. The co-evolution of capabilities and transaction costs: explaining the institutional structure of production. Working paper, London Business School.
Jap, S. 2001. 'Pie sharing' in complex collaboration contexts. *Journal of Marketing Research*, 38: 86–99.

Jobber, D. and O'Reilly, D. 1998. Industrial mail surveys: a methodological update. *Industrial Marketing Management* 27: 95–107.
Jobber, D. and Saunders, J. 1988. An experimental investigation into cross-national mail survey response rates. *Journal of International Business Studies* 19: 483–489.
Jobson, JD. 1992. *Applied Multivariate Data Analysis. Volume II: Categorical and Multivariate Methods.* Springer-Verlag: New York.
John, G. and Reve, T. 1982. The reliability and validity of key informant data from dyadic relationships in marketing channels. *Journal of Marketing Research* 19(4): 517–524.
Johnson, JL., Cullen, JB., Sakano, T. and Takenouchi, H. 1996. Setting the stage for trust and strategic integration in Japanese–U.S. cooperative alliances. *Journal of International Business Studies* 27: 981–1004.
Johnson, G., Melin, L. and Whittington, R. 2003. Guest editors' introduction: Micro strategy and strategizing: towards an activity-based view. *Journal of Management Studies* 40(1): 3–22.
Kale, P., Dyer, JH. and Singh H. 2002. Alliance capability, stock market response, and long-term alliance success: the role of the alliance function. *Strategic Management Journal* 23(8): 747–767.
Kale, P. and Singh, H. 1999. Alliance capability and success: a knowledge-based approach. Working paper, Wharton School, University of Pennsylvania.
Kale, P., Singh, H. and Perlmutter, H. 2000. Learning and protection of proprietary assets in strategic alliances: building relational capital. *Strategic Management Journal*, Special Issue 21(3): 217–237.
Kalmbach, C. and Roussel, C. 1999. *Dispelling the Myths of Alliances.* Andersen Consulting. http://www.ac.com/ideas/Outlook/special99/over_specialed_intro.html. Accessed 18 August 2000.
Kanter, R. 1983. *Change Masters: Innovation and Entrepreneurship in the American Cooperation.* Simon & Schuster: New York.
Kanter, RM. 1994. Collaborative advantage. *Harvard Business Review* 72(4): 96–108.
Kanuk, L. and Berenson, C. 1975. Mail surveys and response rates: a literature review. *Journal of Marketing Research* 12: 440–453.
Karim, S. and Mitchell W. 2000. Path-dependent and path-breaking change: reconfiguring business resources following acquisitions in the US medical sector, 1978–1995. *Strategic Management Journal*, Special Issue 21(10–11): 1061–1081.
Karnoe, P. 1995. Competence as process and the social embeddedness of competence building. Academy of Management, Best Papers Proceedings: 7–11.
Katz, R. and Allen, TJ. 1982. Investigating the not invented here (NIH) syndrome: a look at the performance, tenure, and communication patterns of 50 R&D projects. *R&D Management* 12(1): 7–19.
Khanna, T., Gulati, R. and Nohria, N. 1998. The dynamics of learning alliances: competition, cooperation, and relative scope. *Strategic Management Journal* 19(3): 193–210.
Killing, JP. 1983. *Strategies for Joint Venture Success.* Praeger: New York.
Kim, D. 1993. The link between individual and organizational learning. *Sloan Management Review* 35(1): 37–50.
Kim, JO. and Mueller, CW. 1978. *Factor Analysis: Statistical Methods and Practical Issues.* Sage: Newbury Park, CA.

King, AW. and Tucci, CL. 2002. Incumbent entry into new market niches: the role of experience and managerial choice in the creation of dynamic capabilities. *Management Science* **48**(2): 171–186.

King, AW. and Zeithaml, CP. 2001. Competencies and firm performance: examining the causal ambiguity paradox. *Strategic Management Journal* **22**(1): 75–99.

Klecka, WR. 1980. *Discriminant Analysis*, Series: Quantitative Applications in the Social Sciences, No. 07–019. Sage Publications: London.

Kleiner, A. and Roth, G. 1987. How to make experience your company's best teacher. In *Harvard Business Review on Knowledge Management*. Harvard Business Review Press (ed). Harvard Business School Press: 137–151.

Knott, AM. 2003. The organizational routines factor market paradox. *Strategic Management Journal* **24**(10): 929–943.

Kogut, B. 1988. A study of the life-cycle of joint ventures. *Management International Review*, Special Issue **28**: 39–52.

Kogut, B. 1989. The stability of joint ventures: reciprocity and competitive rivalry. *The Journal of Industrial Economics* **38**: 183–198.

Kogut, B. and Zander, U. 1992. Knowledge of the firm, combinative capabilities, and the replication of technology. *Organization Science* **3**: 383–397.

Kogut, B. and Zander, U. 1993. Knowledge of the firm and evolutionary theory of the multinational corporation. *Journal of International Business Studies* **24**: 625–645.

Kogut, B. and Zander, U. 1996. What firms do? Coordination, identity, and learning. *Organization Science* **7**(5): 502–518.

Kogut, B. and Zander, U. 1997. Knowledge of the firm, combinative capabilities, and the replication of technology. In *Resources, Firms and Strategies, A Reader in the Resource-Based Perspective*. Foss, NJ. (ed). Oxford University Press: Oxford: 306–326.

Koka, BR. and Prescott, JE. 2002. Strategic alliances as social capital: a multidimensional view. *Strategic Management Journal* **23**(9): 795–816.

Kotabe, M., Martin, X. and Domoto, H. 2003. Gaining from vertical partnerships: knowledge transfer, relationship duration, and supplier performance improvement in the U.S. and Japanese automotive industries. *Strategic Management Journal* **24**(4): 293–316.

Koza, MP. and Lewin, AY. 1998. The co-evolution of strategic alliances. *Organization Science* **9**(3): 255–264.

Koza, MP. and Lewin, AY. 2000. Managing partnerships and strategic alliances: raising the odds of success. *European Management Journal* **18**(2): 146–151.

Kuder, GF. and Richardson, MW. 1937. The theory of the estimation of test reliability. *Psychometrika* **2**: 151–160.

Kumar, BN. 1995. Partner-selection-criteria and success of technology transfer: a model based on learning theory applied to the case of Indo-German technical collaborations. *Management International Review*, Special Issue **1**: 65–78.

Kumar, BN. and Nti, KO. 1998. Differential learning and interaction in alliance dynamics: a process and outcome discrepancy model. *Organization Science* **9**(3): 356–367.

Kusunoki, K., Nonaka, I. and Nagata, A. 1998. Organizational capabilities in product development of Japanese firms: a conceptual framework and empirical findings. *Organization Science* **9**(6): 699–718.

Lambe, CJ., Spekman, RE. and Hunt, SD. 2002. Alliance competence, resources, and alliance success: conceptualization, measurement, and initial test. *Journal of the Academy of Marketing Science* 30(2): 141–158.
Lambin, J-J. 1993. *Marketing Strategy: A New European Approach.* McGraw-Hill: New York.
Lambin, J-J. 2000. *Market-Driven Management: Strategic and Operational Marketing.* Palgrave-Macmillan: New York.
Lane, PJ. and Lubatkin, M. 1998. Relative absorptive capacity and interorganizational learning. *Strategic Management Journal* 19(5): 461–477.
Lane, PJ., Salk, JE. and Lyles, MA. 2001. Absorptive capacity, learning, and performance in international joint ventures. *Strategic Management Journal* 22(12): 1139–1161.
Langlois, RN. 1997. Transaction-cost economics in real time. In *Resources, Firms and Strategies, A Reader in the Resource-Based Perspective.* Foss, NJ. (ed). Oxford University Press: Oxford: 286–305.
Lapré, MA., Mukherjee, AS. and Van Wassenhove, LN. 2000. Behind the learning curve: linking learning activities to waste reduction. *Management Science* 46(5): 597–611.
Lapré, MA. and Van Wassenhove, LN. 2001. Creating and transferring knowledge from productivity improvement in factories. *Management Science* 47(10): 1311–1325.
Larson, PD. and Chow, G. 2003. Total cost/response rate trade-offs in mail survey research impact of follow-up mailings and monetary incentives. *Industrial Marketing Management* 32(7): 533–537.
Larsson, R., Bengtsson, L., Henriksson, K. and Sparks, J. 1998. The interorganizational learning dilemma: collective knowledge development in strategic alliances. *Organization Science* 9(3): 285–305.
Lawley, DN. and Maxwell, AE. 1971. *Factor Analysis as a Statistical Method.* Butterworths: London.
Lehmann, DR., Gupta, S. and Steckel, JH. 1998. *Marketing research.* Addison-Wesley-Longman: Reading, MA.
Lehtonen, J. 2003. Alliance capability. White paper. Helsinki University of Technology.
Lei, D. and Slocum, JW. jr. 1992. Global strategy, competence-building and strategic alliances. *California Management Review* 31(1): 81–97.
Lei, D., Hitt, MA., Bettis, R. 1996. Dynamic core competencies through meta-learning and strategic context. *Journal of Management* 22(4): 549–569.
Lei, D., Slocum, JW. jr. and Pitts, RA. 1997. Building cooperative advantage: managing strategic alliances to promote organizational learning. *Journal of World Business* 32(3): 203–223.
Lemmens, C. 2003. Network dynamics and innovation. The effects of social embeddedness in technology alliance blocks. PhD thesis. Eindhoven Centre for Innovation Studies. Eindhoven University Press, the Netherlands.
Lenox, M. and King, A. 2004. Prospects for developing absorptive capacity through internal information provision. *Strategic Management Journal* 25(4): 331–345.
Leonard-Barton, D. 1992. Core capabilities and core rigidities: a paradox in managing new product development. *Strategic Management Journal*, Special Issue 13: 111–125.

Leonard-Barton, D. 1995. *Wellsprings Of Knowledge*. Harvard Business School Press: Boston, MA.

Leonard, D. and Swap, W. 2004. Deep Smarts. *Harvard Business Review* **82**(9): 88–97.

Levin, DZ. 2000. Organizational learning and the transfer of knowledge. *Organization Science* **11**(6): 630–647.

Levinthal, D. 2000. Organizational capabilities in complex worlds. In *The Nature and Dynamics of Organizational Capabilities*. Dosi, G., Nelson, RR. and Winter, SG. (eds). Oxford University Press: Oxford, New York: 363–379.

Levinthal, DA. and March, JG. 1993. The myopia of learning. *Strategic Management Journal*, Special Issue **14**: 95–112.

Levitt, B. and March, J. 1988. Organizational learning. *Annual Review of Sociology* **14**: 319–340.

Lewin, AY. and Volberda, HW. 1999. Prolegomena on coevolution: a framework for research on strategy and new organizational forms. *Organization Science* **10**(5): 519–534.

Lewis-Beck, MS. 1994. *Basic Measurement*. Sage Publications, Toppan Publishing: London.

Li, SX. and Rowley, TJ. 2002. Inertia and evaluation mechanisms in interorganizational partner selection: syndicate formation among U.S. investment banks. *Academy of Management Journal* **45**(6): 1104–1119.

Lippman, S. and Rumelt, R. 1982. Uncertain imitability: an analysis of inter-firm differences in efficiency under competition. *Bell Journal of Economics* **13**: 418–438.

Littler, D., Leverick, F. and Bruce, M. 1995. Factors affecting the process of collaborative product development: a study of UK manufacturers of information and communications technology products. *Journal of Product Innovation Management* **12**(1): 16–32.

Long, JS. 1997. *Regression Models for Categorical and Limited Dependent Variables*. Sage Publications: Thousand Oaks, CA.

Lorange, P. 1997. Black-box protection of your core competencies in strategic alliances. In *Cooperative Strategies: European Perspectives*. Beamish, PW. and Killing, JP. (eds). New Lexington Press: San Francisco, CA: 59–73.

Lorange, P. and Roos, J. 1990. *Strategic Alliances, Formation, Implementation and Evolution*. Blackwell: Cambridge. MA.

Lorenzoni, G. and Baden-Fuller, C. 1995. Creating a strategic center to manage a web of partners. *California Management Review* **37**(3): 146–163.

Lorenzoni, G. and Lipparini, A. 1999. The leveraging of inter-firm relationships as a distinctive organizational capability: a longitudinal study. *Strategic Management Journal* **20**(4): 317–338.

Lorino, P. 2001. A pragmatic analysis of the role of management systems in organizational learning. In *Knowledge Management and Organizational Competence*. Sanchez, R. (ed). Oxford University Press: New York: 177–209.

Luo, Y. 2002a. Building trust in cross-cultural collaborations: toward a contingency perspective. *Journal of Management* **28**(5): 669–694.

Luo, Y. 2002b. Contract, cooperation, and performance in international joint ventures. *Strategic Management Journal* **23**(10): 903–919.

Lyles, MA. 1988. Learning among joint venture sophisticated firms. *Management International Review*, Special Issue **28**: 85–97.

Madhok, A. 2002. Reassessing the fundamentals and beyond: Ronald Coase, the transaction cost and resource-based theories of the firm and the institutional structure of production. *Strategic Management Journal* **23**(6): 535–550.

Madhok, A. and Tallman, SB. 1998. Resources, transactions and rents: managing value through inter-firm collaborative relationships. *Organization Science* **9**(3): 326–339.

Mahoney, JT. and Pandian, JR. 1992. The resource-based view within the conversation of strategic management. *Strategic Management Journal* **13**(5): 363–380.

Mahoney, JT. and Sanchez, R. 1997. Competence theory building: reconnecting management research and management practice. In *Competence-Based Strategic Management*. Heene, A. and Sanchez, R. (eds). John Wiley & Sons: Chichester: 43–64.

Maidique, MA. and Zirger, BJ. 1985. The new product learning cycle. *Research Policy* **14**(6): 299–309.

Makadok, R. 2001. Toward a synthesis of the resource-based and dynamic-capability views of rent creation. *Strategic Management Journal* **22**(5): 387–401.

Makhija, MV. and Ganesh, U. 1997. The relationship between control and partner learning in learning-related joint ventures. *Organization Science* **8**(5): 508–527.

Malone, T. and Crowston, K. 1994. The interdisciplinary study of coordination. *Computing Surveys* **26**(1): 87–119.

Mankins, MC. 2004. Stop wasting valuable time. *Harvard Business Review* **82**(9): 56–67.

March, JG. 1991. Exploration and exploitation in organizational learning. *Organization Science* **2**(1): 71–87.

March, JG. 1994. *A Primer on Decision Making: How Decisions Happen*. Free Press: New York.

March, JG., Sproull, LS. and Tamuz, M. 1991. Learning from samples of one or fewer. *Organization Science* **2**: 1–13.

Margulis, M. and Pekar, P. 2001. The next wave of alliance formations: forging successful partnerships with emerging and middle-market companies. Houlhan Lokey Howard & Zukin: Los Angelos, CA.

Maritan, CA. and Brush, TH. 2003. Heterogeneity and transferring practices: implementing flow manufacturing in multiple plants. *Strategic Management Journal* **24**(10): 945–959.

Markides, C. and Williamson, PJ. 1994. Related diversification, core competences and corporate performance. *Strategic Management Journal* **15**: 149–157.

Martin, de Holan P. and Phillips, N. 2003. Organizational forgetting. In *Handbook of Organizational Learning and Knowledge Management*. Easterby-Smith, M. and Lyles, MA. (eds). Blackwell: Oxford: 393–409.

Mason, CH. and Perreault, WD. 1991. Collinearity, power, and interpretation of multiple regression analysis. *Journal of Marketing Research* **28**: 268–280.

McCullagh, P. and Nelder, JA. 1989. *Generalized Linear Models*. Chapman & Hall: London.

McDonald, RP. 1981. The dimensionality of tests and items. *British Journal of Mathematical and Statistical Psychology* **34**: 100–117.

McEvily, SK. and Chakravarthy, B. 2002. The persistence of knowledge-based advantage: an empirical test for product performance and technological knowledge. *Strategic Management Journal* **23**: 285–305.

McLachlan, GJ. 1992. *Discriminant Analysis and Statistical Pattern Recognition.* John Wiley & Sons: New York.

McLeod, LD., Swygert, KA. and Thissen, S. 2001. Factor analysis for items scored in two categories. In *Test Scoring*. Thissen, D. and Wainer, H. (eds). Lawrence Erlbaum: Mahwah, NJ: 189–216.

Medcof, JW. 1997. Why too many alliances end in divorce. *Long Range Planning* **30**(5): 718–732.

Menard, S. 1995. *Applied Logistic Regression Analysis*. Sage: Thousand Oaks, CA.

Merali, Y. 1997. Information, systems and dasein. In *People, Organizations, and Environment*. Stowell, F. (ed). New York: Plenum.

Merali, Y. 2001. Building and developing capabilities: a cognitive congruence framework. In *Knowledge Management and Organizational Competence*. Sanchez, R. (ed.). Oxford University Press: New York: 41–62.

Metcalfe, JS. and James, A. 2000. Knowledge and capabilities. A new view of the firm. In *Resources, Technology and Strategy*. Foss, NJ. and Robertson, PL. (eds). Routledge: London: 31–52.

Miller, KD. 2003. An asymmetry-based view of advantage: towards an attainable sustainability. *Strategic Management Journal* **24**(10): 961–976.

Mintzberg, H., Ahlstrand, B. and Lampel, J. 1998. *Strategy Safari: A Guided Tour through the Wilds of Strategic Management*. Free Press: New York.

Mohr, J. and Spekman, R. 1994. Characteristics of partnership success: partnership attributes, communication behavior and conflict resolution. *Strategic Management Journal* **15**: 135–152.

Moll, WAW. 1995. http://www.euronet.nl/users/warnar/itemanalyse.html. Accessed 12 June 2003.

Montealegre, R. 2002. A process model of capability development: lessons from the electronic commerce strategy at Bolsa de Valores de Guayaquil. *Organization Science* **13**(5): 514–531.

Montgomery, CA. and Wernerfelt, B. 1997. Diversification, Ricardian rents and Tobin's q. In *Resources, Firms and Strategies, A Reader in the Resource-Based Perspective*. Foss, NJ. (ed.). Oxford: Oxford University Press: 173–186.

Moorman, C. and Miner, AS. 1997. The impact of organizational memory on new product performance and creativity. *Journal of Marketing Research* **34**(2): 91–106.

Morgan, RN. and Hunt, SD. 1994. The commitment-trust theory of relationship marketing. *Journal of Marketing* **58**, 20–38.

Mowery, DC. (ed.). 1988. *International Collaborative Ventures in U.S. Manufacturing*. Ballinger: Cambridge, MA.

Mowery, DC., Oxley, JE. and Silverman, BS. 2002. The two faces of partner-specific absorptive capacity: learning and cospecialization in strategic alliances. In *Cooperative Strategies and Alliances*. Contractor, FJ. and Lorange, P. (eds). Elsevier Science: Oxford: 292–319.

Mukherjee, AS., Lapré, MA. and Van Wassenhove, LN. 1998. Knowledge driven quality improvement. *Management Science* **44**(11): S35–S49.

Muthen, B. 1978. Contributions to factor analysis of dichotomous variables. *Psychometrika* **43**(3): 551–560.

Muthen, B. 1983. Latent variable structural equation modeling with categorical data. *Journal of Econometrics* **22**(9): 48–65.
Muthen, B. 1984. A general structural equation model with dichotomous, ordered categorical, and continuous latent variable indicators. *Psychometrika* **49**(11): 115–132.
Muthen, B. 2004. Mplus, Statistical analysis with latent variables. Technical appendices. Version 3.www.statmodel.com. Accessed 17 December 2003.
Muthen, B. and Christoffersson, A. 1981. Simultaneous factor analysis of dichotomous variables in several populations. *Psychometerika* **48**: 485–500.
Narula, R. and Hagedoorn, J. 1999. Innovating through strategic alliances: moving towards international partnerships and contractual agreements. *Technovation* **19**: 283–294.
Nault, BR. and Tyagi, RK. 2001. Implementable mechanisms to coordinate horizontal alliances. *Management Science* **47**(6): 787–799.
Nelson, R. 1997. Why do firms differ, and how does it matter? In *Resources, Firms and Strategies, A Reader in the Resource-Based Perspective*. Foss, NJ. (ed). Oxford University Press: Oxford: 257–267.
Nelson, R. and Winter, S. 1982. *An Evolutionary Theory of Economic Change*. Harvard University Press: Cambridge, MA.
Nohria, N. and Eccles, RG. 1992. *Networks and Organisations, Structure, form and action*. Harvard Business School Press: Boston, MA.
Nonaka, I. 1988. Toward middle-up-down management: accelerating information creation. *Sloan Management Review* **29**(3): 9–18.
Nonaka, I. 1990. Redundant, overlapping organization: a Japanese approach to managing the innovation process. *California Management Review* **32**(3): 27–38.
Nonaka, I. 1991. The knowledge-creating company. *Harvard Business Review* **69**(6): 96–104.
Nonaka, I. 1994. A dynamic theory of organizational knowledge creation. *Organization Science* **5**(1): 14–37.
Nonaka, I. and Takeuchi, H. 1995. *The Knowledge-Creating Company: How Japanese Companies Create the Dynamics of Innovation*. Oxford University Press: New York.
Nonaka, I. and Takeuchi, H. 1999. A theory of the firm's knowledge-creation dynamics. In *The Dynamic Firm: The Role of Technology, Strategy, Organization, and Regions*. Chandler, AD. jr., Hagström, P. and Solvell, O. (eds). Oxford University Press: New York: 214–241.
Nonaka, I., Toyama, R. and Konno, N. 2001. SECI, Ba and leadership: a unified model of dynamic knowledge creation. In *Managing Industrial Knowledge, Creation, Transfer and Utilization*. Nonaka, I. and Teece, DJ. (eds). Sage: London: 13–43.
Nooteboom, B., Berger, J. and Noorderhaven, NG. 1997. Effects of trust and governance on relational risk. *Academy of Management Journal* **40**(2): 308–338.
Nti, KO. and Kumar, R. 2001. Differential learning in alliances. In *Cooperative Strategy, Economic, Business, and Organizational Issues*. Faulkner, D. and De Rond, M. (eds). Oxford University Press: New York: 119–134.
Nunally, JC. 1978. *Psychometric Theory*, 2nd edn. McGraw Hill: New York.
Nunally, JC. and Bernstein, IH. 1994. *Psychometric Theory*, 3rd edn. McGraw-Hill: New York.
Oliver, AL. 2001. Strategic alliances and the learning life-cycle of bio-technology firms. *Organization Studies* **22**(3): 467–489.

Olk, P. 2002. Evaluating strategic alliance performance. In *Cooperative Strategies and Alliances*. Contractor, FJ. and Lorange, P. (eds). Elsevier Science: Oxford: 119–143.

Oppenheim, AN. 1966. *Questionnaire Design and Attitude Measurement*. Heinemann: London.

Oxtoby, B., McGuiness, T. and Morgan, R. 2002. Developing organisational change capability. *European Management Journal* 20(3): 310–320.

Pacheco-de-Almeida, G. and Zemksy, P. 2001. Resource accumulation under uncertainty. Working paper, INSEAD.

Parise, S. and Casher, A. 2003. Alliance portfolios: designing and managing your network of business-partner relationships. *Academy of Management Executive* 17(4): 25–39.

Park, SO. and Ungson, GR. 2001. Inter-firm rivalry and managerial complexity: a conceptual framework of alliance failure. *Organization Science* 12(1): 37–53.

Parkhe, A. 1993. Strategic alliances structuring: a game theoretic and transaction cost examination of inter-firm cooperation. *Academy of Management Journal* 36(4): 794–829.

Parkhe, A. 1998. Understanding trust in international alliances. *Journal of World Business* 33(3): 219–240.

Paxson, MC. 1992. Follow-up mail surveys. *Industrial Marketing Management* 21(3): 195–201.

Pekar, P. jr. and Allio, R. 1994. Making alliances work – guidelines for success. *Long Range Planning* 27(4): 54–65.

Pennings, JM., Barkema, H. and Douma, S. 1994. Organizational learning and diversification. *Academy of Management Journal* 37(3): 608–640.

Penrose, ET. 1959. *The Theory of the Growth of the Firm*. Oxford University Press: Oxford.

Peter, JP. and Olson, JC. 2004. *Consumer Behavior and Marketing Strategy*. McGraw-Hill: New York.

Peteraf, M. 1993. The cornerstones of competitive advantage: a resource-based view. *Strategic Management Journal* 14(3): 179–191.

Pfeffer, J. and Salancik, GR. 1978. *The External Control of Organizations: A Resource Dependence Perspective*. Harper & Row: London.

Pfeffer, J. and Sutton, RI. 1999. Knowing 'what' to do is not enough: turning knowledge into action. *California Management Review* 42(1): 83–108.

Philips, LW. 1981. Assessing measurement error in key informant reports: a methodological note on organizational analysis in marketing. *Journal of Marketing Research* 18(November): 395–415.

Pisano, GP. 1984. Knowledge, integration, and the locus of learning: an empirical analysis of process development. *Strategic Management Journal* 15: 85–100.

Pisano, GP. 1989. Using equity participation to support exchange: evidence from the biotechnology industry. *Journal of Law, Economics, and Organization* 5: 109–126.

Pisano, GP. 2000. In search of dynamic capabilities: the origins of R&D competence in biopharmaceuticals. In *The Nature and Dynamics of Organizational Capabilities*. Dosi, G., Nelson, RR. and Winter, SG. (eds). Oxford University Press: Oxford, New York: 129–154.

Pisano, GP., Bohmer, RMJ. and Edmondson, AC. 2001. Organizational differences in rates of learning: evidence from the adoption of minimally invasive cardiac surgery. *Management Science* 47(6): 752–768.

Polanyi, M. 1962. *Personal Knowledge: Towards a Post-critical Philosophy*. University of Chicago Press: Chicago, IL.
Polanyi, M. 1967. *The Tacit Dimension*. Routledge: London.
Poppo, L. and Zenger, T. 2002. Do formal contracts and relational governance function as substitutes or complements? *Strategic Management Journal* **23**(8): 707–725.
Porter, ME. 1980. *Competitive Strategy*. The Free Press: New York.
Powell, WW., Koput, KW. and Smith-Doerr, L. 1996. Interorganizational collaboration and the locus of control of innovation: networks of learning in biotechnology. *Administrative Science Quarterly* **41**(1): 116–145.
Prahalad, CK. and Hamel, G. 1990. The core competence of the corporation. *Harvard Business Review* **66**(3): 79–91.
Prahalad, CK. and Hamel, G. 1993. Strategy as stretch and leverage. *Harvard Business Review* **71**(2): 75–84.
Pressley, MM. 1980. Improving mails survey responses from industrial organizations. *Industrial Marketing Management* **9**(3): 231–235.
Priem, RL. and Butler, JE. 2000. Is the resource-based 'view' a useful perspective for strategic management research?. *Academy of Management Review* **26**(1): 22–40.
Probst, G., Büchel, B. and Raub, S. 1998. Knowledge as a Strategic Resource. In *Knowing in Firms, Understanding, Managing and Measuring Knowledge*. Von Krogh, G., Roos, J. and Kleine, D. (eds). Sage: London: 240–252.
Ranft, AL. and Lord, MD. 2002. Acquiring new technologies and capabilities: a grounded model of acquisition implementation. *Organization Science* **13**(4): 420–441.
Ray, G., Barney, JB. and Muhanna, WA. 2004. Capabilities, business processes, and competitive advantage: choosing the dependent variable in empirical tests of the resource-based view. *Strategic Management Journal* **25**(1): 23–37.
Rea, LM. and Parker, RA. 2002. *Designing and Conducting Survey Research, A Comprehensive Guide*. Jossey-Bass Publishers: San Francisco, CA.
Remenyi, D., Williams, B., Money, A. and Swartz, E. 1998. *Doing Research in Business and Management, An Introduction to Process and Method*. Sage Publications: London.
Reuer, JJ., Park, KM. and Zollo, M. 2002a. Experiential learning in international joint ventures: the roles of experience heterogeneity and venture novelty. In *Cooperative Strategies and Alliances*. Contractor, FJ. and Lorange, P. (eds). Elsevier Science: Oxford: 321–344.
Reuer, JJ., Zollo, M. and Singh, H. 2002b. Post-formation dynamics in strategic alliances. *Strategic Management Journal* **23**(2): 135–151.
Rindova, VP. and Kotha S. 2001. Continuous 'morphing': competing through dynamic capabilities, form, and function. *Academy of Management Journal* **44**(6): 1263–1281.
Robins, JA., Tallman, S. and Fladmoe-Lindquist, K. 2002. Autonomy and dependence of international cooperative ventures: an exploration of the strategic importance of U.S. ventures in Mexico. *Strategic Management Journal* **23**(10): 881–901.
Robinson, JP., Shaver, PR. and Wrightsman, LS. 1991. Criteria for scale selection and evaluation. In *Measures of Personality and Social Psychological Attitudes*. Robinson, JP., Shaver, PR. and Wrightsman, LS. (eds). Academic Press: San Diego, CA: 1–15.

Rotter, J. 1966. Generalized expectancies for internal versus external control of reinforcements. *Psychological Monographs* **80**(609), whole number.

Rugman, AM. and Verbeke, A. 2002. Edith Penrose's contribution to the resource-based view of strategic management. *Strategic Management Journal* **23**(8): 769–780.

Rule, E. 1999. *High-Performing Strategic Alliances, In the Pharmaceutical, Biotechnology and Medical Device and Diagnostic Industries*. PricewaterhouseCoopers.

Rumelt, RP. 1984. Towards a strategy theory of the firm. In *Competitive Strategic Management*. Lamb, R. (ed.). Prentice-Hall: Englewood Cliffs, NJ: 556–570.

Rummel, RJ. 1970. *Applied Factor Analysis*. Northwestern University Press: Evanston, IL.

Salk, JE. and Simonin, BL. 2003. Beyond alliances: towards a meta-theory of collaborative learning. In *Handbook of Organizational Learning and Knowledge Management*. Easterby-Smith, M. and Lyles, MA. (eds). Blackwell: Oxford: 253–277.

Sampson, RC. 2002. Do firms learn to manage? Experience and collaborative returns in R&D alliances. Academy of Management Proceedings [CD-ROM].

Sanchez, R. 2001a. Building blocks for strategy theory: resources, dynamic capabilities and competences. In *Rethinking Strategy*. Volberda, HW. and Elfring, T. (eds). Sage Publications: London: 143–157.

Sanchez, R. (ed.) 2001b. *Knowledge Management and Organizational Competence*. Oxford University Press: New York.

Sanchez, R. 2001c. Managing knowledge into competence: the five learning cycles of the competent organization. In *Knowledge Management and Organizational Competence*. Sanchez, R. (ed.). Oxford University Press: Oxford, New York: 3–37.

Sanchez, R. 2002. Industry standards, modular architectures, and common components: strategic incentives for technological cooperation in the new economy. Paper presented at the 6th International Conference on Competence-Based Management, IMD, Lausanne, Switzerland.

Sanchez, R. and Heene, A. 1997. Reinventing strategic management: new theory and practice for competence-based competition. *European Management Journal* **15**(3): 303–317.

Sanchez, R., Heene, A. and Thomas, H. 1996a. *Dynamics of Competence-Based Competition: Theory and Practice in the New Strategic Environment*. Elsevier Pergamon: Oxford.

Sanchez, R., Heene, A. and Thomas, H. 1996b. Introduction: towards the theory and practice of competence-based competition. In *Dynamics of Competence-Based Competition*. Sanchez, R., Heene, A. and Thomas, H. (eds). Pergamon: 1–35.

Sarkar, MB., Aulakh, PS. and Madhok, A. 2004. A process view of alliance capability: generating value in alliance portfolios. White paper presented at KUN seminar, Nijmegen, the Netherlands.

Sarkar, MB., Echambadi, RAJ. and Harrison, JS. 2001. Alliance entrepreneurship and firm market performance. *Strategic Management Journal* **22**: 701–711.

Scharmer, CO. 2001. Self-transcending knowledge: organizing around emerging realities. In *Managing Industrial Knowledge, Creation, Transfer and Utilization*. Nonaka, I. and Teece, DJ. (eds). Sage: London: 68–90.

Schendel, D. 1996. Editor's introduction to the 1996 summer special issue: evolutionary perspectives on strategy. *Strategic Management Journal*, Special Issue **17**: 1–4.

Schoonhoven, CB. 2002. Evolution of the special issue on knowledge, knowing, and organizations. *Organization Science* **13**(3): 223.

Schreiner, M. 2003. Collaborative capability in interorganizational relationships: a preliminary model. Working paper. St. Gallen University.

Schreiner, M. and Corsten, D. 2003. Collaborative capability: a dynamic capability view. White paper. University of St. Gallen.

Schwab, DP. 1980. Construct validity in organization behavior. In *Research in Organizational Behavior*. Staw, BM. and Cummings, LL. (eds). JAI Press: Greenwich, CT.

Senge, P. 1990a. *The Fifth Discipline*. Century Business: London.

Senge, P. 1990b. The leader's new work: building learning organizations. *Sloan Management Review* **32**(1): 7–23.

Shafer, SM., Nembhard, DA. and Uzumeri, MV. 2001. The effects of worker learning, forgetting, and heterogeneity on assembly line productivity. *Management Science* **47**(12): 1639–1653.

Sharma, S., Durand, RM. and Gur-Arie, O. 1981. Identification and analysis of moderator variables. *Journal of Marketing Research* **18**: 291–300.

Shenkar, O. and Li, J. 1999. Knowledge search in international cooperative ventures. *Organization Science* **10**(2): 134–143.

Simonin, BL. 1997. The importance of collaborative know-how: an empirical test of the learning organization. *Academy of Management Journal* **40**(5): 1150–1174.

Simonin, BL. 2002. The nature of collaborative know-how. In *Cooperative Strategies and Alliances*. Contractor, FJ. and Lorange, P. (eds). Elsevier Science: Oxford: 237–263.

Sims, NM., Harrison, RG. and Gueth, A. 2003. An army of diplomats – Eli Lilly. In *Mastering Alliance Strategy: A Comprehensive Guide to Design, Management, and Organization*. Bamford, JD., Gomes-Casseres, B. and Robinson, MS. (eds). Jossey-Bass: San Francisco, CA: 382–395.

Singh, H. 2003. The relational organization: from relational rents to alliance capability. In *The SMS Blackwell Handbook of Organizational Capabilities*. Helfat, C. (ed.). Blackwell: Oxford: 257–263.

Sivadas, E. and Dwyer, RF. 2000. An examination of organizational factors influencing new product development in internal and alliance-based processes. *Journal of Marketing* **64**(1): 31–49.

Snow, CC. and Thomas, JB. 1994. Field research methods in strategic management: contributions to theory building and testing. *Journal of Management Studies* **31**: 457–479.

Spanos, YE. and Lioukas, S. 2001. An examination into the causal logic of rent generation: contrasting Porter's competitive strategy framework and the resource-based perspective. *Strategic Management Journal* **22**(10): 907–934.

Spector, PE. 1991. *Summated Rating Scale Construction: An Introduction*. Sage: London.

Spekman, RE., Isabella, LA. and MacAvoy, TC. 1999. *Alliance Competence, Maximizing the Value of Your Partnerships*. John Wiley & Sons: New York.

Spender, J-C. 1996. Organizational knowledge, learning, and memory: three concepts in search of a theory. *Journal of Organizational Change* **9**: 63–78.

Stata, R. 1989. Organizational learning – the key to management innovation. *Sloan Management Review* **30**(3): 63–74.

Stein, J. and Ridderstrale, J. 2001. Managing the dissemination of competences. In *Knowledge Management and Organizational Competence*. Sanchez, R. (ed.). Oxford University Press: Oxford, New York: 63–76.

Steiner, GA. 1968. *Strategic Factors in Business Success*. University of California Graduate School of Business Administration: Los Angeles.

Suhr, D. 2004. Reliability, exploratory and confirmatory factor analysis for the scale of athletic priorities. White paper. University of Northern Colorado.

Szulanski, G. 1996. Exploring internal stickiness: impediments to the transfer of best practice within the firm. *Strategic Management Journal*, Special Issue **17**: 27–43.

Szulanski, G. 2000. The process of knowledge transfer: a diachronic analysis of stickiness. *Organizational Behavior and Human Decision Processes* **82**(1): 9–27.

Szulanski, G., Winter, SG., Cappetta, R. and Van den Bulte, C. 2002. Opening the black box of knowledge transfer: the role of replication accuracy. Working paper, The Wharton School, University of Pennsylvania.

Tabachnick, BG. and Fidell, LS. 2001. *Using Multivariate Statistics*, 4th edn. Allyn and Bacon: Needham Heights, MA.

Takeishi, A. 2001. Bridging inter and intra-firm boundaries: management of supplier involvement in automobile product development. *Strategic Management Journal* **22**(5): 403–433.

Takeishi, A. 2002. Knowledge partitioning in the interfirm division of labor: the case of the automotive development. *Organization Science* **13**(3): 312–338.

Tanner, JF. 1999. Organizational buying theories: a bridge to relationships theory. *Industrial Marketing Management* **28**: 245–255.

Teece, DJ. 1982. Towards an economic theory of the multiproduct firm. *Journal of Economic Behavior and Organization* **3**: 39–63.

Teece, DJ. 1997. Economies of scope and the scope of the enterprise. In *Resources, Firms and Strategies, A Reader in the Resource-Based Perspective*. Foss, NJ. (ed.). Oxford: Oxford University Press: 103–116.

Teece, DJ. and Pisano, G. 1994. The dynamic capabilities of firms: an introduction. *Industrial and Corporate Change* **3**(3): 537–556.

Teece, DJ., Pisano, G. and Shuen, A. 1997. Dynamic capabilities and strategic management. *Strategic Management Journal* **18**(7): 509–533.

Teece, DJ., Rumelt, R., Dosi, G. and Winter, S. 1994. Understanding corporate coherence: theory and evidence. *Journal of Economic Behavior and Organization* **23**(1): 1–30.

Thomke, S. and Kuemmerle, W. 2002. Asset accumulation, interdependence and technological change: evidence from pharmaceutical drug discovery. *Strategic Management Journal* **23**(7): 619–635.

Thompson, JD. 1967. *Organizations in Action*. New York: McGraw-Hill.

Tippins, MJ. and Sohi, RS. 2003. IT competency and firm performance: is organizational learning a missing link? *Strategic Management Journal* **24**(8): 745–761.

Tripsas, M. and Gavetti, G. 2000. Capabilities, cognition, and inertia: evidence from digital imaging. *Strategic Management Journal*, Special Issue **21**(10–11): 1147–1161.

Tsang, EWK. 2002a. Acquiring knowledge by foreign partners from international joint ventures in a transition economy: learning-by-doing and learning myopia. *Strategic Management Journal* 23(9): 835–854.
Tsang, EWK. 2002b. Sharing international joint venturing experience: a study of some key determinants. *Management International Journal* 42(2): 183–205.
Tsoukas, H. 2003. Do we really understand tacit knowledge?. In *Handbook of Organizational Learning and Knowledge Management*. Easterby-Smith, M. and Lyles, MA. (eds).Blackwell: Oxford: 410–427.
Tucci, CL. 2002. Withholding proprietary information from alliance partners: an empirical exploration. Working paper, NYU Stern School of Business.
Tuchi, C. 1996. Firm heterogeneity and performance of strategic alliances: a synthesis of conceptual foundations. Working paper, MIT Sloan School of Management.
Tucker, LR. and MacCallum, RC. 1997. Introduction to exploratory factor analysis. In *Exploratory factor analysis*. Tucker, LR. and MacCallum, RC. (eds). pp. 144–178. Downloaded from: http://www.unc.edu/~rcm/book/factornew.htm.
Uebersax, JS. 2000. *Binary Data Factor Analysis and Multidimensional Latent Trait/ Item Response Theory (IRT) Models*. http://ourworld.compuserve.com/homepages/jsuebersax/binary.htm. Accessed 19 June 2003.
Van der Bij, H., Song, M. and Weggeman, M. 2003. An empirical investigation into the antecedents of knowledge dissemination at the strategic business unit level. *Journal of Product Innovation Management* 20: 163–179.
Van de Ven, AH. and Ferry, DL. 1980. *Measuring and Assessing Organizations*. John Wiley & Sons: New York.
Van de Ven, AH., Hudson, R. and Schroeder, DM. 1984. Designing new business start-ups: entrepreneurial, organizational, and ecological considerations. *Journal of Management* 10(1): 87–107.
Vanhaverbeke, W., Duysters, G. and Noorderhaven, N. 2002. External technology sourcing through alliances or acquisitions: an analysis of the application specific integrated circuits industry. *Organization Science* 13: 714–733.
Venkatraman, N. and Ramanujam, V. 1986. Measurement of business performance in strategy research: a comparison of approaches. *Academy of Management Review* 11(4): 801–814.
Vera, D. and Crossan, M. 2003. Organizational learning and knowledge management: toward an integrative framework. In *Handbook of Organizational Learning and Knowledge Management*. Easterby-Smith, M. and Lyles, MA. (eds). Blackwell: Oxford: 122–141.
Vera, D. and Crossan, M. 2004. Strategic leadership and organizational learning. *Academy of Management Review* 29(2): 222–240.
Verdin, PJ. and Williamson, PJ. 1994. Core competences, competitive advantage and market analysis: forging the links. In *Competence-Based Competition*. Hamel, G. and Heene, A. (eds). John Wiley & Sons: Chichester: 77–110.
Verschuren, P. and Doorewaard, H. 1999. *Designing a Research Project*. Lemma: Utrecht.
Vicari, S. and Troilo, G. 1998. Errors and learning in organizations. In *Knowing in Firms, Understanding, Managing and Measuring Knowledge*. Von Krogh, G., Roos, J. and Kleine, D. (eds). Sage: London.
Von Hippel, E. 1984. 'Sticky information' and the locus of problem solving: implications for innovation. *Management Science* 40(4): 429–439.

Von Krogh, G., Roos, J. and Kleine, D. (eds). 1998. *Knowing in Firms, Understanding, Managing and Measuring Knowledge*. Sage: London.

Walsh, JP. and Ungson, GR. 1991. Organizational memory. *Academy of Management Review* **16**(1): 57–92.

Wernerfelt, B. 1984. A resource-based view of the firm. *Strategic Management Journal* **5**(2): 171–180.

Westney, DE. 1988. Domestic and foreign learning curves in managing international cooperative strategies. In *Cooperative Strategies in International Business*. Contractor, FJ. and Lorange, P. (eds). Lexington Books: Lexington, MA: 339–346.

Whipple, JM. and Frankel, R. 2000. Strategic alliance success factors. *Journal of Supply Chain Management* **36**(3): 21–28.

Williamson, OE. 1975. *Markets and Hierarchies: Analysis and Antitrust Implications*, Free Press: New York.

Williamson, OE. 1985. *The Economic Institutions of Capitalism: Firms, Markets, Relational Contracting*. Free Press: New York.

Williamson, OE. 1991. Comparative economic organization: the analysis of discrete structural alternatives. *Administrative Science Quarterly* **36**: 269–296.

Williamson, OE. 1993. The logic of economic organization. In *The Nature of the Firm. Origins, Evolution, and Development*. Williamson, OE. and Winter, SG. (eds). Oxford University Press: New York: 90–116.

Williamson, OE. 1999. Strategy research: governance and competence perspectives. *Strategic Management Journal* **20**(14): 1087–1108.

Williamson, OE. and Winter, SG. (eds). 1993. *The Nature of the Firm. Origins, Evolution, and Development*. Oxford University Press: New York.

Winter, SG. 1987. Knowledge and competence as strategic assets. In *The Competitive Challenge*. Teece, D. (ed.). Ballinger Publishing: Cambridge, MA: 159–184.

Winter, SG. 1995. Four Rs of profitability: rents, resources, routines and replication. In *Resource-based and Evolutionary Theories of the Firm*: Towards a Synthesis. Montgomery, CA. (ed.). Kluwer: Norwell, MA: 147–178.

Winter, SG. 2000. The satisficing principle in capability learning. *Strategic Management Journal* **21**(10–11): 981–996.

Winter, SG. 2003. Understanding dynamic capabilities. *Strategic Management Journal* **24**: 991–995.

Xie, Y. 1989. Structural equation models for ordinal variables. *Sociological Methods & Research* **17**: 325–352.

Yaffee, RA. 1998. Enhancement of Reliability Analysis: Applications of the Intraclass Correlation With SPSS V8. March 11, 1998. http://www.nyu.edu/acf/socsci/Docs/intracls.html. Accessed 21 June 2003.

Yin, RK. 1994. *Case Study Research: Design and Methods*, 2nd edn. Sage: Thousand Oaks, CA.

Yoshino, MY. and Rangan, US. 1995. *Strategic Alliances. An Entrepreneurial Approach to Globalization*. Harvard Business School Press: Boston, MA.

Young-Ybarra, C. and Wiersema. M. 1999. Strategic flexibility in information technology alliances: the influence of transaction cost economics and social exchange theory. *Organization Science* **10**(4): 439–459.

Zaheer, A., McEvily, B. and Perrone, V. 1998. Does trust matter? Exploring the effects of interorganizational and interpersonal trust on performance. *Organization Science* **9**(2): 141–159.

Zahra, SA. and George, G. 2002. Absorptive capacity: a review, reconceptualization, and extension. *Academy of Management Review* 27(2): 185–203.

Zahra, SA. and Nielsen, AP. 2002. Sources of capabilities, integration and technology commercialization. *Strategic Management Journal* 23(5): 377–398.

Zander, U. and Kogut, B. 1995. Knowledge and the speed of the transfer and imitation of organizational capabilities: an empirical test. *Organization Science* 6(1): 76–92.

Zeng, M. and Hennart, J-F. 2002. From learning races to cooperative specialization: towards a new framework for alliance management. In *Cooperative Strategies and Alliances*. Contractor, FJ. and Lorange, P. (eds). Elsevier Science: Oxford: 189–210.

Zollo, M. 1997. Strategies or routines? Knowledge codification, path-dependence and the evolution of post-acquisition integration practices in the U.S. banking industry. Working paper, Wharton Financial Institutions Center.

Zollo, M. and Reuer, JJ. 2003. Experience spillovers across corporate development activities. Working paper, INSEAD.

Zollo, M., Reuer, JJ. and Singh, H. 2002. Interorganizational routines and performance in strategic alliances. *Organization Science* 13(6): 701–713.

Zollo, M. and Winter, SG. 2002. Deliberate learning and the evolution of dynamic capabilities. *Organization Science* 13(3): 339–351.

Zott, C. 2003. Dynamic capabilities and the emergence of intraindustry differential firm performance: insights from a simulation study. *Strategic Management Journal*, 22(2): 97–125.

Index

Note: Page numbers in *italics* refer to tables or figures

3M   83
4I framework   149n9

absorptive capacity   38, 56, 61–62, 92, 94
Afuah, A.   132
Aldrich, HE.   46, 55, 108
Alliance Analyst   53
alliance experience   7–8, 12, 13, 48, 76, 80–81, 94, 99–100, 106, 108, 117, 121
  levels of   54–56
  proxying   53, 101
alliance function, dedicated   5–6, 21
alliance goals and outcomes   125
alliance mechanism   66, 96, 101, 106, 121
alliance metrics   55, 63, 64, 80, 98
alliance performance   3, 4–6, 8, 12, 13, 14, 18, 20, 22, 35, 36, 49, 94, 99, 108, 111, 112–113, 116, 124, 135
  enhancing   60, 61, 63, 67, 68, 79, 82, 115, 117, 121
  heterogeneity   120
  measuring   134
  positive effect on   21, 57, 59, 100
alliance research
  contribution of theories to   *40*
  developments in   3–9
  literature review   17;
    inter-firm   17–20;
    intra-firm   20–22
Alza   6
Amit, R.   119
Anand, BN.   9, 13, 24, 119
Anand, J.   6, 13, 100, 135
Argote, L.   37
Arrow, KH.   37
assimilation   60–61
Association of Strategic Alliance Professionals (ASAP)   15, 128

Baden-Fuller, C.   6
Bakker, HJC.   47
Bamford, JD.   6, 13, 48
Baron, RM.   105, 108
Bartholomew, DJ.   72
Bartlett, CA.   83
Barton, RM.   67
BellSouth   48
Bernstein, IH.   128, 148n.5
binominal semantic differential scale   132
Boddy, D.   47
Boisot, MH.   86
Boone, PF.   46
Borker, M.   46
Brown, JS.   81

canonical correlation   78
capability lifecycle   53, 83
capability, meaning of   50–51
Carlile, PR.   83
Casher, A.   6, 46
Chrysler   49
Churchill, GA.   128
Cockburn, I.   51
codified knowledge   61, 86, 119–120
coefficient alpha   72–73
Cohen, MD.   149n.3
Cohen, WM.   38
collaborative advantage   4
Collis, DJ.   50
combination   34
commitment   4, 12, 62, 65, 83, 96, 98, 112, 121, 122, 129
communities of practice   46
competence   51
competence-based view (CBV)   27–28, 29, 32–34
  application of   33–34
competitive advantage   3, 20, 29, 30, 31, 32, 83, 89, 90

competitive heterogeneity 119
complementarity 4, 18
concurrent validity 73–74
confirmatory factor analysis (CFA) 71
Conner, KR. 147n.4
construct validity 72
content/face validity 74–75
Contractor, FJ. 111
control and management processes 63, 80
cooperation 3, 4, 64
cooperative competence 42
coordination 33, 35–36, 56, 61, 62, 64, 80, 82, 97, 108
core competence 33
Coriat, B. 39, 98, 149n.3
Corning 7, 48
Corporate Strategy Board 48, 49
Cote, J. 108
criterion-related validity 73
Cronbach, LJ. 72
Cronbach's alpha 72, 73
cross fertilization, of theories 39
Crossan, MM. 54, 81, 83, 89
cultural sensitivity 63
Cyert, RM. 36

Das, TK. 147n.3
database 15, 56, 63, 80, 94, 97, 101, 128
Davies, H. 71
De Leo, F. 147n.8
dependent variable 133–135
descriptive discriminant analysis 67
development process 91, 116–118
  of alliance capabilities 12–14, 57–59
  analysis and results 102–107
  data collection and methodology 100–102
  discussion 107–110
  hypotheses 92–100;
    capabilities 95–99;
    experience 93–94;
    interaction between experience and capabilities 99–100
discriminant analysis 67, 76, 148
discriminant function analysis 67–68
  effectiveness of 78

Dosi, G. 148n.1
Douma, MU. 150n.1
Dow Chemical 48, 115, 121
Draulans, J. 53, 54, 82, 83, 131
Drucker, Peter 2
Duguid, P. 81
Dutch Internet Society (ISOC) 15
Dutton, JM. 36, 37
Duysters, GM. 18, 67, 76, 127, 149n.1
Dwyer, RF. 25, 42
dyadic issues 12, 87, 112, 124, 127
dyadic logic 4, 20
Dyer, JH. 5, 23, 25, 42, 48, 61, 83, 98
dynamic capability view (DCV) 27–28, 29, 31–32

effective resource-picking mechanism 30
eigenvalue 68, 75, 78
Eisenhardt, KM. 52, 95, 99
Eli Lilly 6, 49
embedding knowledge 81
Epple, D. 37
equifinality principle 7
Ernst, D. 6, 13, 48
evaluation techniques 63
evolutionary economics 28, 29, 35, 51, 58, 119, 120
  coordination 35–36
  routines 35, 36
evolution cycle 58
ex ante limits, to competition 30
experience 7–8, 53, 58, 93–94, 112, 113, 117
expert interviews 131
explanatory variables 131–133
explicit knowledge 50
exploratory factor analysis (EFA) 70–71, 81, 89
externalization 34
external parties 64–65

Financial Times 48
firms 3–4, 45, 76, 80
  ability of 52
  absorptive capacity 62
  alliance competence 47
  alliance experience 7–8
  alliance portfolio 6, 21

firms – *continued*
  as a collection of resources 30
  competitive advantage 3, 30
  dyadic factors 4
  experience 91
  institutional mechanisms 47
  internal mechanisms 48
  resources, characteristics of 30
  routines 36
first-rate communication systems 48
The Forbes Magnetic 40 47
formalization of knowledge exchange 64
Frechtling, J. 150n.1
Freidheim, C. 48
Fujimoto, T. 13, 29, 96
functions 60, 61, 62, 78, 79–80, 85

Geringer, JM. 134
Ghoshal, S. 83
Gittell, JH. 13, 58, 75, 92, 108, 117, 118, 119, 132
GlaxoSmithKline 115, 121
Grant, RM. 50, 52, 58, 122
group-level learning 81, 82, 86
group level mechanism 85, 86, 87
Gulati, R. 23

Hagedoorn, J. 67, 76
Hamel, G. 5, 147n.8, 149n.3
Harbison, JR. 48, 52, 54, 95
Hebert, L. 134
Heene, A. 147n.5, 147n.8
Heimeriks, KH. 127, 147n.2, 149n.1
Helfat, C. 13, 39, 51, 52, 53, 57, 58, 83, 92
Helmink, JWA. 47
Henderson, R. 51
Hewlett Packard 48, 49
higher-order resource 52
Hirsch, WZ. 37
Hoang, HT. 5, 8, 25
Huberty, CJ. 67
Hunt, SD. 25, 51, 52

Iacobucci, D. 128
IBM 83
information provision 57

Inkpen, AC. 54
institutionalization 81, 89
integrated alliances 48–49
integration, of knowledge 81
inter-firm factors 4, 5, 6, 17–20
inter-firm learning 38
internal evolutionary mechanism 96
internalization 34–35
Internet Society (ISOC) 128
intra-firm antecedents 4–5, 6, 112
  alliance experience 7–8
  recent contribution to literature 6
intra-firm learning 38
intra-firm mechanisms 11–12, 14, 21, 45, 49, 57, 58, 60, 95, 109, 117, 120, *132*
  role in developing alliance capabilities 114–116
Ireland, RD. 5
item-based testing of mechanisms 65–70
item-level analysis 79–81

John, G. 150n.1
joint venture experience sharing among managers 8

Kale, P. 5, 13, 24, 25, 52, 58, 75, 95, 108, 109, 119, 132
Kenny, DA. 105, 108
Khanna, T. 9, 13, 24, 119
King, AW. 12, 57, 93, 108, 109, 120
Kleiner, A. 7, 83
KLM 115, 121
Knott, AM. 11, 13, 29, 45, 89, 109, 118, 119, 120, 133
know-how skill 50
knowledge-based view (KBV) 28, 29, 34–35, 42
  transfer and integration of knowledge 35
knowledge evolution cycle 37
knowledge sharing 35
knowledge transference 37, 46, 64
knowledge transformation cycle *see* knowledge evolution cycle
Kuemmerle, W. 52
Kumar, R. 7, 61
Kusunoki, K. 50

Lambe, CJ. 25, 47
learning 38, 58, 81, 82, 86, 92
  definition of 37
  learning curve notion 38
Lei, D. 50
Lenox, M. 57, 108, 109, 120
Leonard, D. 85
Levinthal, DA. 38
Lewin, AY. 148n.11
Likert scale 133
limitations and future research 121–124
linear regression 104
Lipparini, A. 24
literature review
  early research alliance 17–20
  recent research alliance 20–22
  theoretical underpinnings of 22
logistic regression model, ordinal 102–106
log likelihood ratio test 103, 104
Lorange, P. 111
Lorenzoni, G. 6, 24
Luo, Y. 18, 28
Lyles, MA. 23, 51

Madhok, A. 119
Mahoney, JT. 42
Maidique, MA. 7
Makadok, R. 51, 52, 119
managerial implications 121
March, JG. 36
Martin, JA. 52, 95, 99
McKinsey 83
McLeod, LD. 148n.5
mechanisms 13, 47, 48, 65–70, 85, 86, 87, 96, 97–98, 99, 108, 109, 112, 113, 117, 118–119, 121, 122
  see also individual entries
Meehl, PE. 72
micro-level understanding
  of alliance capabilities 11–12
  analysis and results: item-based testing of mechanisms 65–70; scale-based testing of mechanisms 70–79

groups of mechanisms 60–65
interpretation and discussion: item-level analysis 79–81; scale-level analysis 81–88
micro-mechanisms 96
Miller, KD. 13, 45, 132
Miner, AS. 107
Mintzberg, H. 149n.9
Montealegre, R. 123
Moorman, C. 107
Morgan, RM. 51, 52
Motorola 48
Mplus statistical package 72
Mukherjee, AS. 93

Nagelkerke pseudo R-square 103–104
Nelson, RR. 42, 52, 149n.3
Nielsen, AP. 97
Nobeoka, K. 42, 61
Nonaka, I. 34, 35, 96, 148n.1, 148n.2
Nortel 48
Nti, KO. 7, 61
Nunally, JC. 73, 128, 148n.5

oblique rotation see PROMAX
Oracle 115, 121
organizational economics 42, 52
organizational learning theory 28, 29, 36–38, 81–82
  knowledge transference 37
organizational routines 35, 36, 51, 53, 58, 92, 99
organization-level mechanism 87
original replacement follow-up (ORF) technique 129
orthogonal method see VARIMAX

Pandian, JR. 42
Parise, S. 6, 46
Parkhe, A. 135
partner programme 66
partner selection programmes 80, 87
Pekar, P. 48, 54
Penrose, ET. 29, 30, 95
personnel instability 46
Peteraf, MA. 13, 39, 51, 52, 53, 57, 58, 83

Pfeffer, J. 122
Philips 115, 121
Philips, LW. 150n.1
Polanyi, M. 50, 148n.2
portfolio of alliances 6, 21, 46, 49, 55, 86
practice 53
Prahalad, CK. 147n.8, 149n.3
predictive discriminant analysis 67
problem definition, in alliance capabilities 9–14
productivity gains 37
progress function 36
progress principle 37
PROMAX 72
proxying, of alliance experience 53

Ramanujam, V. 133
Ray, G. 134
Rebentisch, ES. 83
relational advantage 4
resource-based view (RBV) 27, 29, 30, 31
dynamic resource-based view 39
resources 50, 51
Reuer, JJ. 25, 101
Reve, T. 150n.1
reward and bonus system 46, 55, 63, 64
Roth, G. 7, 83
Rotter, J. 132
routines 35, 36, 45–46, 97, 98–99, 108, 120, 121, 122, 123
types 52–53
routinization of activities 45
Rumelt, RP. 33

Sanchez, R. 50, 51, 147n.5, 148n.1, 149n.1
Sarkar, MB. 13, 75, 83, 109, 118
scale-based testing of mechanisms 70–79
scale-level analysis 81–88
Schoemaker, PJH. 119
Schreiner, M. 147n.2
Senge, P. 35
Sharma, S. 150n.9

Simonin, BL. 5, 11, 12, 13, 23, 58, 95, 108, 117, 122, 150n.10
Singh, H. 5, 23, 24, 25, 98, 108
Sivadas, E. 25, 42
socialization 34
Sohi, RS. 128
Spekman, RE. 25
Spender, J-C. 148n.2
standardization of alliance procedures 55
strategic alliances 1
development in 2
reasons for failure 19, 127
see also individual entries
structure matrix 69, 70, 78
study design, of alliance capabilities 14–16
summated scale 75, 76, 81, 101–102, 119
survey 127–131
Sutton, RI. 122
Swap, W. 85

tacit knowledge 50, 64
Tallman, SB. 119
Teece, DJ. 149n.1
Teng, B-S. 147n.3
theoretical implications 118–120
Thomas, A. 36, 37
Thomke, S. 52
Tippins, MJ. 128
tools 62–63, 80
Toyota 61
traditional strategy perspectives 17–20
transfer mechanisms 85
trust 4, 12, 18, 112, 124
Tsang, EWK. 8, 95, 97, 122
Tucci, CL. 93

Uebersax, JS. 72
Unisys 49

value creation 63
Van de Ven, AH. 46
VARIMAX 72
Vassalo, RS. 6, 13, 100, 135
Venkatraman, N. 133

Volberda, HW. 148n.11
Von Hippel, E. 50

Walters, P. 71
weak liaison 56
Winter, SG. 42, 50, 52, 53, 58, 148n.2, 149n.3

Xerox 49

Zahra, SA. 97
Zeithalm, CP. 12
Zirger, BJ. 7
Zollo, M. 13, 25, 29, 50, 58, 110